KEATS THE POET

KEATS THE POET

STUART M. SPERRY

PRINCETON UNIVERSITY
PRESS

Published by Princeton University Press, 41 William Street,
Princeton, New Jersey 08540
In the United Kingdom: Princeton University Press,
Chichester, West Sussex

Library of Congress Cataloging-in-Publication Data

Sperry, Stuart M.
Keats the poet / Stuart M. Sperry.
p.   cm.
Originally published: 1973.
Includes bibliographical references (p.   ) and index.
ISBN 0-691-00089-1
1. Keats, John, 1795–1821—Criticism and interpretation.
I. Title.
PR4837.S57   1994
821'.7—dc20   93-11443

First Princeton Paperback printing, 1994

10 9 8 7 6 5 4 3

Printed in the United States of America

For Sophie

CONTENTS

PREFACE

THIS BOOK attempts to trace the intellectual and poetic development of John Keats from the beginning to the end of his career. In order to fulfill this task, it seemed desirable to sketch by way of background some of the major problems he inherited from the century preceding his own and which he had finally in his own way, and within the terms of his own art, to confront—problems that (in my view) find their genesis in the main evolution of British empirical philosophy. As I make clear hereafter, I have no intention of claiming for Keats anything like a formal commitment to or knowledge of philosophy, a discipline he often regarded with misgiving. Nevertheless the questions that, directly or indirectly, came steadily to engross him—the question of the relationship between mind and object or the manner in which the imagination operates upon its materials—are ultimately philosophical and are best taken up not as if they were (or ever could be) peculiar to Keats alone, or to any of his contemporaries, but as they remained of broad consequence throughout the age. It seemed also necessary, even at the risk of violating chronology, to devote a second preliminary chapter to the emergence, relatively soon in his career, of what might be called an early theory of the imagination, a set of analogies for conceiving the poetic process that are tentative and metaphoric. The remaining chapters take the form of a critical discussion of the major poems or creative periods of his life. The reader whose interests lie primarily in the interpretation of the poetry is always free, if he so chooses, to turn directly to the poems that most engage him. Nevertheless I hope that the central problems adumbrated in the opening chapters—the whole complex relationship, for example, between sensation and thought—can be seen as basic to the later discussions and as the ones that give distinctive shape not only to Keats's poetry but to his career as a whole.

ix

Beyond most English writers, certainly beyond any English writer of the nineteenth century, Keats has benefited from a distinguished line of scholars and critics, British and American, who have devoted attention to him. I have tried to give some indication, both in the text and footnotes, of the great debt I owe this tradition. However, it is impossible to acknowledge in detail the host of general and special studies that has shaped my sense of Keats and his achievement over many years and to which I can only pay a general tribute of thanks. Some special obligations, however, are of a more personal kind. Professor Carlos Baker first introduced me as a student to the study of the Romantic poets and has consistently encouraged my efforts. Undoubtedly my greatest debt is to Professors Douglas Bush and Walter J. Bate, whose extraordinary learning, insight, and humanity, both as teachers and writers, have been steadily inspiring. I have benefited from conversations with the late Hyder E. Rollins, a scholar generous with his time for any project involving Keats. My colleagues, Alfred David and Charles Forker, talked with me helpfully about particular problems. My debt to Edgar F. Harden is of long standing, while Mary Elizabeth David provided advice and encouragement at many stages. Professors David Perkins and Bishop Hunt read the book in typescript and made valuable suggestions. Not the least of my debts is to my wife, who not only did all the typing but often paused to criticize.

The fine study by Morris Dickstein, *Keats and His Poetry: A Study in Development* (Chicago, 1971), appeared after my own typescript was completed and too late for me to take into account. Sections of my book have been previously published, but I have, in every case, modified them, if only slightly, in adapting them. The first half of Chapter Two was published originally as "Keats and the Chemistry of Poetic Creation," *PMLA*, LXXXV (1970), 268-77. Chapter Four is "The Allegory of *Endymion*," *Studies in Romanticism*, II (1962), 38-53, entirely rewritten. Chapter Five appeared as "Keats's *Epistle to John Hamilton Reynolds*," *ELH: A Jour-

PREFACE

nal of English Literary History, xxxvi (1969), 562-74, copyright The Johns Hopkins Press. Chapter Eight was published as "Romance as Wish-Fulfillment: Keats's *The Eve of St. Agnes,*" *Studies in Romanticism,* x (1971), 27-43, but has been restructured and revised. Chapter Twelve is "Keats, Milton, and *The Fall of Hyperion,*" PMLA, lxxvii (1962), 77-84, but substantially rewritten and revised. I am grateful to these journals and their editors for permission to republish or rework the earlier pieces.

Bloomington, Indiana
May 1972

KEATS THE POET

CHAPTER ONE

A POETRY OF
SENSATION

KEATS'S CRY, "O for a Life of Sensations rather than of
Thoughts!"[1] is the most characteristic of his utterances in
the letters. He might equally well have written, "O for a
Poetry of Sensations," for the word is basic not only to his
poetic vocabulary but to his conception of the source and
end of verse. Poetry, for Keats, finds its origin in what he
means by "sensation." At the same time, poetry exists to
express and to communicate sensation. Throughout his
thought and writing, there is a looseness and ambiguity in his
use of the word, a fact that is hardly surprising. The term, as
he inherited it, carried with it a long history of confusion and
debate running back through the annals of late seventeenth-
and eighteenth-century philosophy and aesthetics.

Critics of Keats have seen the fundamental importance of
sensation to his conception of poetry. Yet past discussion has
not necessarily brought us any closer to the significance he
attached to the term or the importance it assumes in his
poetry and letters. The fact is there exists no general agreement as to what he meant by the word. The point can be
demonstrated by comparing two quite different glosses of his
famous declaration by scholars whose approaches to the poet,
nevertheless, have much in common. By "sensations," Clarence Thorpe writes in his study of the poet's mind, Keats
meant "feelings or intuitions, the pure activity of the imagi-

---

[1] *The Letters of John Keats, 1814-1821*, ed. Hyder Edward Rollins,
2 vols. (Cambridge, Mass., 1958), I, 185. References by volume and
page number to this edition are hereafter included in the text. Unless
otherwise noted, italics are mine.

3

nation."[2] Much more recently, W. J. Bate has noted of the passage that "Hazlitt's constant use of the word 'sensations' in the traditional empirical sense—as virtually equivalent to concrete experience—added a new term to Keats's own habitual vocabulary."[3] The two interpretations are significantly different in emphasis. The first asserts the primacy of the mind and its own intuitions. The second stresses the evidence of the senses and the contact they provide with material phenomena. Dissimilar as they appear with regard to Keats, the two readings together give some indication of the wide range of meanings the term actually possesses both in modern and in late eighteenth- and early nineteenth-century critical or aesthetic discussions.

Keats's approach to poetry was far from philosophical, and he more than once expressed strong if qualified distrust of the value of such discipline. To subject his adoption of a term he used casually throughout his letters to rigorous analysis may seem at first a questionable procedure. Furthermore it involves us rapidly in so much else—the whole fabric of his thinking. Nevertheless his notion of "sensation" is the logical point of departure for any study of his development, for the conception bears directly on his sense of the nature of the materials from which poetry springs, the way it operates upon them, and the manner in which it differs from or transcends them. It also takes us to the center of certain problems he was to return to over and over again and that might almost be said, as they develop in implication, to determine the course of his poetic career.

Keats defines the word only once—in the anatomical and physiological notes he took while attending lectures as a

[2] Clarence Dewitt Thorpe, *The Mind of John Keats* (New York, 1926), p. 64. Thorpe cites Sir Sidney Colvin's statement (*John Keats: His Life and Poetry, His Friends, Critics, and After-Fame* [London, 1920], p. 155) that "what [Keats] means are intuitions of the mind and spirit . . . independent of all consecutive stages and formal processes of thinking." See similar statements in Thorpe, pp. 12, 111n., 118.

[3] Walter Jackson Bate, *John Keats* (Cambridge, Mass., 1963), p. 240.

4

medical student at Guy's Hospital. One can imagine him
copying down the stiffly-worded phrases almost mechanically
amid a host of other technical terms. "Sensation," he notes,
"is an impression made on the Extremities of the Nerves
conveyed to the Brain. . . . Volition is the contrary of sensation it proceeds from the internal to the external parts."[4]
Like many others, the definition attempts to maintain careful
boundaries between material phenomena, sense impression,
and inner consciousness. Keats uses the term more loosely in
his letters. At first glance one might be tempted to assume he
employs it as a general synonym for sense experience. Such
a passage as the following comes to mind as typical: "For
instance suppose a rose to have sensation, it blooms on a
beautiful morning it enjoys itself—but there comes a cold
wind, a hot sun—it can not escape it, it cannot destroy its
annoyances" (II, 101). The passage suggests quite specific
impressions of cold and heat; nevertheless these are clearly
subordinate to the effects of pleasure and pain the flower is
fated to experience. The example can be taken as typical of
the way in which Keats's use of the word, while denoting
specific physical impressions, moves beyond the realm of
sense experience. A friend of Fanny Brawne's, to take another
instance, "plays the Music without one sensation but the
feel of the ivory at her fingers" (II, 13). Here the significance
of the word is restricted with deliberate irony to the physical
impression of touch in order to suggest missing qualities it
should ideally include—hearing, taste (in its broader meaning), and sensibility. On yet another occasion Keats describes
how young men should learn to greet uneasiness "as an
habitual sensation, a pannier which is to weigh upon them
through life" (I, 270). The sense of physical strain and pressure, the cut of the strap into the shoulder blade, serves by
analogy to suggest a quality of interior discomfort, as unmistakable and as enduring. Even where it draws its force
directly from the evidence of the senses, the term "sensation,"

[4] *John Keats's Anatomical and Physiological Notebook*, ed. Maurice
Buxton Forman (Oxford, 1934), pp. 55-56.

as Keats uses it, habitually encompasses much more—feeling, sensibility, and the world of interior consciousness.

More frequently still Keats uses "sensation" as a synonym for feeling or emotion. He can, for example, adopt it to refer to aesthetic experience, as when he inquires of his brother and sister-in-law: "With what sensation do you read Fielding?" (II, 18). Often the term has at best only a tenuous connection with any source in external reality. "My sensations are sometimes deadened for weeks together" (I, 325). "I went the other day into an ironmonger's shop, without any change in my sensations" (II, 43). "Either that gloom overspred me or I was suffering under some passionate feeling, or if I turn'd to versify that acerbated the poison of either sensation" (II, 260). In such typical cases the word stands for states of feeling that appear almost entirely subjective. Sometimes the tie between emotion and the senses is suggested by figure or analogy: "I have a sensation at the present moment as though I was dissolving" (II, 223). At other times the connection is missing, as when, in a moment of despondency, he writes Reynolds that he has scarcely anything to say, "except I was to give you a history of sensations, and day-night mares" (II, 146). Such states, in their autonomy and aloofness from communicable experience, often possessed an extraordinary and disturbing reality for the poet.

It is notable that Keats never uses "sensation" to refer to anything that might be described as immediate apprehension of a higher reality. It has, as we have partly seen, been frequently asserted that his use of the word includes, at times refers directly to, this kind of intuition. Such an interpretation can rest at best upon a single passage in the letters. That is a part of the famous letter to Bailey of November 1817, in which he asserts the "holiness of the Heart's affections," calls into question the value of "consequitive reasoning," and compares the imagination in its operation to Adam's dream. "However it may be," he goes on, "O for a Life of Sensations rather than of Thoughts! It is 'a Vision in the form of

Youth' a Shadow of reality to come" (1, 185). To interpret
"sensation" as pure intuition of some transcendental reality
on the basis of these words alone is to overlook every other
occasion on which Keats uses the word and to fix on this.
It is, moreover, to freeze a metaphor into metaphysics. For
he does not refer to any kind of intuition. He writes of "a
Life of Sensations" and compares it to "a Shadow of reality
to come." His meaning, interpreted most directly, is that our
consciousness can and inevitably must contain at any given
moment of our experience the seed or embryo of realization
that will come to birth in future and that we are at certain
times aware of this process of development as it proceeds.
Hence the pleasure of "the simple imaginative Mind" in
experiencing "the repeti[ti]on of its own silent Working
coming continually on the spirit with a fine suddenness," or
the surprise we feel in rediscovering an old melody, sung by
a new and enchanting voice. The phenomenon is one that
had a continual fascination for Keats: the sudden realization
of distinct but continuously interrelated levels of growth
within the evolution of his own awareness. However, such
growth is spontaneous and natural, and there is no need for,
nor does Keats's metaphor advance, any transcendental hypothesis to account for it.

We are apt, without reflecting, to conceive of sensation
as something simple and immediate—the prick of a pin or
the odor of a rose. The more we study the phenomenon the
more obvious it becomes, even leaving aside the complications introduced by memory and imagination, that it is in
fact temporal and complex. It is, indeed, a *process*, an assimilation of outer stimulus and inner response that proceeds
through time, and by Keats's day the notion of sensation as a
continuum was, in one way or another, assuming ever greater
relevance to poetry. The literature of the Romantic age is,
above most things, a literature involved with the conception
of process, and among nineteenth-century poets one can account in great measure for the centrality of Wordsworth as

7

well as the eccentricity of Blake by the degree to which each attempted to assimilate his generation's understanding of the complexity of the mind and its operations.

Wordsworth's preoccupation with the nature of sensation is too well known to require extensive citation. One has only to recall "Tintern Abbey" and its apostrophe to

> sensations sweet,
> Felt in the blood, and felt along the heart;
> And passing even into my purer mind,
> With tranquil restoration:—feelings too
> Of unremembered pleasure. . . .
>
> (27-31)

Like Keats, Wordsworth is beguilingly vague in his use of the word, as we can readily see if we but pause to examine the elements it involves. It encompasses, first of all, the "beauteous forms" of nature (from a few lines earlier) and the way in which these impressions, felt along the blood-stream, enter into heart and mind to unite with intellect and feeling. As with Keats, "sensation" here cannot be identified as any single form or action. It is, rather, insepa-rable from a highly complicated process, sensory, emotional, and intellectual. In its plural form it is roughly equivalent to consciousness, stimulated in part from without but also molded or colored from within. Born of the interplay be-tween mind and nature, it is, moreover, a growing and ex-panding awareness, a kind of intelligence that, for Words-worth at least, can lead on to "that blessed mood" of "aspect more sublime" in which "we see into the life of things." Behind the generality with which both Keats and Words-worth use the term, one can sense a characteristic unwilling-ness to isolate or overemphasize any single element in a continuing and complex process of perception.

Throughout much Romantic poetry, but especially Keats's, the poetic process—that is the way in which poetry is created or conceived—is more than ever bound up, at times indis-tinguishably, with the processes of human perception. The two kinds of growth or progression, or the conception of them, become interlocking and analogous. Such interdependence, paradoxically, is even more the case with a poet like Keats who never cared to formulate a deliberate, detailed idea of such concepts, whose notion of them was in large part subliminal and metaphoric. His antipathy for the abstractions of systematic or "consequitive" reasoning was ingrained and brought with it definite advantages. It permitted him the freedom to ignore technical, philosophic questions and to found his approach to poetry on the inherent value and interest of sensation itself. His conception of verse is founded on the primacy of sense experience. However it necessarily assumes, if only unconsciously, an orderly relationship between the various levels of human awareness which sensation, as an evolving process of realization, includes. That Keats was never at pains to crystallize his idea of that process in any systematic way, that his approach to the problems surrounding it was consistently tentative and figurative, does not indicate that they were any less important. The analogies by which he thought of the spirit of poetry, its origins and methods of operation, were ones he quietly absorbed from the intellectual climate of his age.

No less than Wordsworth's, Keats's genius as a poet is rooted in the nature of sensation. The word describes both the source of his verse and the main region of his song. Perhaps this is only to say that what is vital for all poetry is more than usually so for his: the nature of our primary grasp over material reality, the way our sense impressions are channeled and combined in consciousness, and the way in which such states of perception assimilate with feeling and emotion. Keats's absorption with the nature of sensation clearly engages all these areas of experience. This is not to say that his approach to these concerns was ever abstract or analytic but rather that they together constitute the life and interest of his verse. The once fashionable cliché of Keats as a poet uninterested in or incapable of ideas has been, one hopes, exploded. Nevertheless the "speculations" in the letters come

9

into being gradually, as if through a process of original discovery, and are inseparable from the chain of feelings and
perceptions that give rise to them. As virtually every critic
has in one way or another acknowledged, Keats's approach
to art is primitive and constructive: it begins with what is
most fundamental to human experience and proceeds from
there. To put the matter more simply, his poetry before
everything else explores the way we prove the essential truths
of life upon our pulses, a metaphor that suggests a link between the avenues of sense perception and the higher faculties of heart and head.

The benefits of Keats's approach to poetry are thoroughly
apparent. They account in large part for its rich concreteness
and immediacy, the fullness of its range of sympathies, its
abhorrence of the merely doctrinaire and openness to various
points of view—qualities that organize themselves generally
around the criterion of "Negative Capability." The approach, however, is also one that contains certain inherent
problems and dangers. These become clear if we pause to
look somewhat more broadly at the background of philosophic and aesthetic thinking that dominates the age. If the
conception of sensation is a chief premise of Keats's art, it is
central also to the major problem with which late eighteenth-
and early nineteenth-century philosophy was above all concerned and to a whole complex of ensuing questions. While
Wordsworth and Keats, with typical Romantic comprehensiveness, were finding a broad and fluid notion of sensation
ever more fundamental to their sense of poetry and its basis
in human experience, their philosophic contemporaries were
becoming steadily more dissatisfied with the inexactness of
the concept yet were discovering the extraordinary difficulties
of defining it with any precision. The poetry of the Romantic
age attempts to render the experience of sensation as a vital
process. At the same time, the major intellectual concern of
the period was to define and explain scientifically the progression and the elements composing it. The two efforts, the
poetic and the analytic, were necessarily interdependent in

innumerable ways, even for a poet like Keats who was apparently so far removed from more abstruse involvements. Although they begin from opposite poles, the two attempts to explore the nature of sensation have much to reveal about each other, especially in the kinds of problem they ultimately must confront.

II

Much of the impetus behind the precise investigation of the nature of sensation undoubtedly came from John Locke and is reflected in the tremendous influence he exerted on the age that followed him. It was Locke's examination of our grounds of knowledge that required every writer who followed him to discriminate more accurately between the qualities actually possessed by material objects and the perceptions or sensations these qualities occasion in the human mind. Our awareness of life is, for Locke, something basically constructed from a stock of sense impressions gained from material reality. At the same time, his analysis of human consciousness raises serious questions regarding the ability of our sense impressions to convey a true notion of the real identity of the objects they perceive. Here the term "sensation" takes on a pivotal significance. In his *Essay Concerning Human Understanding* Locke first defines "sensation" as *"such an impression or motion made in some part of the body, as produces some perception in the understanding."*[5] At first glance "sensation" here seems roughly equivalent to sense impression. Yet it also relates to and depends upon the actual transmission of perception to consciousness. Thus it is both a quality of bodily experience and a condition of consciousness or mind; or rather it relates to both at once. The somewhat equivocal nature of Locke's idea of sensation is seen again, some pages later, when he declares that "the

[5] John Locke, *An Essay Concerning Human Understanding*, ed. Alexander Campbell Fraser (rpt. New York, 1959), I, 141 (Locke's italics).

perception or thought which actually accompanies, and is annexed to, any impression on the body, made by an external object, being distinct from all other modifications of thinking, furnishes the mind with a distinct idea, which we call *sensation;*—which is, as it were, the actual entrance of any idea into the understanding by the senses."[6] Here "sensation" appears more clearly equivalent to "idea"—an idea of sense experience. While, however, the term appears to designate a relatively distinct and individual perception, Locke's definition, like the earlier one, clearly involves the notion of a *process.* It is "the actual *entrance* of any idea into the understanding by the senses" that constitutes sensation.

It is understandable that throughout the century following Locke's death the major questions that engaged philosophers had to do with the way perceptions or thoughts "accompany" or become "annexed to" sense impressions and the precise way this process operates in conveying physical sensations to the mind. Even if we imagine the mind as a *tabula rasa* or some other impressionable substance, it is hard to imagine its ideas and feelings as being the result of certain forms and pressures transmitted directly upon it. As one writer of the eighteenth century was moved to inquire: "Does the roar of a cannon bear any resemblance to the ball, or to the powder, in shape, in weight, or in magnitude? What figure has the pain of the toothach, and our remembrance of that pain? Is it triangular, or circular, or of a square form?" Even "supposing impressions to be made on the brain," he went on to ask, "I would ask, *how* the mind perceives them."[7]

There is a fundamental paradox involved in Locke's analysis of human understanding that was to manifest itself throughout much of the theoretical and critical writing that followed along the channels he laid out. On the one hand he conceives of the human intelligence as the steady outgrowth of a progressive assimilation of sense experience into more

[6] *Ibid.,* p. 298 (Locke's italics).

[7] James Beattie, *Dissertations Moral and Critical* (Dublin, 1783), I, 14 (Beattie's italics).

complex units through the mind's organizing and concep-
tualizing abilities. The development from sense impression
to complex idea is gradual and unbroken. On the other hand,
Locke's psychology postulates a decisive gap between the
actual identity of external objects and the impressions we
form of them. Certain qualities we experience in the face of
natural objects are directly attributable to those objects;
others as we experience them are not. Among the impressions
we gain from external objects, some qualities can be directly
identified as properties of the objects themselves. Yet there
are other qualities of sensation that, however much they
characterize our perception of reality, enjoy no demonstrable
connection with external forms. The complexities introduced
by Locke's division between primary and secondary qualities
were to become more obvious and troubling when carried one
step further by Berkeley in his subtle argument that all
qualities are imputed, not inherent. Locke transmitted to the
generations that followed him an outline or schema of the
human understanding and its operations that was able effectively to account for the organic growth of the mind from
sense perception to higher intelligence. Yet his criticism of
the grounds of human awareness laid the basis for a significant dichotomy between such knowledge as the mind can
possess of reality and the actual identity of what it beholds,
a division that was fated to become more evident and disturbing as time passed.

It is not surprising that by the mid-eighteenth century one
finds many writers and critics following Locke in using the
word "sensation" more deliberately and in such a way as to
preserve a distinction between the mind's knowledge and the
reality of the external world. David Hartley, for example,
defines "sensations" as "those internal Feelings of the Mind,
which arise from the Impressions made by external Objects
upon the several Parts of our Bodies."[8] Similarly Francis
Hutcheson writes that "those *Ideas* which are rais'd in the

[8] David Hartley, *Observations on Man, His Frame, His Duty, and His Expectations* (London, 1749), p. ii.

Mind upon the Presence of external Objects, and their acting upon our Bodies, are call'd *Sensations.*"[9] Such definitions testify to a growing dichotomy, at least in one area of human inquiry, between nature and mind. To be sure, one frequently finds the word used as a loose synonym for sense experience; however, Lord Kames is again more typical in his desire to use the term more strictly:

> *Perception* and *sensation* are commonly reckoned synonymous terms, signifying the consciousness we have of objects; but, in accurate language, they are distinguished. The consciousness we have of external objects, is termed *perception.* Thus we are said to perceive a certain animal, a certain colour, sound, taste, smell, &c. The consciousness we have of pleasure or pain arising from external objects, is termed *sensation.* Thus we have a sensation of cold, of heat, of the pain of a wound, of the pleasure of a landscape, of music, of beauty, of propriety, of behaviour, &c. The consciousness we have of internal action, such as deliberation, resolution, choice, is never termed either a perception or a sensation.[10]

Such a passage is typical in the way it distinguishes radically between sense impression and the broader range of human response that we are apt to include within the general terms of feeling and emotion.

Later in the century the division between the objective and subjective worlds, nature and mind, became even more categorical in the work of Thomas Reid, one of the founders of the so-called Scottish school of common sense philosophy. While working to bridge the gap by appealing to the common testimony of man's practical experience, Reid in some ways only emphasized it more by rigorously observing the critical distinctions drawn by predecessors such as Hume.

[9] Francis Hutcheson, *An Inquiry into the Original of our Ideas of Beauty and Virtue,* 5th ed. (London, 1753), p. 2 (Hutcheson's italics).
[10] Henry Home, Lord Kames, *Elements of Criticism* (Edinburgh, 1762), III, 378-79 (Kames's italics).

"Sensation," he writes, "is a name given by Philosophers to an act of mind, which may be distinguished from all others by this, that it hath no object distinct from the act itself."[11] Realizing, as Archibald Alison was shortly to argue, that matter is essentially dead and its qualities are "in themselves incapable of producing emotion, or the exercise of any affection,"[12] Reid saw that, strictly speaking, sensation could be defined in terms of the mind alone. "Sensation," he writes, "taken by itself, implies neither the conception nor belief of any external object. It supposes a sentient being, and a certain manner in which that being is affected, but it supposes no more."[13] Conceived in terms of such a definition, sensation becomes entirely subjective.

Of course, as Reid and others saw, it remained impossible in practice to make any final separation between external objects and sensation. Even if, as Hutcheson wrote, "Beauty," properly speaking, denotes not "any Quality suppos'd to be in the Object" but rather "the *Perception* of some Mind," just as "*Cold, Hot, Sweet, Bitter,* denote the Sensations in our Minds, to which perhaps there is no Resemblance in the Objects, which excite these Ideas in us," still, he observed, "we generally imagine otherwise."[14] More important was the notion, a commonplace of later eighteenth-century aesthetic criticism, of a vital accommodation between mind and object, perception and sensation, operating in a way most

[11] Thomas Reid, *Essays on the Intellectual Powers of Man* (Edinburgh, 1785), p. 33.

[12] Archibald Alison, *Essays on the Nature and Principles of Taste* (Edinburgh, 1790), p. 127.

[13] Reid, *Essays*, p. 233. Cf. the assertion of Berkeley, as cited by Reid's chief disciple, Dugald Stewart, that "as there can be no notion or thought but in a thinking being, so there can be no sensation but in a sentient being; it is the act or feeling of a sentient being; its very essence consists in being felt. Nothing can *resemble* a sensation, but a similar sensation in the same, or in some other mind. To think that any quality in a thing inanimate can *resemble* a sensation is absurd, and a contradiction in terms" (*Philosophical Essays* [Philadelphia and New York, 1811], p. 86).

[14] Hutcheson, *Original of our Ideas*, p. 14 (Hutcheson's italics).

analogous to a kind of instinct. Far from being merely incidental to the objects we observe, the sensations we experience
in the face of nature, it was argued, arise through a process
in which the mind both modifies and adjusts itself to the
identity of what it perceives. As Alexander Gerard phrased
it: "The law of sensation which we have in view, is this:
When an object is presented to any of our senses, the mind
conforms itself to its nature and appearance, feels an emotion, and is put in a frame suitable and analogous; of which
we have a perception by consciousness or reflection."[15] The
hypothesis of such a process of accommodation, in which the
mind instinctively "conforms itself" to the character of what
it observes, encouraged the notion of sensation as a vital
coalescence of mind with nature, in which the identity of the
external world is faithfully grasped and realized through the
modifications of the perceiving consciousness. Sensation is
regulated by laws inherent in the mind that bring impression
and response into ideal accordance. So, as Wordsworth was
to write, "feeling comes in aid / Of feeling"[16] in ways that
cannot logically be justified, yet which strike us as truthful
to the grounds of our experience. The premise that there is a
kind of instinct in control of sensation is fundamental to
much British associationism of the eighteenth century. Such
an explanation offered a practical bulwark against the extreme skepticism of Hume, who, following Locke, had driven
the wedge ever deeper between the mind and certain knowledge of reality.

Nevertheless, the notion of some inherent instinct adjust-
ing sensation to perception and mediating between the world
of consciousness and that of external reality was tenuous at
best and subject to continual question. For one thing, it
looked back to the old Shaftesburian idea of an inherent
"moral sense" and, more generally, to the whole doctrine of
innate ideas Locke had attacked so successfully in the open-

[15] Alexander Gerard, *An Essay on Taste*, 2nd ed. (Edinburgh, 1764),
p. 153.
[16] *The Prelude*, xii.269-70.

ing chapter of his *Essay*. For another thing, it was advanced and elaborated most influentially by those who were, at the same time, keenly aware of its difficulties and the possible objections to it. Thomas Reid, for example, relied on a persistent and deeply felt sense of some logical continuity linking perception and consciousness to defend his common-sense approach to the problem of epistemology. "We have reason to conclude in general," he declared, "that as the impressions on the organs, nerves, and brain, correspond exactly to the nature and conditions of the objects by which they are made; so our perceptions and sensations correspond to those impressions, and vary in kind, and in degree, as they vary."[17] Thus, he continued: "Every different perception is conjoined with a sensation that is proper to it. The one is the sign, the other the thing signified. They coalesce in our imagination. They are signified by one name, and are considered as one simple operation. The purposes of life do not require them to be distinguished."[18] Reid saw that analysis, were it carried far enough, could ultimately challenge the most fundamental kinds of relationship necessary to carrying on a day-to-day existence. In order to perform even the simplest operations one had to assume the consistency and reliability of his impressions. At the same time, however, Reid took care, as we have seen, to define "sensation" in such a way as to remove it from any necessary dependence on the world of objects, and in this, as in many other aspects of his argument, he revealed his unwillingness to challenge the fundamental distinctions drawn up by Hume. In adapting a passage from D'Alembert, Dugald Stewart, Reid's pupil and most influential defender, summed up what he thought to be the main principles of his master's philosophy "in point of doctrine as well of phraseology" so as to reveal the essential dilemma with which both struggled:

> The truth is, that as no relation whatever can be discovered between a sensation in the mind, and the object by which

[17] Reid, *Essays*, p. 81.   [18] *Ibid.*, p. 233.

it is occasioned, or at least to which we refer it, it does not appear possible to trace, by dint of reasoning, any practicable passage from the one to the other. Nothing but a species of *instinct,* more sure in its operation than reason itself, could so forcibly transport us across the gulf by which mind seems to be separated from the material world.[19]

If reasoning by itself is helpless to establish the grounds of our connection with the external universe, we can only fall back on some notion such as instinct to provide a satisfactory explanation. Yet it is, in philosophy at least, a rather questionable method of procedure to predicate a faculty in order to account for capacities that cannot be fully admitted to exist.

The logic of Stewart's argument reveals a fundamental paradox whose importance needs to be emphasized. The primary task of British empiricism followed Locke, like that of Wordsworth in his greatest poem, had been to explain the growth of the human mind from sense to reason. Like Wordsworth, too, philosophers and writers on aesthetics had conceived of that growth as a total process, a complex development from sense experience through imagination and reason to an organic and harmonious integration of the human faculties. In the *Essay Concerning Human Understanding* Locke provided those who followed him with a framework for visualizing the growth of human consciousness as an unbroken chain of development. Yet he also encouraged the propensity to examine the chain piece by piece, to break it into separate links, and to examine each with rigorous care and insistency. While treating the understanding and its evolution as a whole, he nevertheless encouraged writers to analyze its methods in terms of certain fixed operations. While he conceived of sensation, for example, as essentially the result of a single process, he resolved it into various stages of transference that have the effect of dividing the

[19] Stewart, *Philosophical Essays,* pp. 132-33 (Stewart's italics).

mind into separate areas of consciousness. Sense impressions are internalized as "ideas of sensation" along a single train of perception that both unites them and preserves them as distinct. As Reid characteristically observed, "The perception of external objects is one main link of that mysterious chain which connects the material world with the intellectual."[20] Like Stewart, one could emphasize the chain either as an unbroken progression or as a series of mysterious and inexplicable links, depending on whether one were more preoccupied with the practical or with the technical and theoretical aspects of the problem.

Such developments were to exercise an important bearing on the growth of English Romanticism where, as we have partly seen, the notion of sensation and the related idea of process were from the first primary. We often refer, especially in discussing Romantic poetry, to various stages in a process of growth or development. If, however, we are using our words with any strictness, there is bound to be an element of contradiction in such a notion. "Process" denotes movement and continuity; "stage" requires us to think in terms of fixed divisions. One of the major tendencies of British empiricism, and more especially the associationism that was its offspring, was to conceive of the development of the human mind in both ways simultaneously. While there was growing incentive for visualizing the evolution of human intelligence as the gradual organization and refinement of the elements of man's perception of the natural world, that assimilation was continually endangered by a dissolving realization of the inexplicable nature of the ties uniting matter and mind. There is a fundamental irony here: the ascending chain connecting the two worlds becomes increasingly the common metaphor for explaining the mind and its operations, even while its individual links are being tested and placed under the strain of intense and often skeptical investigation.

Various solutions to the problem of bridging the gap were advanced, and the history of late eighteenth- and early nine-

[20] Reid, *Essays*, p. 75.

teenth-century philosophy and aesthetics is in large measure
the record of attempts to investigate the most promising.
There was, to begin with, the attempt of David Hartley to
materialize the elements of Locke's system by explaining its
operations in purely physical terms. Hartley based his theory
on the notion of a very subtle and elastic fluid or "Aether"
diffused throughout space and occupying even "the Pores of
gross Bodies," an idea deriving primarily from some later
speculations of Sir Isaac Newton that were, by Hartley's day,
receiving increasing attention from investigators in a variety
of fields.[21] Sense impressions, he explained, were actually
minuscule vibrations radiating from physical objects and
transferring themselves to the nerve ends of the human body
through the medium of the aether. These vibrating motions
were then conveyed by aether surrounding the capillary substance of the nerves and impressed upon the brain, where
they tended to linger as "vestiges." By dint of repetition, such
vestiges became transformed in time to "vibratiuncles" possessing a certain permanence and autonomy. Essentially intellectual in nature, they nevertheless corresponded in everything except intensity to the sensory vibrations that gave rise
to them. By postulating an unbroken physical medium or
aether connecting objects and the brain and a series of vibrations passing across it, Hartley established for his system a
direct relationship between the world of natural objects and
the operations of the human intellect. Yet his conception of
the human organism as a kind of aeolian harp vibrating complexly but passively beneath the impulses of nature was repel-
lent to many of his contemporaries and involved considerable
difficulties, not the least of which was the question of free will.

If Hartley's materialism exploited, at the expense of some
apparent oversimplification, the dynamic and constructive
aspects of Locke's formulations, the immaterialism of Berkeley was the logical result of Locke's methods of decomposition and analysis carried to an extreme. The two were, as

[21] *Observations on Man*, pp. 13ff., 56ff.

Abraham Tucker perceived, largely opposite sides of a single coin. If Hartley reduced man to a parcel of vibrating vapors, "the late bishop of Clogher," Tucker wrote, "goes into a contrary extreme, for he allows us neither ether nor nerves nor organs nor limbs nor external substances nor space nor distance."[22] Berkeley, of course, never denied the phenomena of sense perception; it was sufficient for him to argue merely that they bear no necessary or verifiable correspondence to an external reality. The fact that we, in common with our fellows, daily depend and act on a wealth of sense impressions was one Berkeley preferred to attribute to the controlling intelligence of a divine mind in whom we live and move and have our being than to account for by postulating a world of material objects. While Hartley sought to bridge the gap between substance and intelligence by evolving a conception of matter that would gradually encompass mind, Berkeley annihilated the gap categorically, subsuming matter in mind through the logic of a seemingly irrefutable argument. Neither account of sensation, however supported by science or reasoning, could ultimately prevail over the dictates of common sense or the deeper instincts of human nature. Johnson's vulgar but effective "refutation" of Berkeley and Coleridge's more laborious extrication from the toils of Hartley's materialism express dissatisfactions that are basic. Primarily, neither account of sensation accorded the human mind that active and vital role in shaping experience that we feel to be an inalienable part of our day-to-day reality. Neither sufficiently accounted for such elements as taste, discrimination, sensitivity, and intuition—qualities that ultimately came to be united in the single term "imagination."

The chief effort of most later eighteenth-century aesthetic theorizing was, in effect, directed toward the discovery of some middle ground between the two extremes that would respect both the creativity of the mind and the identity of matter in accounting for the nature of aesthetic experience.

[22] Abraham Tucker [Edward Search], *The Light of Nature Pursued* (London, 1768), I, 51.

If one could not agree with Hartley in materializing Locke's outline of the process or with Berkeley in subsuming the whole question in an enveloping idealism, it was necessary to provide some alternative account. The most influential of such attempts concentrated, as we have partly seen, around the effort to define "sensation" as a vital coalescence in which the qualities of both mind and matter were subsumed and realized. Through continual association, sense impressions not only called up but ultimately merged with the mental images or "ideas" that corresponded to them. While in theory it might remain necessary to discriminate between the object itself and its image in the mind, in actuality they ran together so inseparably as virtually to fuse. In all but abstract terms it was impossible to distinguish between them. Among comments one might cite from a variety of writers of different emphasis, those of Thomas Reid seemed, in their moderation and reasonableness, especially persuasive:

> The number and quick succession of the operations of the mind make it difficult to give due attention to them. It is well known, that if a great number of objects be presented in quick succession, even to the eye, they are confounded in the memory and imagination. We retain a confused notion of the whole, and a more confused one of the several parts, especially if they are objects to which we have never before given particular attention. No succession can be more quick than that of thought. The mind is busy while we are awake, continually passing from one thought, and one operation, to another. The scene is constantly shifting.[23]

Reid argues tellingly that, even with the utmost concentration, our powers of introspection never permit us to divide consciousness into neat categories like "perception" or "image," "outer" or "inner." Moreover his argument approaches a further point. It is typical that, while writing from the standard associationist premise of a succession of images or

[23] Reid, *Essays*, p. 62.

ideas, Reid nevertheless approaches the notion that the mind takes in and organizes what it perceives as wholes. Through memory and imagination, any single impression may call up a whole group of related elements—feelings, ideas, recollections—that actively respond to and enlarge it, merging with it as a complex totality. For a philosopher like Reid, habituated by temperament to preserving, as far as possible, orderly distinctions between the human faculties, such complexity was bound to seem disconcerting in its "confusion" and resistance to analysis. In the field of aesthetics, on the other hand, the growing realization of the complicated nature of sensation was more openly welcome, for it tended to support, if somewhat vaguely, the evolution toward a more organic approach to the problem of perception that would respect both the fundamental truths of sense experience and the active, shaping powers of the mind.

The purpose of this introductory chapter is not to provide a general review of the development of the theory of coalescence, a subject treated at length by other writers, most notably by W. J. Bate.[24] It is rather to define certain key problems surrounding the idea of sensation with which philosophers and aestheticians, following Locke, had increasingly to deal and which were to take on practical importance for poets in the Romantic period. Once broadly outlined, such problems can be best exemplified and pursued in terms of the work of a single writer, Abraham Tucker. For one thing it was his lengthy and prolix *The Light of Nature Pursued* that Keats's intellectual mentor, William Hazlitt, was to champion, abridge, and absorb, in certain

[24] *From Classic to Romantic: Premises of Taste in Eighteenth-Century England* (Cambridge, Mass., 1946). Although I differ in points of emphasis, I am throughout this chapter indebted to Bate's discussion as well as to Samuel H. Monk's *The Sublime: A Study of Critical Theories in XVIII-Century England* (New York, 1935), a work that emphasizes a growing subjectivism in the period in a way that contrasts usefully with Bate. Ernest Lee Tuveson's *The Imagination as a Means of Grace: Locke and the Aesthetics of Romanticism* (Berkeley and Los Angeles, 1960) has also been highly suggestive.

ways, into the current of his own thinking. While difficult and frequently obscure, Tucker's treatise is remarkable for the vigor of its attempt to develop the basic premises of associationism in such a way as to enable him to push beyond them toward a more vital conception of the growth of human intelligence. Like a number of others, Tucker began by emphasizing the quality of instinct, starting from the behavior of many insects and beasts whose unreasoning capacity to perform complex acts necessary to their survival precisely at the moment required had been a source of admiration in the ancient world. Such knowledge, variously described as instinct, intuition, insight, and sympathy, had from the time of antiquity often been likened to a kind of sixth sense, essentially mysterious in its origins and method of operation. Tucker, however, preferred to explain it as an outgrowth or coalescence of the other five and in accord with the principal laws of association.

Although working toward a unified view of human intelligence, Tucker was led by his preoccupation with the nature of instinct to draw a distinction between the faculties of imagination and understanding, a division he himself was quick to acknowledge as artificial but also to find useful, one that in some ways looked forward to Coleridge's more famous discrimination. Imagination is that whole store of impressions and sensations of which the mind has cognizance, together with all the images and associations connecting them. It is synonymous, in other words, with the total contents of the mind and its faculties as they have developed through time and as they exist in their capacity fully to respond to new experience. An act of understanding, on the other hand, is the deliberate use of our faculties for some particular end or purpose. It is the limited and directed use of our physical and mental powers and therefore inevitably falls, to some degree, within the province of the more inclusive faculty. At the same time imagination is crucially dependent on the excursive and more specialized powers of

24

the understanding for its sources of fresh knowledge and experience. The distinction Tucker draws between the two, as well as his sense of the necessary cooperation that exists between them, emerges in the following passage:

> Understanding commonly draws imagination after it, but not always nor immediately. . . . A discovery that we have worked out by a consideration of various particulars often loses its force as soon as the proofs whereon it depended have slipped out of our sight: the next time we employ our thoughts upon it we arrive at the conclusion sooner, and upon every repeated trial our process grows shorter and shorter, until in time we learn to discern the thing so discovered to be true upon a very little reflection without the suggestion of any proof: upon further acquaintance it takes the nature of a self-evident truth, the judgement arising instantaneously in the same assemblage with the terms, and then becomes a property of imagination.[25]

At first glance Tucker seems to be describing merely the telescoping of the associative process, one of the commonplaces of associationist theory. Yet it is clear that something more than a restatement of the familiar mechanism is involved, for the end result, the point at which a truth arises in the mind "instantaneously" with its terms, implies an immediacy that is distinct in kind from the various stages of the process giving rise to it. It is just this point, the way in which understanding passes over into imagination, that is critical to the originality and logic of Tucker's theorizing. We have seen that associationism had for some time developed the idea that the mind, through habit and training, naturally acquires an ingrained responsiveness that gives it an essentially creative rather than merely passive role in consciousness. Yet Tucker pushes the tendency one stage further by arguing that, after a point, such store of knowledge can acquire an autonomy of its own, a freedom from any mechan-

[25] Tucker, *Light of Nature Pursued*, I, 352-53.

ical dependence on the trains of association through which it has been achieved. Such knowledge that has become habitual and spontaneous he describes as "instinct."

It would be misleading to overstate Tucker's actual importance in the period. Nevertheless his treatise represents a fascinating attempt to elaborate a more dynamic concept of the graduated and accumulative pattern of the growth of human intelligence that associationism and its analysis of the mind's various operations had set forth. While distinguishing between imagination and understanding, he never actually divides them. The two are mutually embracing and cooperate continuously and "contribute to enlarge one another's stores."[26] While it draws upon and digests the findings of the understanding, the imagination at the same time directs the reasoning of the other faculty in its quest for logical certainty. Here Tucker argues the pervasiveness of instinct more subtly and from a different direction. Is it really possible, he asks, to suppose that our powers of concentration and reflection, the chief faculties of understanding, ever act independently of influences that are more profound? Even while we are applying our power of reasoning to a problem under investigation, we are subtly guiding it along the path to some conclusion, for there must be some deeper insight at work to explain the direction it takes among the bewildering possibilities that confront it at every turn. The imagination, as a kind of instinct, must be latent and play "an under part"[27] in guiding the intelligence even in its more customary and methodical operations, just as the understanding must act to "transfer over some part of her treasures to imagination" in return.[28] Yet such reciprocity cannot be described so much as a process of transference as an act of genuine coalescence, for it involves for Tucker a *qualitative* change supported by his notion, borrowed from chemistry, that "a compound may have properties resulting from the composition which do not belong to the parts

[26] *Ibid.*, p. 353.   [27] *Ibid.*, p. 346.   [28] *Ibid.*, p. 353.

singly whereof it consists."[29] Several of these interrelated ideas have, as we shall shortly see, a suggestive relationship to Keats's metaphoric notion of the operation of the spirit of poetry.

Tucker's development of the doctrine of coalescence and his view of imagination as the functioning of the whole mind in all its faculties represents a remarkable attempt to adapt the mechanism of association to a more organic view of human experience. His analysis of the workings of imagination and understanding as distinct yet complementary functions of the mind looks forward in certain ways to the dynamics of modern psychology. Yet it also looks back to Locke's discrimination between sensation and reflection as the two great functions of the mind. It is, in short, a moot question to what degree Tucker genuinely succeeds in freeing himself from the mechanism of association and to what degree he merely complicates it. Insofar as his efforts were characteristic of a general need to expand the capabilities of associationist thinking, they provide a telling comment on much that was to follow. Certainly his ideas about the independence of the imagination and its controlling influence over the mechanical operation of the understanding and about their capacity for a kind of chemical synthesis are striking and suggestive. The problem, however, remained whether such notions could prove compatible with the pragmatic and empirical foundations on which the main outline of associationism rested. There comes to mind again the statement Dugald Stewart adapted from D'Alembert: "Nothing but a species of instinct, more sure in its operation than reason itself, could so forcibly transport us across the gulf by which mind seems to be separated from the material world." Faced with the mysterious nature of such a power, one could either resign oneself to its inscrutability or, like Tucker, develop various hypotheses to explain it. What remained to be seen was how far such explanations could proceed with-

[29] *Ibid.*, p. 338.

out recourse to arguments of a mystical or transcendental kind or to evident illogic.

III

The concerns of this chapter may seem a far cry from the poetry of the Romantic era, especially that of John Keats. Such is not, however, the case. There has always been an important tie between philosophy and poetry, one that can be self-conscious and deliberate but which is more fundamentally revealed through their common use of metaphor. Both poets and (until, perhaps, very recently) philosophers have relied on metaphor to express their awareness of the phenomena and processes with which they must inevitably concern themselves. No poet, not even one so disinclined to any systematic theorizing as Keats, can do without the means of explaining, if only to himself, the nature of certain basic processes: the manner in which poetry originates, the method of its operation, and the way it appeals to other minds and achieves its effects. If, as in Keats's case, the understanding of these relationships remains largely metaphoric and unconscious, it can for that very reason assume greater importance.

It is here that some awareness of the major problem confronting English philosophy in the Enlightenment is most useful: the task of rendering a satisfactory account, sufficiently definite and at the same time inclusive, of sensation. For one finds that, in a somewhat different way, this was also the task of poets in the main movement of English Romanticism. In philosophy the work proceeded through the attempt to abstract and define the nature of sensation by analyzing the channels and processes connecting the mind and the external world. In verse it took the form of an attempt to infuse a new vitality into poetry itself by drawing out and realizing to the full the complex powers of human response in a way that had not been sought after by an earlier poetry of wit, a poetry that conceived of sensation largely in terms of the stereotype of the Lockean "image" or "idea." The two efforts to extend the boundaries of sensation were bound to overlap, whether for poets who deliberately set out to observe and illustrate "the primary laws of our nature"[30] or those whose intentions were less formalized and still emergent. The two tasks have, moreover, much to reveal about each other, especially in the kinds of problems they encounter and the resolutions or expedients they adopt. One may be justified in taking Keats, as is usually done, simply within the context of his poems and letters. Even here, however, there is some use in knowing that the problems with which he struggled and which became critical to the course of his career were more than the offspring of his own imagination; they were fundamental to his age.

[30] William Wordsworth, Preface to the second edition of *Lyrical Ballads, The Poetical Works of William Wordsworth*, ed. Ernest de Selincourt (Oxford, 1952), II, 386.

CHAPTER TWO

THE CHEMISTRY OF
THE POETIC PROCESS

ALTHOUGH the major premises underlying Keats's view of poetry as an art have been extensively examined in recent years, critics have never made the attempt to define his conception of the poetic process, that is, the way in which poetry is created or conceived, with the exactness it deserves. The question is of more than theoretic interest, for, beyond the work of any other major English poet in the nineteenth century, Keats's verse can be read throughout as a deepening investigation of the sources of creative inspiration. As everyone knows, poetry originates for Keats in a contemplation of the natural world and in a full awareness of the various sense impressions it affords. Indeed poetry both arises from and distills a heightened sense of external reality. Yet it is at this point that certain major questions begin to arise concerning the pattern of his thinking about the poetic processes that are of fundamental consequence to his evolution as a poet. For example, Keats is often inclined to view natural objects as only various starting points "towards all 'the two-and thirty Pallaces'" of the mind and to regard poetry as a kind of "voyage of conception" (I, 231) that withdraws the poet from the material world into some higher or imaginative realm. As Clarence Thorpe, elucidating Keats's youthful view of the imagination, has put it in his sane and useful study of the poet's mind: "In the presence of natural objects of unusual beauty or significance, the poet becomes oblivious of the present world. He loses himself in contemplation, becomes detached from his surroundings, as 'fainter-gleamings' shoot over his fancy, and visions of human form appear, until presently his imagination takes wing, and poetic creation is accomplished."[1] Sleep and dreaming are the most frequent analogues for imaginative experience in Keats's work. Thorpe allows, of course, for an element of growth in such a formulation, corresponding to his sense of Keats's development as poet and thinker. As he puts it, summarizing Keats's more mature view: "The poet must still fly to his dream world, but in his flight he does not escape reality; rather he carries with him, to shape and inform his vision, the stored-up experiences of a life spent in sympathetic contact with his fellow-men."[2] The creation of poetry begins with an awareness of the real world but culminates only in flight to some higher or imaginative realm, although in what sense the poet can be thought to "carry" his experience of the actual world with him is not altogether clear.

If Thorpe emphasizes the way in which the poet, in Keats's view, withdraws the elements of reality into the dreamworld of his own consciousness, W. J. Bate sees the creative process as an imaginative penetration or vitalization of the concrete and actual. Following his broader study of the backgrounds of the Romantic imagination in the philosophy and aesthetic theorizing of an earlier age, Bate interprets the nature of creative apprehension, as Keats describes and conceives it, as a harmonious coalescence of the perceiving mind and its objects within a common ground they share between them.[3] Far from withdrawing the poet into distant realms,

---

[1] Clarence Dewitt Thorpe, *The Mind of John Keats* (New York, 1926), p. 50. The notion of poetic creation as imaginative release has been examined recently within the context of Keats's imagery by Mario L. D'Avanzo in *Keats's Metaphors for the Poetic Imagination* (Durham, N.C., 1967). See esp. ch. 3.

[2] Thorpe, *Mind of John Keats*, p. 94.

[3] See the important discussion in "Negative Capability," Walter Jackson Bate, *John Keats* (Cambridge, Mass., 1963), ch. 10, reprinted in somewhat abbreviated form in *Keats: A Collection of Critical Essays*, ed. Walter Jackson Bate (Englewood Cliffs, N.J., 1964), pp. 51-68. It is, of course, impossible to summarize adequately Bate's views, drawing

31

the imagination, in Bate's view, acts to supplement, to channel, even in a sense to create the sensory qualities we apprehend in nature or in art. Working, like Hazlitt's "gusto," through an immediacy of response, the imagination is habituated, through long experience, to construct from least suggestions, to seize in a moment of intuition an aspect of reality in its full complexity and richness. It selects and reinforces, without necessarily distorting, our primary impressions of nature. While for Thorpe the imagination conveys the poet to a world apart, analogous to the real world, for Bate it acts chiefly as an extension and heightening of our powers of sense experience.

The two views, emphasizing alternately abstraction from and immersion in the world of material phenomena, are equally central to Keats's conception of the nature of aesthetic experience. Yet they raise certain basic questions, in particular the problem of how two such different ideals of the imagination, while not necessarily irreconcilable, can be thought compatible. The problem is one most important criticism of the poet has, in one way or another, touched on, if only in passing. It accounts, for example, for the way in which Earl Wasserman, in the opening pages of his influential study, borrows Kenneth Burke's term, the "mystic oxymoron," to describe a kind of "paradoxical essence" that is "the central principle of Keats' visions"—the way in which the poet, through use of metaphor, "invests the physical with the ethereal."[4] It is intimately related to Albert Gérard's broader conception of Romantic poetry as the product of a *tertium quid* between the human mind and matter.[5] If poetry is the result of such a vital coalescence,

---

as they do on his interpretation of the main current of eighteenth- and earlier nineteenth-century aesthetics. See esp. the later chapters of his *From Classic to Romantic* (Cambridge, Mass., 1946).

[4] Earl R. Wasserman, *The Finer Tone: Keats' Major Poems* (Baltimore, 1953), pp. 15-16 and n.

[5] See Albert S. Gérard, *English Romantic Poetry: Ethos, Structure, and Symbol in Coleridge, Wordsworth, Shelley, and Keats* (Berkeley and Los Angeles, 1968), pp. 6, 8.

what, more exactly, are the grounds and logic of its processes? The intention of this chapter is to show how Keats approached such problems, in fact the whole question of the imagination and its activity, with the help of certain fundamental analogies borrowed from contemporary science. An understanding of these analogies, their interrelationships and capacity for change and evolution, provide a basic means for grasping the significance of particular works within the broad current of his intellectual development.

II

Keats consistently grants a fundamental reality to the forms and beings of the natural world. For Wordsworth there were times, as he recalled from his youth, when "I was often unable to think of external things as having external existence, and I communed with all that I saw as something not apart from, but inherent in, my own immaterial nature. Many times while going to school have I grasped at a wall or tree to recall myself from this abyss of idealism to the reality."[6] There were no such moments, as far as we know, for Keats, and it is hard to imagine there being any. His response to the objects and movements around him was too open and immediate and his grasp on experience too particular and concrete. "The Sun, the Moon, the Sea and Men and Women who are creatures of impulse," he writes in a typical passage, "are poetical and have about them an unchangeable attribute" (I, 387). Keats's favorite term for this "attribute" is "identity," by which he means a nucleus of individual traits or distinct characteristics perceivable, in the first place, by the senses and held in close association in imagination. "All God's Creatures"—inanimate objects within a landscape, animals, and human beings—possess for him such identity, growing and changing, perhaps, through time as their natures are more fully borne home to him. Much of the

[6] *The Poetical Works of William Wordsworth*, ed. Ernest de Selincourt and Helen Darbishire (London, 1947), IV, 463.

joyousness of his verse and letters arises from a pure delight in observing and amplifying such discriminations, a pleasure that strikes him as poetical in the most fundamental way and which links him with Chaucer.

However strong and insistent Keats's sense of the identity of the particular forms of life around him may be, his conception of poetry involves much more than observation alone. For one thing, the universe of material phenomena is both multitudinous and commonplace, and there is a sense in which Keats, like any poet, would agree with Coleridge that "objects (*as* objects) are essentially fixed and dead," and that "images, however beautiful, though faithfully copied from nature, and as accurately represented in words, do not of themselves characterize the poet."[7] Objects are primarily of concern to a poet or his readers only insofar as their identities are extended or modified by feeling and emotion, and this process (or the conception of it) can differ radically in different poets. It is at this point that a number of questions are apt to arise of critical importance in any discussion of Romantic art but of particular relevance to Keats, a poet whose sensibility is so much grounded in the senses. Very broadly, those questions concern the way in which the images of sense experience are transformed to those of verse.

From the outset of his career Keats realized the poetical process transcends the separate identities of the objects or beings it involves and that the poet's role is essentially creative, not merely imitative. In an early letter to Haydon he writes of "looking upon the Sun the Moon the Stars, the Earth and its contents as materials to form greater things— that is to say ethereal things" (1, 143). In another letter, written from the Lake District at the outset of his walking tour with Brown, he comments: "I shall learn poetry here and shall henceforth write more than ever, for the abstract endeavor of being able to add a mite to that mass of beauty

[7] Samuel Taylor Coleridge, *Biographia Literaria*, ed. J. Shawcross (London, 1907), 1, 202; 11, 16.

34

which is harvested from these grand materials, by the finest spirits, and put into etherial existence for the relish of one's fellows" (I, 301). Both these passages refer to an underlying idea of a creative process, although its precise nature is far from clear. One important clue, however, is Keats's use of the words "material" and "ethereal." One finds the two terms, continual favorites, frequently juxtaposed throughout the poetry and letters. Indeed one can go further and say that "etherealization," or the way in which material forms are "put into etherial existence," is close to the heart of his notion of poetic creativity.

Keats may have been familiar from his reading with the classical conception of ether as a thin, subtle matter, finer and rarer than air, comprising the whole of outer or heavenly space. The classical distinction between elementary and ethereal matter postulated a world of flux and mutability and, beyond it, a domain of perfect substance or "quintessence," homogeneous, transcendent, and unchanging.[8] Yet the traditional division between the two realms of being seems at odds with Keats's conception in one important respect. Keats imagines a differentiation but not a complete separation between the two domains, for the ethereal or poetic elements are in some way compounded out of the material phenomena that provide their basis for existence. In his use of "ethereal" it is far more likely that Keats was drawing on a general awareness of various theories, derived in England primarily from Newton, concerning certain imponderable or subtle fluids diffused throughout the atmosphere, theories that were becoming ever more common in the science of his day as a means of explaining the transmission and operation of light, heat, and other chemical forces throughout the universe.[9]

---

[8] Although to some degree prefigured in earlier Greek thought, the conception derives largely from the cosmology of Aristotle. See George Sarton, A History of Science (Cambridge, Mass., 1952), I, 242, 452, 475, 509.

[9] See in particular the discussion of Hartley, p. 20 above.

More specifically, we should remember that Keats spent several years immediately preceding his break for freedom and for poetry at medical school in close study of the sciences. At Guy's Hospital he took two courses in chemistry,[10] and the degree to which his sense of the poetic processes is conditioned by his knowledge of that discipline has never been appreciated. In the course of a letter to Haydon, for example, he refers in a famous phrase to the "innumerable compositions and decompositions which take place between the intellect and its thousand materials before it arrives at that trembling delicate and snail-horn perception of Beauty" (1, 265). It is interesting to note on the first page of the syllabus he probably used for his chemistry courses, by William Babington and William Allen, and again in the manuscript of Babington's lectures from which the syllabus was in part drawn up, the following definition: "CHEMISTRY [is] therefore defined, *The Science of the Composition and Decomposition of the heterogeneous particles of Matter.*"[11] The definition is a standard one, repeated in one form or another over and again in late eighteenth- and early nineteenth-century manuals of chemistry. Keats no doubt adopted the phrase more immediately from a passage in Hazlitt's lecture "On Shakespeare and Milton," a work he knew intimately, where its chemical context is fully apparent. Hazlitt declared:

[10] The courses are noted as a part of Keats's record on a page of the register of Apothecaries' Hall. See Amy Lowell, *John Keats* (Boston, 1925), I, 154.

[11] William Babington, M.D., and William Allen, F.L.S., *A Syllabus of a Course of Chemical Lectures Read at Guy's Hospital* (London, 1802), p. 1. The same definition appears on the second page of the MS of Babington's lectures preserved in the Wills Library, Guy's Hospital. Keats attended lectures in 1815-1816. I am indebted to Mr. A. H. Burfoot, Clerk to the Governors, and to Mr. W.H.G. Hills, Librarian of the Wills Library, for the information that, since Allen was traveling on the Continent in 1816, Keats may have attended lectures given by either Babington or Alexander Marcet, who joined Babington and Allen in bringing out a revised edition of the syllabus in 1816. According to Robert Gittings the courses in chemistry that Keats attended were given by Marcet (*John Keats* [London, 1968], p. 49).

"In Chaucer we perceive a fixed essence of character. In Shakspeare there is a continual composition and decomposition of its elements, a fermentation of every particle in the whole mass, by its alternate affinity or antipathy to other principles which are brought in contact with it. Till the experiment is tried, we do not know the result, the turn which the character will take in its new circumstances."[12] As Keats undoubtedly realized, the basic analogy Hazlitt was relying on to convey his sense of the poetical process was that of an experiment in chemistry, while Hazlitt's major terms retained a strong tincture of their exact chemical significance. Indeed it is worth observing how many of Keats's favorite words for referring to poetry or the process by which it is created— "abstract" and "abstraction," "spirit" and "spiritual," "essence" and "essential," "intense" and "intensity," "distill" and "distillation," "empyreal," "ethereal," "sublime"—all have more or less exact meanings in the chemistry of his day. If a study of Plato, Locke, and Freud each in its way throws a certain light on Keats's mind and art, such a work as Sir Humphry Davy's *Elements of Chemical Philosophy* (1812) is also highly revealing.

Keats often uses such a common poetic word as "ethereal" only in its loosest sense. However, by his day the term, and a number of others like it, had begun to acquire an increasing range of exact, scientific denotations.[13] More important,

[12] *The Complete Works of William Hazlitt*, ed. P. P. Howe (London, 1930), v, 51.

[13] In *Newton Demands the Muse* (Princeton, N.J., 1946) Marjorie Nicolson has shown how for poets the two contexts, the general and the scientific, had already begun to overlap and interassimilate well before Keats's day. See particularly her discussion of such a central poet as Thomson and his use of "ether" (pp. 48-50). One could cite, more specifically, Keats's copy of John Bonnycastle's *An Introduction to Astronomy*, a school prize which, as Bate remarks (*John Keats*, p. 26n.), there is no reason to doubt the poet read. The word is there used in its general or classical sense at least four times in quotations from Ovid and Homer (in translation) and Milton (4th ed. [London, 1803], pp. 146, 161, 314). Yet Bonnycastle also defines the word in his glossary of scientific terms (p. 428) and explains its relevance to Newton's ideas,

Keats himself at times uses such words with obvious awareness of their technical or scientific meaning. In the famous
letter to Bailey of November 1817, in which he compares
the imagination in its mode of operation to Adam's dream,
he asserts that "Men of Genius are great as certain ethereal
Chemicals operating on the Mass of neutral intellect—by
[*for* but] they have not any individuality, any determined
Character" (1, 184). Here again one encounters an important
figure drawn from chemistry and evidence that Keats is
using the term "ethereal" in a far more exact context than
has been commonly assumed. That context becomes plainer
if one turns to Sir Humphry Davy's discussion "Of Radiant
or Ethereal Matter," a section he introduces with the words:

> In treating of the different substances which, by their
> agencies, combinations, or decompositions, produce the
> phenomena of chemistry—*radiant* or *ethereal matters* will
> be first considered, as their principal effects seem rather to
> depend upon their communicating motion to the particles
> of common matter, or modifying their attractions, than to
> their actually entering into combination with them; and
> as from the laws of their motions, or from their extreme
> subtileness, they are incapable of being weighed.[14]

It is a notable fact that Sir Isaac Newton, developing certain
ideas of the existence of an ether persisting from the Greeks
through Descartes, advanced the notion of a universal
medium rarer and more elastic than air that was basic to the

---

albeit in a much oversimplified and skeptical fashion (pp. 95-96). See
also George Bornstein's "Keats's Concept of the Ethereal," *Keats-
Shelley Journal*, xviii (1969), 97-106, an article that discusses Keats's
use of the term within a different context.

[14] Sir Humphry Davy, *Elements of Chemical Philosophy*, *The Collected Works of Sir Humphry Davy*, ed. John Davy (London, 1839-
1840), iv, 140 (Davy's italics). For purposes of convenience references
are to this edition rather than that of 1812, the text of which is virtually identical to that cited. Unless otherwise noted, quotations from
Davy are from the *Elements of Chemical Philosophy* and are included
in parentheses within the text.

earth's atmosphere and had the power to effect changes on the earth's surface through the action of light, heat, and other rays of an indefinable nature. Not so much a theory as a loose hypothesis tantalizingly thrown out at the end of the *Principia* and amplified to some degree in the Queries at the end of the *Opticks*, the notion became steadily more intriguing to eighteenth-century scientists as a way of accounting for a number of the otherwise mysterious phenomena of optics, physics, and chemistry.[15] The conception of an ether passed into the mainstream of earlier nineteenth-century science and became of primary concern to so central a figure as Davy, the teacher of Michael Faraday, the friend and correspondent of Coleridge and Wordsworth, a poet in his own right, and one of the most celebrated scientists of his generation. Davy explains such "imponderable" or "subtle" fluids:

Besides these [other] forms of matter [solids, fluids, gases] which are easily submitted to experiment, and the parts of which may be considered as in a state of apparent rest, there are other forms of matter which are known to us only in their states of motion when acting upon our organs of sense, or upon other matter, and which are not susceptible of being confined. They have been sometimes called *etherial substances*, which appears a more unexceptionable name than *imponderable substances*. It cannot be doubted that there is matter in motion in space, between the sun and the stars and our globe, though it is a subject of discussion whether successions of particles be emitted from these heavenly bodies, or motions communicated by them, to particles in their vicinity, and transmitted by successive

[15] Perhaps the best discussions of ethereal fluids and their influence following Newton are contained in "The Education of a Philosopher," ch. 2 of L. Pearce Williams's *Michael Faraday* (New York, 1964), and in the earlier chapters of I. Bernard Cohen's *Franklin and Newton* (Philadelphia, 1956). See also Carl Grabo's *A Newton Among Poets* (Chapel Hill, N.C., 1930), esp. chs. 6 and 7, which discuss the theories of Newton, Davy, and others and their effect on Shelley.

impulses to other particles. *Etherial* matter differs either in its nature, or in its affections by motion; for it produces different effects; for instance, as radiant heat, and as different kinds of light.   (IV, 45-46; Davy's italics)

The notion of an ethereal matter forever at work in the world's atmosphere and bringing about continual changes in its elements offered Keats a useful and suggestive parallel to the operation of the spirit of poetry. Thus, near the beginning of Book Three of *Endymion*, for example, he pauses to pay tribute to those

> *ethereal things* that, unconfin'd,
> Can make a ladder of the eternal wind,
> And poise about in cloudy thunder-tents
> To watch the abysm-birth of elements.
> Aye, 'bove the withering of old-lipp'd Fate
> A thousand Powers keep religious state,
> In water, fiery realm, and airy bourne;
> And, silent as a consecrated urn,
> Hold sphery sessions for a season due.
> Yet few of these far majesties, ah, few!
> Have bared their operations to this globe.[16]

Here, as elsewhere, Keats's use of "ethereal," and, indeed, the meaning of the passage as a whole, is illuminated by some understanding of contemporary science.

More broadly, what the sciences, and in particular chemistry, provided Keats was a set of analogies useful in ex-

---

[16] *Endymion*, iii.25-35. Unless otherwise noted, all quotations from Keats's poetry are from *John Keats: Selected Poems and Letters*, ed. Douglas Bush (Boston, 1959), and are hereafter included in the text. Unless otherwise noted, italics are mine. In *The Consecrated Urn* (London, 1959) Bernard Blackstone discusses this passage and Keats's use of "ethereal" generally within the context of the Hermetic and alchemical philosophy of Agrippa, Burton, and the *Timaeus*. In my view the parallels between Keats's poetic theory and contemporary chemistry are more fundamental and revealing. See Blackstone, *The Consecrated Urn*, pp. 101, 112-13, 149-50, and passim.

plaining the origin and operation of poetry as an immaterial or "spiritual" power active throughout the universe. As Davy asserts, "The forms and appearances of the beings and substances of the external world are almost infinitely various, and they are in a state of continued alteration: the whole surface of the earth even undergoes modifications." He goes on to explain how "a series of decompositions and recombinations are constantly occurring in the phenomena of nature, and in the operations of art" by which "one variety of matter becomes as it were transmuted into another." "The object of Chemical Philosophy," therefore, "is to ascertain the causes of all phenomena of this kind, and to discover the laws by which they are governed" (IV, 43, 374-75, 1). In a similar way poetry can be said to operate through the laws by which the mind, and more especially the imagination, assimilates and transmutes the impressions it derives from nature and the way, in turn, such distillations react upon general consciousness once they have been brought into existence. As Davy observes during the course of an introductory lecture:

A certain portion of physical knowledge is essential to our existence; and all efficient exertion is founded upon an accurate and minute acquaintance with the properties of the different objects surrounding us. The germ of power indeed is native; but it can only be nourished by the forms of the external world. The food of the imagination is supplied by the senses, and all ideas existing in the human mind are representations of parts of nature accurately delineated by memory, or tinged with the glow of passion, and formed into new combinations by fancy.[17]

For Keats, certain fundamental analogies between the laws of physical change and the processes of the imagination were

[17] "A Discourse Introductory to a Course of Lectures on Chemistry" (1802), *Works*, II, 324-25. Cf. Woodhouse's remarks to Keats in a letter of October 1818, *Letters*, I, 380.

current and readily available in the chemical theory of his day.

Of course the poet, like the chemist, does more than merely observe the existence of such principles. He makes use of them and puts them into practice. As Babington asserts, the "Natural Phylosopher is not content with observing the appearances which these bodies exhibit when left to themselves but interrogates nature more closely, & exercises his invention by putting them into a variety of new & artificial situations."[18] In practice this means, following the logic of Hazlitt's metaphor, experimentation on the state of substances or their ability to separate, combine, or react upon each other ("till the experiment is tried, we do not know the result, the turn which the character will take in its new circumstances").

Chemical changes come about in several ways. First, substances may separate or unite to form new compounds, for, as Davy observes, "That bodies differing in nature blend or unite with each other into a common mass possessed of new properties, is the most simple and ancient fact of chemical affinity."[19] Bodies can also assume different states or forms: solids can become fluids and fluids gases, or vice versa. All such changes, however, come about primarily through the agency of heat or "caloric" (to use the term increasingly favored by chemists to distinguish it from mere sensation) in compliance with the fundamental law that "in all chemical changes there is an alteration of temperature" (IV, 64).[20] Such changes, too, are closely interrelated, for just as heat, when applied to bodies, brings about "changes in their forms of aggregation," so it "is possessed of most extensive powers in producing chemical combinations, and decompositions."[21] Such principles are summarized by the well-known

[18] MS of Babington's lectures, Wills Library, Guy's Hospital, p. 4.

[19] *Miscellaneous Lectures*, Works, VIII, 283.

[20] See also IV, 60-61, where Davy cites Black's law.

[21] A *Syllabus of a Course of Lectures on Chemistry* (1802), Works, II, 387.

French chemist, A. F. Fourcroy, in the form of several laws that Keats would have been familiar with from his own studies:

> There is not a single experiment in chemistry in which one or the other of the two following phenomena does not happen. 1. Caloric [heat] is disengaged or fixed. 2. An elastic fluid is formed, or absorbed, or its base passes from one fluid into another.
>
> These two general facts being once established and clearly known, it will be seen, that the foundation of chemical theory depends on the properties and the action of heat, the formation and fixation of elastic fluids.[22]

As the primary agent of physical change throughout the universe, heat is of the utmost importance to chemical science. As Davy remarks from a broader viewpoint:

> Upon the various operations of the radiant heat of the sun absorbed, or rendered sensible in bodies, almost all the phaenomena which are the subjects of *meteorological science* depend. . . . By this agent likewise are most of the new combinations, and decompositions, of substances produced, by which they are rendered capable of organization, and of becoming parts of living beings. . . . In short, the agency of heat in nature is almost universal; and it either primarily occasions, or materially influences, all the different changes that take place upon our globe.[23]

Indeed it was primarily the necessity to explain the mysterious operation of heat and light, among the foremost problems confronting nineteenth-century science, that gave rise, as we have seen, to various theories concerning the existence of "subtle fluids" or an ethereal matter dispersed throughout the atmosphere.

[22] A. F. Fourcroy, *Elements of Chemistry and Natural History* (Edinburgh, 1800), III, 476.
[23] A *Syllabus of a Course of Lectures on Chemistry*, Works, II, 393 (Davy's italics). Cf. also II, 445.

Such principles shed important light on another of Keats's favorite terms for discussing the creative process. On the opening page of his *First Principles of Chemistry* (1792) William Nicholson asserts: "Heat expands solids, then renders them fluid, and afterwards converts them into vapour; and these changes succeed each other as the *intensity* of the heat is rendered greater."[24] Such a use of the term to refer to the degree of energy, most often caloric, involved in physical reactions is common throughout chemical dictionaries and treatises of the day. Davy himself notes that "almost all cases of vivid chemical action are connected with the increase of temperature of the acting bodies, and a greater radiation of heat from them. . . . The strength of the attraction of the acting bodies determines the rapidity of combination, and in proportion as this is greater, so likewise is there more *intensity* of heat and light" (IV, 165-66). Yet the interesting relationship between the significance of the term in its scientific context and Keats's adoption of it in the realm of aesthetics has never been explored. Keats expresses his sense of intensity and its importance to art in a letter of December 1817 which analyzes the failure of Benjamin West's painting, *Death on the Pale Horse*, a work where, as he complains, "there is nothing to be *intense* upon." "The excellence of every Art," he goes on to declare, "is its *intensity*, capable of making all disagreeables evaporate, from their being in close relationship with Beauty & Truth" (I, 192). Now the process of creation Keats seems to have in mind here as an ideal, the process that has failed to materialize in the case of West's painting, must strike one as closely akin to that of chemical distillation. Among the diverse elements present to the artist's perception, those essential to his conception are fused and refined through an intensity of imaginative power, while those that are incidental or unsuitable—the "disagreeables"— are expelled or "evaporated." The latter term, like a number of other favorites of Keats's, is one regularly defined in

[24] *The First Principles of Chemistry*, 2nd ed. (London, 1792), pp. 1-2.

44

chemical dictionaries and treatises. "Evaporation" is merely an open or uncovered form of distillation wherein the unwanted properties or "disagreeables" are driven off by heat.[25] "Distillation," on the other hand, occurs "when evaporation is performed in vessels either perfectly or nearly closed, so that the volatile parts which are raised in one part of the apparatus, may be received and condensed in the other part."[26] "Abstraction" refers specifically to the process of distillation. "The volatile products which come over, and are condensed in the receivers, are sometimes said to be *abstracted* from the more fixed part which remains behind."[27] "Sublimation" "is founded on the same principles as distillation, and its rules are the same, as it is nothing but a dry distillation."[28] All these operations are closely related in chemistry and require, moreover, varying intensities of heat.[29] Similarly the volatile elements abstracted during such processes are commonly referred to as "spirits" or "essences."[30] Like "empyreal" air, a term used by chemists to describe

[25] See Andrew Ure, A *Dictionary of Chemistry*, 1st ed. (London, 1821), "Evaporation." The term is also defined by Nicholson, *First Principles of Chemistry*, p. 34, and used throughout Babington's lectures, pp. 41, 43, 60, 65, and passim.

[26] Nicholson, *First Principles of Chemistry*, p. 34. The term is similarly defined in Babington's lectures, p. 65. Cf. Ure, "Distillation."

[27] Ure, "Abstraction."

[28] Ure, "Sublimation." The term is also defined by Nicholson, *First Principles of Chemistry*, pp. 34-35.

[29] In the *Syllabus of a Course of Lectures Read at Guy's Hospital*, Babington and Allen note, under the topic of "Caloric," that "to the head of *Evaporation* may also be referred the process of *Distillation*, and *Sublimation*" (pp. 8-9; authors' italics).

[30] Spirits are of various kinds but usually produced by exposing wine, beer, or other fermented liquors to distillation (see Nicholson, *First Principles of Chemistry*, p. 466). Cf. Keats's remarks to Woodhouse on wines "of a heavy and spirituous nature" compared with "the more ethereal Part" of the grape which "mounts into the brain, not assaulting the cerebral apartments" (II, 64). Ure asserts (under "Essences") that "several of the volatile or essential oils are called essences by the perfumers," and Babington and Allen note (p. 134) that they are obtained by distillation.

oxygen,[31] the more vital part of the earth's atmosphere, such distillations possess unusual powers.

Keats's idea of the creative processes of art can best be illuminated by understanding the analogies that exist between the terms he habitually uses and their significance within the context of certain physical operations or experiments studied by the science of his day. During an interval of particular creativeness, in the autumn of 1818, he writes to tell George and Georgiana how "my Solitude is *sublime*," how, despite his loneliness, "there is a *Sublimity* to welcome me home." "The roaring of the wind is my wife and the Stars through the window pane are my Children," he goes on to explain. "The mighty *abstract* Idea I have of Beauty in all things stifles the more divided and minute domestic happiness—an amiable wife and sweet Children I contemplate as a part of that Beauty" (1, 403). The comments clearly relate to his earlier remarks to Haydon about looking upon sun, moon, and stars as "materials to form greater things—that is to say ethereal things," for what he is attempting to convey is the tremendous joy and power latent in the poetical process, its ability to distill higher or ideal elements that transcend the limited aspects of any particular stage of human experience. Again, in the famous letter to Bailey in which he compares the imagination to Adam's dream he asserts that "I have the same Idea of all our Passions as of Love they are all in their *sublime*, creative of *essential* Beauty" (1, 184). Here again Keats is describing the poetic process, the way in which the materials of earthly beauty are condensed "by the finest spirits, and put into etherial existence for the relish of one's fellows" (1, 301), and his language once more suggests the analogy with the chemical art of distillation. What Keats means by "essence" begins with his whole sense of the par-

[31] The term is defined as a synonym for oxygen gas by Babington and Allen (*Syllabus*, p. 10). See also Fourcroy, *Elements*, III, 479, and Davy's section "Of Empyreal Undecompounded Substances," *Works*, IV, 165-80.

ticular "identities" of the material forms that confront the poet; yet the two terms are not, as they have sometimes been made to appear, synonymous.[32] Although the process may begin with the realization of particular identities, these are nevertheless synthesized and purified by the intensity of the poet's imagination which transforms them to a higher state, akin to the "ethereal." Through the poet's "abstract endeavor" (1, 301) an ideal of beauty is refined and released from such common ingredients by the imagination which, through its energies, bestows a kind of "finer tone" on what it perceives. The process involves not merely a separation and release of elements but a superior degree of concentration. Thus, in the same letter, Keats recommends to Bailey "this old Wine of Heaven which I shall call the *redigestion* of our most *ethereal* Musings on Earth" (1, 186). Nicholson (p. 34) defines "digestion" as "keeping bodies for a considerable time immersed in a fluid at a higher temperature than that of the atmosphere, in order that combinations may take place that could not else have been effected." In its operation the imagination is both analytic or selective and synthetic. Moreover Keats conceives of the process as a moral, not merely an aesthetic, one. A few weeks earlier he had written, again to Bailey, how "there are no Men thouroughly wicked—so as never to be self *spiritualized* into a kind of *sublime* Misery" (1, 173). The ideals of Beauty, Truth, and Misery (in its higher, disinterested sense) are abstractions that derive their qualities from the total sum of human experience. At the same time, however, the essential forms of poetry are refined and liberated from the world of material

[32] A number of the terms considered in this section have been usefully tabulated and examined by Newell F. Ford in *The Prefigurative Imagination of John Keats* (Stanford, Calif., 1951). While he is right in attacking transcendental interpretations of "essence," Ford is not sufficiently exact when he takes the term as virtually equivalent to natural forms or objects or when he writes that "if Keats had written 'An essense [sic] of beauty is a joy forever' . . . his meaning would not have been missed" (pp. 14-15).

CHEMISTRY OF THE POETIC PROCESS

identity by the intensifying power of the poet's imagination. Paradoxically, perhaps, they maintain a reality relative to both the worlds of nature and the mind.

Slightly over a month after his remarks on West's painting, Keats returned to the subject of intensity in a letter to his publisher, John Taylor, in which he forwarded his revision of a passage for inclusion in the first book of *Endymion*. The lines were ones he described as "a regular stepping of the Imagination towards a Truth" and which he thought might "be of the greatest Service to me of anything I ever did":

> Wherein lies Happiness? In that which becks
> Our ready Minds to fellowship divine;
> A fellowship with essence, till we shine
> Full alchymized and free of space. Behold
> The clear Religion of heaven—fold &c—.
> (*Letters*, I, 218; *Endymion*, i.777-81)

These lines and the passage that follows, too long and familiar to be quoted in full, are vital to the argument, and thus to any interpretation, of Keats's poem. They have frequently been read, largely on the basis of the use of "essence," as an affirmation of belief in a Platonic or transcendental reality. Such metaphysical interpretations have, more recently, been vigorously attacked.[33] What has gone unnoticed, however, is the fact that it is the creative process the passage describes, and that the chief key to its significance, as indicated by the word "alchymized," is its relation to chemical theory. Once again the process begins with the

---

[33] The Neoplatonic reading, which has its roots in the criticism of Sir Sidney Colvin, Robert Bridges, and Ernest de Selincourt, is most systematically advanced by Claude L. Finney, *The Evolution of Keats's Poetry* (Cambridge, Mass., 1936), I, 291-305. Ford's attack, beginning with "The Meaning of 'Fellowship with Essence' in *Endymion*," *PMLA*, LXII (1947), 1061-76, was combined with an erotic reading of the poem in "*Endymion*—a Neo-Platonic Allegory?" *ELH*, XIV (1947), 64-76, an interpretation expanded in the book-length study cited above. See also E. C. Pettet, *On the Poetry of Keats* (Cambridge, 1957), pp. 123-202.

48

realization of particular impressions—the feel of a rose leaf pressed against the lips. Yet "fellowship with essence" is born of more than mere awareness of such identities or "things" of beauty. The material elements of perception must first be concentrated and distilled through an intensity of imaginative effort:

> *Feel* we these *things?*—that moment have we stept
> Into a sort of oneness, and our state
> Is like a floating *spirit's.*
>
> (i.795-97)

Friendship, love, and the values akin to them are abstractions derived from the elements of human experience even as, depending on their place in the scale of rising intensities, they transcend those elements in unity and power. What, in short, the first book of *Endymion* expresses is Keats's "mighty abstract Idea I have of Beauty in all things" (1, 403), his faith in the poetic chemistry of the imagination which, "spreading in this dull and clodded earth / Gives it a touch ethereal—a new birth" (*Endymion,* i.297-98). In this connection it is worth noting the exact relevance of the simile Keats used in describing the passage to Taylor: "It set before me at once," he wrote, "the gradations of Happiness even like a kind of Pleasure Thermometer" (1, 218). That device, incongruous in most discussions of metaphysical or poetic theory, is here precisely apt, for it is of all instruments the one most fundamental to chemistry and essential to the scientist for determining those intensities at which specific reactions occur.

III

It would be wrong to argue that the analogies by which Keats regularly visualizes the imagination and its operations ever constituted a coherent, fully developed theory. He himself nowhere provided so detailed or abstract an analysis of the poetic process, nor is there any reason to imagine he ever attempted to formulate such a conception in any deliberate way. His sense of artistic creativity was partly subliminal and largely metaphoric. Nevertheless, there emerges in his letters of the winter of 1817-1818, when he was revising *Endymion* for the press, a series of comments on the subject of the imagination that organize themselves around the chemical metaphor with such consistency as to justify one's speaking of an early conception of the poetic process. The notion must be described as an *early* one not because Keats ever rejected or abandoned it but rather because it undergoes a remarkable course of change and qualification throughout the whole of his career. Indeed it is not too much to say that his deepening criticism of the imagination and the role it plays in human awareness explains a major part of the fascination his career holds for us today. This is, however, to anticipate. For the moment it is necessary to examine his primary conception with somewhat more thoroughness and with an eye to some of its more significant implications.

The chemical analogy was useful to Keats in providing a means of visualizing poetry both as a spirit active throughout the universe and as a quality of particular objects or events; the two ways of conceiving poetry were both habitual to him. As the prototype of the creator, the poet distills the stuff of beauty from the perception of a myriad of divergent elements—the whispering of the reeds, the rising of the moon, his sympathies and feelings, and his knowledge of and love for his fellow man. Yet his creations—myth, legend, verse itself—come, if they are worthy, to enjoy a permanence, autonomy, and influence of their own. "Nor do we merely feel these essences / For one short hour," Keats declares at the outset of *Endymion* (i.25-26), a poem that begins with a description of the creative process. They exert their own power over human souls and, like a vital ferment, help to inspire and perpetuate the creative cycle. Poetry is "A drainless shower / Of light . . . the supreme of power" ("Sleep and Poetry," 235-36), "An endless fountain of immortal drink, / Pouring unto us from the heaven's brink" (*Endym-*

ion, i.23-24). Keats is able to conceive of verse in terms that are substantial and material and, more abstractly, as a kind of supernal energy. "The poetry of earth is never dead": the combination and refinement of minute, concrete particulars never ceases. Nevertheless the process is aided and fomented by the power of creative genius active throughout the world and those "far majesties"

> whose benevolence
> Shakes hand with our own Ceres; every sense
> Filling with spiritual sweets to plenitude.
> (*Endymion,* iii.37-39)

Poetry ranges freely "From the clear space of ether, to the small / Breath of new buds unfolding" ("Sleep and Poetry," 168-69), discovering the analogies that connect the material world and the spiritual.

During the winter of 1817-1818 Keats was studying Milton intensively, and his comments on *Paradise Lost* reveal how fully the chemical metaphor had established itself within his thinking. Milton, he writes, "*refines* on his descriptions of beauty, till the sense aches at them." Or again, the older poet's treatment of the image of the vale "is a sort of Delphic *Abstraction*—a beautiful thing made more beautiful." Beyond these general instances, a striking comment on Milton himself illustrates Keats's ability to develop the chemical image in a more vital way and in conjunction with a series of related images. Milton, he declares, "is 'sagacious of his Quarry,' he sees Beauty on the wing, pounces upon it and gorges it to the producing his *essential* verse."[34] Although Keats's figure for the creative process is here a biological one, the continuity of the chemical logic is evident. Indeed the figure is especially interesting in the way it combines the notion of chemical process with two other favorite images for creative ex-

---

[34] Keats's annotations are reprinted in Finney, *The Evolution of Keats's Poetry*, 1, 339-40. Finney asserts that they were made in December 1817 and January and February 1818 when Keats was reading *Paradise Lost* with Dilke.

perience—eating and drinking, and spinning and weaving.[35] As has sometimes been pointed out before, eating or drinking is throughout Keats's poetry the common prelude to imaginative experience, for the act of ingestion expresses his primary idea of the way the facts of sense experience become absorbed as the materials of verse. At the same time digestion, but more particularly the airy texture of the insect's weaving, represents his notion of the chemistry by which the imagination rarefies and transforms its objects. "I endeavour'd to drink in the Prospect," Keats writes Reynolds the following summer of some particularly fine scenery on the walking tour with Brown, "that I might spin it out to you as the silkworm makes silk from Mulberry leaves" (1, 323). The sentence illustrates his inclination to conceive of the chemistry of the poetic process in a more organic way, and with, inevitably, certain shifts of emphasis.

The poet's proper nourishment, the "food" of his "delighted fancy," as Keats puts it in the early sonnet, "How Many Bards," is "beauties, earthly, or sublime." Each kind is in its own way sustaining. The difference between food and wine as symbols of sensation is that wine, as the product of prior distillation, is more concentrated and powerful and so often associated with the intenser delights of the imagination and art. The difference is primarily one of degree, although Keats was to become increasingly fascinated by the analogy between intoxication and certain aspects of imaginative experience that came in time to seem more suspect to him. Poetry, like the other arts, offers a limitless source of refined sensation, one that he can look upon, like food or drink, with sensual relish. Writing Reynolds on February 3 to thank him for "your dish of Filberts"—the gift of several sonnets—he goes on to add: "Would we were a sort of ethereal Pigs, & turn'd loose to feed upon spiritual Mast &

---

[35] In *Keats's Metaphors for the Poetic Imagination*, D'Avanzo has helpfully collected and discussed a number of examples under the headings "Wine" (pp. 108-13) and "Weaving" (pp. 160-64).

Acorns" (1, 223). In his following letter of the same month, perhaps as a reaction against the idea of poetry as the occasion for such sybaritism, he is moved to go on to declare "the Benefit done by great Works to the 'Spirit and pulse of good' by their mere passive existence." "Man should not dispute or assert but whisper results to his neighbour," he adds, "and thus by every germ of Spirit sucking the Sap from mould ethereal every human might become great, and Humanity instead of being a wide heath of Furse and Briars with here and there a remote Oak or Pine, would become a grand democracy of Forest Trees" (1, 232-33). If poetry is a pleasurable indulgence, it also provides the nourishment vital to the various forms of human growth and progress and works in its own silent, unobtrusive way toward the political and social betterment of men. Keats's early humanitarianism is generally an instinctive afterthought, an outgrowth of the primary pleasure principle, just as at the end of the central argument of Book One of *Endymion*, the chief essence, Love, while enrapturing men with its "unsating food," nevertheless acts to "bless / The world with benefits unknowingly" and to "Produce more than our searching witnesseth" (i.816, 826-27, 834). The poet indulges his love of sensation, whether in nature or the intenser realm of art, not only for its own sake but to digest and assimilate such pleasures in order to propagate them in a higher, more essential form for the enjoyment and improvement of his fellows.

A number of these strands of metaphor and implication come together in the important letter last touched on, that of February 19 to Reynolds. One can best proceed at once to the center of the letter where Keats expresses his conviction

that almost any Man may like the Spider spin from his own inwards his own airy Citadel—the points of leaves and twigs on which the Spider begins her work are few and she fills the Air with a beautiful circuiting: man should be content with as few points to tip with the fine Webb of his Soul and weave a tapestry empyrean—full of Symbols for his spiritual eye, of softness for his spiritual touch, of space for his wandering of distinctness for his Luxury.

(I, 231-32)

The passage describes again the familiar process by which the poet, or any man of imagination, can refine the stuff of common experience into the fabric of an interior world of harmony and delight analogous to the spiritual. The resulting creation is not, needless to say, "spiritual" in any transcendental sense but simply more intense and unified—a world like that of dreams where the flow of suggestions and associations can elaborate itself freely and endlessly. At the same time the material from which the spider spins her web and the particular points to which she attaches it suggest that the process, however refined, is no merely nebulous one but operates upon and has reference to substantial reality.

The interrelated ideas of consumption and digestion, the concentration and assimilation the productive insect brings to its materials in weaving them into the complex network of its web, were useful to Keats as metaphors that helped him develop the various implications of his chemical analogy. Nevertheless it should by now be clear that his conception of the poetic process must be extended in another way to include the manner in which poetry operates on other minds —those of its readers—in achieving its effects, for Keats visualizes the two processes as analogous and inseparable. Poetry, that is to say, works by arousing in the mind of the reader sensations and associations, a series of speculations and inquiries, similar in kind (which is not to say identical with) those through which it has been created. Just as poetry, the distillation of one's own imaginative endeavor, also exerts its vital influence on others, so the image of spinning or weaving applies equally well to the kind of stimulation and activity it can effect. The point becomes clearer if we return to the commencement of the letter to Reynolds where Keats begins by considering poetry less as a form of creative activity itself and more as the stimulus for exciting it, the food for further speculation and thought:

> I have an idea that a Man might pass a very pleasant life in this manner—let him on any certain day read a certain Page of full Poesy or distilled Prose and let him wander with it, and muse upon it, and reflect from it, and bring home to it, and prophesy upon it, and dream upon it—untill it becomes stale—but when will it do so? Never —When Man has arrived at a certain ripeness in intellect any one grand and spiritual passage serves him as a starting post towards all "the two-and thirty Pallaces" How happy, is such a "Voyage of conception," what delicious diligent Indolence! A doze upon a Sofa does not hinder it, and a nap upon Clover engenders ethereal finger-pointings.
>
> (I, 231)

As the concentrated product of intense imaginative experience, poetry works by generating the creative cycle anew by propelling the reader on his own journey of discovery. What poetry affords, in a superior degree to the natural images it uses, is a network of closely woven and refined associations, "ethereal finger-pointings" in Keats's phrase, a set of advanced and suggestive connections to stimulate the reader and convey him on his way. Poetry is something more than what gets written down. More broadly, it is the power of a form of imaginative thinking that is perpetually active throughout existence and the minds of men. It represents the change we work on our experience merely in the way or ways we perceive it, the organization and refinement of sensation we describe as sensibility. Again more broadly, however, it constitutes a form of communication, the way different minds progressively corroborate, assimilate, and extend the primitive experience they share in common. Using the imagery of the observable universe, poetry achieves effects of concentration and power analogous to man's sense of the spiritual. It embodies one form of the spiritual shorthand or "hieroglyphic visioning" all art uses—the effect created when, as Keats wrote in December in a review of Edmund Kean, "the very letters and points of charactered language show like the hieroglyphics of beauty,"[36] when its "finger-pointings" suddenly disclose a further range of meaning.

IV

There is, no doubt, a certain danger in conforming the sometimes random observations in Keats's poems and letters to the shape of any single pattern. Nevertheless there is present at least by early in 1818 a consistent design to the metaphors he uses to describe the way the imagination operates upon its materials, the way it condenses and refines them into a higher state, and the way in which such essences in turn stimulate the creative processes in others. The whole notion provides an important element of unity within his thought. At the same time, however, it raises a number of obvious questions and problems, difficulties that are not the less significant because Keats was from the first clearly aware of many of their different aspects and because much of his later career can be considered as an attempt to come to terms with them as they grew in importance and implication. Briefly, one must pause to ask:

(1) What is there to ensure that the sensations and trains of association from which poetry arises and that ideally it induces in others ever culminate in some conclusion? What brings the vortex of poetic creation to a close?

(2) What ensures an element of congruence between the sensations and speculations of the poet and his reader, or between different readers of any given work? Or is it simply sufficient that poetry launch the reader on his own imaginative adventure without determining a course or destination?

(3) What is the relationship between poetry, together with the recognitions it yields, considered as a kind of imaginative

[36] *The Poetical Works and Other Writings of John Keats*, ed. Maurice Buxton Forman (the Hampstead edition) (New York, 1939), v, 229.

thinking, and the truths of logic or (to use Keats's phrase) "consequitive reasoning" (1, 185)? Are the two processes distinct, even antipathetic; or is there an area of agreement between them?

The questions overlap in various ways, and one could readily add to them. Indeed it may seem arbitrary, unreasonable, and even contrary to the bent of the poet's temperament to submit a set of loose metaphors and theorems to the scrutiny of formal inquiry. It is only too easy to dismiss the procedure as irrelevant or uncongenial. The fact remains, however, that the questions hold the key to Keats's career and, as much as any other, explain the course of its development. Moreover they are ones that from the start in various ways preoccupied him. Since this is the case, it is far better to take such questions up where they belong, as an important aspect of his early thinking about the imagination, rather than having to deal with them later as inexplicable aberrations or misgivings. More to the immediate purpose, the questions suggest why, virtually from the outset of its clear emergence in late 1817 and early 1818, Keats's conception of the creative process reveals a steady tendency towards qualification and change.

V

Keats early anticipated a number of such problems and objections, and in some cases faces them head on. In the letter of February 19, for example, in which he speculates to Reynolds on the possibility of each man's pursuing his own imaginative voyage, discovering or creating his own spiritual world, he goes on to add:

But the Minds of Mortals are so different and bent on such diverse Journeys that it may at first appear impossible for any common taste and fellowship to exist between two or three under these suppositions—It is however quite the contrary—Minds would leave each other in contrary

directions, traverse each other in Numberless points, and
all [*for* at] last greet each other at the Journeys end—A
old Man and a child would talk together and the old Man
be led on his Path, and the child left thinking.

(I, 232)

Keats recognizes the fact that poetry operates differently on
different minds, that the trains of association it arouses will
never prove identical.[37] The inevitableness of diversity, of an
element of subjectivity, far from disconcerting him, strikes
him as healthy and even delightful because of his faith in a
larger kind of unity and coherence. The various lines of
human speculation may diverge but only to intersect. Less
than a month later he develops the global implications of his
spinning metaphor in a letter to Bailey. "It is an old maxim
of mine," he writes, "and of course must be well known that
eve[r]y point of thought is the centre of an intellectual
world—the two uppermost thoughts in a Man's mind are
the two poles of his World he revolves on them and every
thing is southward or northward to him through their
means—We take but three steps from feathers to iron"
(I, 243). Seemingly divergent points of view are only ter-
mini for a network of fresh discovery and interassimilation.
Moreover this capacity for expansion and creative interrelationship is not merely a characteristic of individual minds.
It is a quality of human perception generally and, potentially
at least, links man with man.

Such assumptions—hardly an organic theory of the imagi-

---

[37] The standard treatment of Keats's relationship to the theory of
association of ideas is James R. Caldwell's *John Keats' Fancy: The Effect on Keats of the Psychology of His Day* (Ithaca, N.Y., 1945).
While usefully establishing connections between many of the poet's
habits and notions and the major tenets of associationist theory, Caldwell's treatment is primarily uncritical. That is, it does not allow for
major differences of emphasis within the general movement of associationism, nor does it come to terms with the particular questions and
difficulties that the theory by itself creates.

nation in any meaningful sense so much as a loose faith in a set of general relationships and correspondences—are basic to most of Keats's early thinking about the creative process. They serve to explain two of his favorite tenets: his insistence on the unobtrusiveness of poetry and the kind of indetermination with which it acts. Works of genius operate like "ethereal Chemicals" on the great "Mass of neutral intellect"; but they do so, Keats insists, without imparting "any individuality, any determined Character" (1, 184). Like a catalyst, they serve to stimulate activity but without determining the nature or course of any individual reaction. They work impersonally, for the energies from which they derive and which they express in concentrated form are not merely their own but those of life itself. "The best of Men have but a portion of good in them," Keats writes Bailey in January, "a kind of spiritual yeast in their frames which creates the ferment of existence—by which a Man is propell'd to act and strive and buffet with Circumstance" (1, 210). Poetry accelerates the progress of this ferment by perpetuating the purest of its tendencies. However it cannot by itself propound the kind of resolution every man must define for himself through his own exertions. Even the great metaphors Keats later evolved against a deepening awareness of human limitation and unhappiness to explain the "burden of the Mystery"—the idea of life as a "Mansion of Many Apartments" and as a "vale of Soul-making"—describe situations where man must make his own way or create his own identity amid a multitude of possibilities. The greater part of his verse and letters expresses the faith in a deepening and progressive vision into the nature of human existence. Such trust, however, was from time to time obscured by his awareness of the labyrinthine aspects of the problem and of the unremitting turbulence and wastefulness of life. "There is an ellectric fire in human nature tending to purify," he writes over a year later, employing another scientific figure, "so that among these human creature[s] there is continually some birth of new heroism—The pity is," he adds in some-what disillusioned fashion, "that we must wonder at it: as we should at finding a pearl in rubbish" (II, 80). If the progressive nature of the arts could come in time to seem doubtful to him, it was always possible to conceive of poetry more naturalistically—as the expression of life and its energies simply at their most instinctive, vibrant, animated, "intense" —without demanding more.

In any case poetry could not succeed by imposing its own goals and solutions. The idea of such control was repugnant because it subverted the vital cooperation of poet and reader, the flow and interassimilation of awareness, the give-and-take of cross-reference and comparison. All that was required was the distilled suggestiveness of works of art and the "ripeness in intellect" necessary to pursue and elaborate them. The question of direction was no doubt important, but one best left to determine itself—an attitude not unsimilar to Wordsworth's early ideal of "wise passiveness." "A strain of musick," he writes Reynolds, may conduct us "to 'an odd angle of the Isle' and when the leaves whisper it puts a 'girdle round the earth.[']" Poetry, he urges in the same February letter, should not proceed "impatiently from a knowledge of what is to be arrived at" (I, 232). To pre-establish fixed goals was only to betray its highest uses. While inspired by particular works, poetry was ideally a form of self-discovery each reader had to carry out in the light of his own unique experience. This same month Keats writes Taylor, as the first of his poetical "Axioms," that "I think Poetry should surprise by a fine excess and not by singularity." Then he adds significantly: "It should strike the Reader as a wording of his own highest thoughts, and appear almost a Remembrance" (I, 238). Ideally poetry proceeded from a genuine coalescence of intelligence, one that should appear, in part at least, as the product of the reader's own imaginative effort, serving to confirm his own perceptions and to encourage him to pursue their ramifications further.

Keats's dislike of the dogmatic strain in art—the "egotistical sublime" as he referred to it—is well known. Words-

CHEMISTRY OF THE POETIC PROCESS

worth's habit of philosophical moralizing, of using poetry as
a means of steadily pushing one in the direction of his own
presuppositions, was paralyzing to the reader's self-respect
and creative independence. "We hate poetry that has a pal-
pable design upon us," he writes Reynolds, again in February, "and if we do not agree, seems to put its hand in its
breeches pocket" (i, 224). In a similar way there was Hunt's
tiresome habit of explaining (and therefore restricting)
some particular effect of beauty, insisting on the importance
of his own intuitions "instead of giving other minds credit
for the same degree of perception as he himself possesses"
(ii, 11). "I don't mean to deny Wordsworth's grandeur &
Hunt's merit," he sums up to Reynolds, "but I mean to say
we need not be teazed with grandeur & merit—when we can
have them uncontaminated & unobtrusive" (i, 224-25).

Even Coleridge was not exempt from this sort of criticism.
The famous statement on Negative Capability in late December, crystallized in part by his sense of the methodology
of Coleridge's approach to poetry and the arts generally, is
best taken up in this context, for it established a whole
cortex of ideas that he would find it necessary to return to
in the coming months and in certain respects to question.
"I had not a dispute but a disquisition with Dilke, on various
subjects," he writes;

> several things dovetailed in my mind, & at once it struck
> me, what quality went to form a Man of Achievement
> especially in Literature & which Shakespeare posessed so
> enormously—I mean *Negative Capability*, that is when
> man is capable of being in uncertainties, Mysteries, doubts,
> without any irritable reaching after fact & reason—Cole-
> ridge, for instance, would let go by a fine isolated verisimili-
> tude caught from the Penetralium of mystery, from being
> incapable of remaining content with half knowledge. This
> pursued through Volumes would perhaps take us no further
> than this, that with a great poet the sense of Beauty over-
> comes every other consideration, or rather obliterates all
> consideration.   (i, 193-94; Keats's italics)

The statement has been often taken to express the prevailing principle of Keats's thought. In recent years especially the very phrase Negative Capability has been, more than any other, identified with the whole direction of his intellectual and poetic commitment. As with so many major metaphors and principles enunciated in the letters, however, one recognizes Keats's attempt to formulate a definition not in order to advance it in any final way but for purposes that are more heuristic—as a way of outlining a position with the end of clarifying it, of discovering its range of possibilities and implications. To accept the statement as any kind of ultimate declaration, moreover, is to overlook the way in which it qualifies itself in the uncertainty it affirms, a kind of irony of which Keats himself was to become increasingly conscious. "It is a wretched thing to confess," he writes Woodhouse in October 1818, "but is a very fact that not one word I ever utter can be taken for granted as an opinion growing out of my identical nature" (1, 387). In theory it was easy to contend that a poet could have no fixed opinions, no settled nature, no "identity"; in practice, however, it remained to be seen whether such an ideal was actually tenable. The whole problem was one he had to return to in the light of his further experience, especially that of composition itself.

For the moment his remarks on Negative Capability were more useful as a way of exploring the kind of knowledge most appropriate to poetry, a form of thinking that a philosophic mind like Coleridge's, as Keats conceived of it, must ultimately find unsatisfactory. For Keats's chief contention is that poetry exists in "half knowledge," in uncertainty and mystery, and that an element of the problematic or probational, however unsettling to certain kinds of temperament, is not only justifiable but vitally necessary to its effects. Here his choice of the word "verisimilitude" instead of "truth" to describe the kind of poetic effect with which Coleridge is unable to remain content is especially revealing. The longer but more exact word suggests the apprehension of truth not in any final or absolute sense but as a partial aspect of some larger reality. It indicates a form of verification that proceeds not through the rules of logic but by means of that imaginative convergence—the intersecting or "dovetailing" of different insights—that by itself leads to no final conclusion but to a deeper awareness of the "Penetralium of mystery" in its perpetually fascinating complexity. It suggests the imaginative perception of a series of interrelationships that lose their real vitality and significance once we attempt to abstract them from the flowing texture of sensations and speculations that embody them, once we seek to freeze them into the settled forms of "fact and reason." Keats's remarks on Negative Capability are more than anything an attempt to justify poetry as a kind of thinking we might consider unconscious or preconscious—a form of apprehension proceeding by relationships and laws distinct from those of the reason. The whole formulation represents a broadly philosophic defense of his commitment to the value and integrity of the poetic process.

What more exactly, however, is the relationship between poetry and other kinds of intellectual activity, such as reasoning? If poetry is a form of communication between different minds, does it also share points of contact and interchange with other modes of human discipline and thought? The importance of these questions was not lost on Keats, although the answer was far from simple. To begin with what was most fundamental, his outcry in the "Adam's dream" letter, "O for a Life of Sensations rather than of Thoughts" (1, 185), represented a central conviction and expressed a dichotomy he basically believed in. His primary impulse was to imagine a total separation between the two realms, to assume the position of being able to dismiss the so-called truths of logic and reasoning as simply irrelevant to the kind of knowledge poetry conveys. In March he writes the sober-minded Bailey: "Now my dear fellow I must once for all tell you I have not one Idea of the truth of any of my speculations—I shall never be a Reasoner because I care not to be in the right, when retired from bickering and in a proper philosophical temper"

(I, 243). Coming at the end of a letter of serious, at times skeptical, theorizing on the nature of the poetic imagination, the statement has a deliberately flippant ring. Nevertheless it is possible to emphasize the tendency it represents—the impulse to conceive of poetry as alien to or withdrawn from the methods of any reasoned, systematic kind of progression. Late the next year, when his career was all but at an end, he could still write of Dilke, in a way reminiscent of his remarks on Wordsworth and Coleridge, as "a Man who cannot feel he has a personal identity unless he has made up his Mind about every thing. The only means of strengthening one's intellect," he goes on, "is to make up ones mind about nothing—to let the mind be a thoroughfare for all thoughts. Not select a party." Then he adds: "All the stubborn arguers you meet with are of the same brood—They never begin upon a subject they have not preresolved on" (II, 213). The best way was to predetermine nothing, to approach each new situation with a mind entirely open to the trains of speculation it naturally suggested. "Dilke will never come at a truth as long as he lives; because he is always trying at it," he continues. The way to insight was to allow oneself to be led, to let the poetic process determine its own direction and to create afresh its network of sensations and perceptions— "Those thoughts that wander through Eternity."[38]

Nevertheless the problem was not so simple. Spontaneity and freedom were no doubt necessary—the spaciousness necessary for imaginative wandering and reflection. However it was possible to be led into the contemplation of different aspects of things without making constructive progress with the major questions that were continually suggesting themselves. Certain resting places and points of reference were vital if one were to keep one's bearing. "What a time! I am continually running away from the subject," he writes Bailey in the "Adam's dream" letter of November, using a phrase

[38] *Paradise Lost*, II. 148.

he was to employ again.[39] "Sure this cannot be exactly the case with a complex Mind—one that is imaginative and at the same time careful of its fruits—who would exist partly on sensation partly on thought—to whom it is necessary that years should bring the philosophic Mind" (1, 185-86). The "simple imaginative Mind" he had described earlier in the same letter, the kind he associated more nearly with his own, was relatively self-contained, bound up in the web of "its own silent Working," habitually pleased by its own intuitions. The ideal of the "complex Mind" that Bailey suggested to him was one of wider scope, a mind where sensation and thought, instead of representing opposing tendencies, actually served to supplement and reinforce each other. Such a mind was both imaginative and at the same time eager to "increase in knowledge and know all things."

The need for some accommodation between the broad and often contradictory demands of sensation and thought and their particular relation to the poetic process were consuming preoccupations throughout the formative months of 1817-1818. However unique and antagonistic to analysis the means of art might prove, it was impossible to consider poetry in separation from the other forms and avenues of knowledge. In the important letter to Reynolds of May 1818, comparing life to a "Mansion of Many Apartments," Keats carries his consideration of the problem one stage further, starting with the conviction that "every department of knowledge we see excellent and calculated towards a great whole." Proceeding from this unifying premise, he goes on to attempt to define further the whole complex relationship between heart and head:

> An extensive knowledge is needful to thinking people—it takes away the heat and fever; and helps, by widening speculation, to ease the Burden of the Mystery: a thing I begin to understand a little. . . . The difference of high Sensations with and without knowledge appears to me

[39] Cf. *Letters*, 1, 279.

this—in the latter case we are falling continually ten thousand fathoms deep and being blown up again without wings and with all [the] horror of a bare shoulderd Creature—in the former case, our shoulders are fledge, and we go thro' the same air and space without fear. This is running one's rigs on the score of abstracted benefit.

(I, 277)

In one sense Keats is only saying that, in developing from the impulse toward imaginative adventure and discovery, the creative processes must seek their materials in a broad awareness of human experience. In this sense an *"extensive* knowledge" helps by *"widening* speculation." However it seems clear that Keats is now concerned not only with the breadth of speculation but with its *stability*, and that by "knowledge" he means not just sensation in its simplest form but rather the superior organization and regularity of the complex mind that is "imaginative and at the same time careful of its fruits." In this connection his nautical metaphor concerning the advantages of "running one's rigs on the score of abstracted benefit" is particularly significant. Instead of merely hampering one's flight, the habits of reflection and deliberation could actually assist it by establishing a series of tentative points of reference throughout the chaotic wilderness of one's spiritual *terra semi incognita*.

There were, after all, two ways of regarding thought. On the one hand it was the distillation of experience, the digestion and coalescence of sensation and speculation, and in this sense the goal and end of all human endeavor, including art. On the other hand, as an abstraction from the sum of living experience, it was alien to the means poetry employed and to the kind of knowledge it imparted. It might consist, for example, merely in the kind of tired maxim that in order to have any poetical significance had to be reexperienced each time anew upon the pulses. One thing was clear: the whole relationship between thought in its various possible mani-

66

festations and sensation and the imagination was no simple one. Considered one way, as a mere extraction of the mind, thought was the sheer opposite of everything poetry stood for. Conceived another way, within the context of his several metaphors for the vital working of the imagination, it was the culmination of the whole creative process and virtually synonymous with the kind of insight or truth of which poetry was capable. The problem was that most of the time it was difficult to avoid seeing thought from both points of view— as process and effect. In short, all these relationships, together with the terms and functions they involved, would have to be reconsidered and worked out as he proceeded.

Such qualifications and elaborations—such distinctions as that between the "simple imaginative Mind" and the "complex," between "high Sensations with and without knowledge"—were all the natural outgrowth of his gradually deepening apprehension of the problems confronting him. The shifts of emphasis we can detect are not attributable to any instability of mind but to a genuine realization of the complexities a thoughtful elaboration of his views on the substance and operation of poetry would involve. Not that he was necessarily interested in theoretical issues for their own sake. It was rather that the practical, day-to-day demands of composition required him continually to visualize his art in terms of processes and functions of genuine application to life. The metaphoric analogies on which he relied fulfilled a basic psychological need. Nevertheless they were still evolving and open to a number of doubts and questions.

For example, there were some second thoughts about the nature of "intensity." Did it act with the absolute impersonality, the "disinterestedness" of a chemical force in distilling ethereal things from the common elements of human experience, as he had earlier maintained? Or did it, in fact, enter into and qualify, perhaps largely determine, the nature of the essences it created? In March 1818, some months after his remarks of November on "Men of Genius" and his

67

December letter on Negative Capability with its discussion of intensity, Keats comes back to the issue in a letter to Bailey:

> I am sometimes so very sceptical as to think Poetry itself a mere Jack a lanthern to amuse whoever may chance to be struck with its brilliance—As Tradesmen say every thing is worth what it will fetch, so probably every mental pursuit takes its reality and worth from the ardour of the pursuer—being in itself a nothing—Ethereal thing[s] may at least be thus real, divided under three heads—Things real—things semireal—and no things—Things real—such as existences of Sun Moon & Stars and passages of Shakspeare—Things semireal such as Love, the Clouds &c which require a greeting of the Spirit to make them wholly exist—and Nothings which are made Great and dignified by an ardent pursuit—Which by the by stamps the burgundy mark on the bottles of our Minds, insomuch as they are able to "consec[r]ate *whate'er they look upon.*"
>
> (I, 242-43; Keats's italics)

There is little if anything here that directly contradicts the substance of Keats's earlier remarks, only a significant shift of emphasis. Now, as he confesses, in a more "sceptical" mood, he is inclined to attribute the primary role in bringing the work of art into reality to the imagination and its "ardour" or intensity. Being also more analytic than usual in this letter (perhaps for the benefit of the logically minded Bailey), he has come to see that the imaginative endeavor can enjoy various degrees of connection with (or abstraction from) material reality and that its link with the world of objects is more substantial in some cases than in others. Keats is not saying that the work of the imagination is necessarily mere illusion. On the contrary, "Ethereal thing[s] may at least be thus real," and he proceeds to explain the nature of this reality by making allowance for the various degrees of abstraction from the concrete that different kinds of beauty require. Nevertheless the passage takes us well beyond his remarks of the preceding May to Haydon about "looking upon the Sun the Moon the Stars, the Earth and its contents as materials to form greater things—that is to say ethereal things" (I, 143). It takes us beyond his revision for Taylor in late January of the "Pleasure Thermometer" with its rising scale of intensities ascending to the higher ideals of friendship and love. All these passages are stepping-stones toward what Keats afterward described as "the mighty abstract Idea I have of Beauty in all things" (I, 403). However the later remarks to Bailey, in their evident preoccupation with the element of subjectivity in human experience, reveal a further range of questions and complexities. Thus Keats sees it is possible to concentrate on the transforming energy of the imagination in such a way as to minimize the importance of the elements on which it operates—the forms of material reality as they exist or as they have already been imaginatively interpreted by others. No doubt the process of creation is the result of "a greeting of the Spirit," a coalescence between the objects of perception and the power of the mind that fulfills and extends them in the act of apprehension. Nevertheless Keats sees that the process can be emphasized from several different aspects —from the point of view of the imagination and its inform-ing, shaping power, or that of the materials on which it operates. The question is one that involves not merely the "reality" but the "worth" of the creative process. It is pos-sible for him to consider the process as chiefly individual and reflexive, a kind of superior amusement, an aspect of what he was afterwards to describe as "the Amusement of Life—to a speculative Mind" (II, 80). On the other hand he can see it, as the closing allusion to Shelley's "Hymn to Intellectual Beauty" suggests, as permanent and universal, a form of spiritual validation. Characteristically the passage settles nothing. It proposes several different contexts for viewing the creative process, the one subjective and skeptical, the other broadly affirmative, and it indicates Keats's unwillingness (in line with his principle of Negative Capability) to choose be-tween them. The passage suggests how Keats's central preoccupation with the nature of the creative process could lead him deeper into a period of critical self-questioning.

VI

During the winter of 1817-1818, Keats proceeded to develop his favorite chemical analogy through a number of related metaphors as a means of exploring the mystery of poetic creation. The formulation was of invaluable service as a way of articulating the kinds of reaction from which poetry sprang and which it in turn occasioned. Nevertheless it raised as many questions as it solved. The scientific operations he found most useful by way of comparison were suggestive in a variety of ways; the very terms they employed were subject to a number of different implications once one sought to adapt or extend them. While science, particularly chemistry, provided a method for understanding the changes and reactions taking place within the world of physical energy and matter, there was no simple or exact means for applying such principles in order to explain imagery, sensation, emotion, thought, and the various combinations and relationships between them. The larger context, one which kept shifting in his mind, was fundamentally poetical and would have to be worked out in terms of his verse itself. It was just here that the problem, far from depressing him, was proving so stimulating. For it was one, as he realized, that could be resolved not merely in terms of the metaphors and speculations that preoccupied him in his letters but through the new inferences and values these were continually assuming in his poetry. The problem, that is to say, could be settled only through the coherence and discipline (the outgrowth of self-discovery) sustained composition demanded—through the act of creation itself. Indeed the shifts and conflicts in his own attitude toward certain major aspects of the question had already begun to provide that kind of dramatic tension from which great poetry often springs. While evident as a recurring theme throughout the letters, Keats's preoccupation with the nature of the poetic process was also becoming, at a more profound level, a principal source of the life and fascination of his verse.

CHAPTER THREE

THE EARLY VERSE

In moving from the theoretical concerns of the last chapter to those of the present, we shift our attention from Keats's letters to his poetry. It is necessary, also, to return to an earlier period of his career. Nevertheless the same questions that reveal themselves throughout the letters in his preoccupation with the creative process are basic to his earliest approach to the demands of composition. More than anything else, Keats's early verse is, in W. J. Bate's phrase, a "poetry about trying to write poetry."[1] The same problems that were to assume theoretical importance reveal themselves from the start in his first creative efforts—only in ways that are more practical and imperative.

A large number of Keats's early poems are occasional pieces—verse that takes its motive and intention from the impulse to pay tribute to a friend or to celebrate some event. In addition, he was quick to discover in the attempt to work toward more extended efforts the adaptability of the verse epistle where a general looseness of form permitted him to rely, as in his letters, on developing a flow of associations sufficient to determine its own point and direction. Even with the help of such expedients, however, there is an evident struggle throughout the early verse for some means to start the creative process flowing. Often Keats's method is simply to amass a series of impressions in the hope they will of themselves create the impetus to carry him forward. "How *many* bards gild the lapses of time!" "*Many* the wonders I this day have seen."

> *Much* have I travell'd in the realms of gold,
> And *many* goodly states and kingdoms seen;
> Round *many* western islands have I been.

[1] *John Keats* (Cambridge, Mass., 1963), p. 70.

Or, by way of variety, "What is more gentle than a wind in summer? / What is more soothing than the pretty hummer . . . ?" For a poetry of sensation nothing was more necessary than sensation itself.

It is worth pausing to examine the technique in one of the most characteristic of the shorter pieces, a sonnet left untitled in the 1817 volume:

> How many bards gild the lapses of time!
>   A few of them have ever been the food
>   Of my delighted fancy,—I could brood
> Over their beauties, earthly or sublime:
> And often, when I sit me down to rhyme,
>   These will in throngs before my mind intrude:
>   But no confusion, no disturbance rude
> Do they occasion; 'tis a pleasing chime.
> So the unnumber'd sounds that evening store:
>   The songs of birds—the whisp'ring of the leaves—
> The voice of waters—the great bell that heaves
>   With solemn sound,—and thousand others more,
> That distance of recognizance bereaves,
>   Make pleasing music, and not wild uproar.

More than anything else, the sonnet describes the creative process itself. It concerns the way in which the sensations first of art, then of nature, are accumulated, then combined or distanced in imagination so as to achieve a unity and harmony of effect. The sonnet proceeds, in octave and sestet, through two complementary stages of aggregation to attain, in the forced rhythm and inverted syntax of the penultimate line, a sense of deliberate compression just before the expansiveness and relaxation of its closing. The effect was one Horace Smith recognized when he exclaimed of the line, "What a well-condensed expression for a youth so young!"[2] when the poem was read aloud to him. The sonnet does not succeed in characterizing the nature of the "chime" or the

[2] Charles and Mary Cowden Clarke, *Recollections of Writers* (London, 1878), p. 133.

greater "music" it distills, nor is there any real effort to do so. It was sufficient for the present for Keats to concentrate his attention on process itself, to let the kind of further definition that would come proceed naturally through a gradual evolution in his grasp and understanding of his own poetic means. Especially at the outset it was understandable that he should find his mode of composition emerging as the subject of his verse. Up to a point the two were inseparable. In the best of his later poetry they were to become if not identical more than ever insolubly combined.

It is significant that the best of the early lyrics spring from particular occasions that serve as catalysts for an exhilarating and powerful but only vague realization of growth and new awareness. Neither the sonnet on Chapman's Homer nor those on the Elgin Marbles attempt to render a clear impression of the works they pretend to celebrate. Any sense of Chapman's translation or of the marble fragments is rapidly subsumed within the feeling of the sublime in its traditional Longinian sense, the sudden shock and wonder that the highest art inspires.[3] The rapt stare of Cortez at the Pacific, multiplied and protracted in the startled glances of his crewmen, or the image of the sun, "a shadow of a magnitude," express, with varying degrees of effectiveness, a realization of infinitely deepening perspectives into the mysterious and unknown. The sonnets convey a sense of sudden elevation and intense excitement but also a certain desolation, a feeling that, especially in the later pair of sonnets, becomes a "dizzy pain" through the overwhelming impression on eye and heart of glories that remain so "dim-conceived" to the mind. Keats was never to lose the impact and astonishment of such experience, its primitive, all-absorbing wonder, the pattern of Adam's awakening in Paradise, a power that was

[3] In *The Mirror and the Lamp: Romantic Theory and Critical Tradition* (rpt. New York, 1958), M. H. Abrams discusses Keats within the context of Longinus and the sublime (pp. 132-38). It seems clear that the more particular, scientific context in which Keats came to think of the sublime is related to the larger tradition.

to renew itself repeatedly throughout his life. In his later poetry, however, and above all in the odes, he was to achieve the ability to command it as an intellectual event, to elaborate its deeper value and significance through a meaningful play of images rather than permitting it to evaporate in blank amazement.

It is revealing to look back on a poem like "How Many Bards" from the prospect of the far better sonnet Keats composed over a year later as a kind of prologue to the writing of *Endymion*. The sonnet "On the Sea" is among the last and best of what we might think of as the "early" lyrics.

It keeps eternal whisperings around
  Desolate shores, and with its mighty swell
  Gluts twice ten thousand caverns, till the spell
Of Hecate leaves them their old shadowy sound.
Often 'tis in such gentle temper found,
  That scarcely will the very smallest shell
  Be moved for days from where it sometime fell,
When last the winds of heaven were unbound.
Oh ye! who have your eye-balls vexed and tired,
  Feast them upon the wideness of the Sea;
     Oh ye! whose ears are dinn'd with uproar rude,
  Or fed too much with cloying melody—
    Sit ye near some old cavern's mouth, and brood
Until ye start, as if the sea-nymphs quired!

Here again Keats's real subject is the poetic process, the natural creativity of the unconscious mind, the "eternal whisperings" of the many caverns the sea gluts and swells, leaving them full of "shadowy sound." Oppressed by his solitude on the Isle of Wight and the necessity of making a beginning with *Endymion*, he had been haunted by an echo from *Lear*: "Do you not *hear* the Sea?" (i, 132). The sonnet represents an obvious invocation, a plea for an inspiration and spontaneousness vital to the larger task confronting him. Again the sonnet builds to its conclusion through an accumulation of images of eye and ear, but they are now more sug-

gestively and complexly related than in the earlier sonnet
"To My Brother George" with its pointless, anticlimactic
cataloguing:

> The ocean with its vastness, its blue green,
>> Its ships, its rocks, its caves, its hopes, its fears,—
>> Its voice mysterious, which whoso hears
> Must think on what will be, and what has been.

"On the Sea" succeeds by endowing the familiar image, the
ocean's voice, with a further range of significance. First suggested by the "eternal whisperings" of the opening line, the
voice is one created within the process of the poem itself,
emerging at the conclusion from an accumulation of detail
chosen to emphasize the changeableness of the sea, the bewildering variety of its moods and appearances, its periods
of alternate calm and turbulence. At the same time the
sonnet expresses a strong movement toward unity and compression. The verbs "gluts," "feast," "fed" build steadily
toward the image of the "old cavern's mouth," a figure partly
geological and partly human, suggesting infinite receptiveness
but also the power of articulation. As in "How Many Bards,"
the sense of gradual concentration is reinforced by a favorite
Keatsian verb, "brood." The process culminates in the "start"
of recognition in the final line when the various sounds of the
sea are suddenly harmonized and it seems to speak as if with
the articulateness of human speech—the song of the sea-
nymphs, mythological creatures partly human and partly
supernatural, partly of the sea and partly of the shore, an
ambivalence that creates its own reverberations. "On the
Sea" perpetuates a whole technique of composition. Nevertheless, in its interplay of detail and power of controlled
suggestiveness, the sonnet transcends such obvious devices as
mere cataloguing to achieve the unity of a symbolic design.

The best of the early verse is characterized by the sudden
start of surprise or recognition, moments when the diverse
strands of sensation and association mysteriously coalesce to
yield a kind of intimation Keats himself can consider only by

analogy with thought. Even in the less successful lyrics, where such realization fails to occur, it can usually be perceived as the desired goal. One can consider as an example the sestet of "After Dark Vapours," another of the early sonnets that reaches its conclusion through the mechanical device of cataloguing:

> The calmest *thoughts* come round us—as of leaves
>   Budding—fruit ripening in stillness—autumn suns
> Smiling at eve upon the quiet sheaves,—
> Sweet Sappho's cheek,—a smiling infant's breath,
>   The gradual sand that through an hour-glass runs,—
> A woodland rivulet—a Poet's death.[4]

In one sense "thoughts" refers simply to the particular images the poem enumerates. In another way, however, it refers to the anticipated effect of the poem as a whole, the way the different images, taken as a progression, interact partly to create, partly to suggest a sum of realization. Although far from the weakest of the early poems, the sonnet fails for the reason that it never creates the grounds for the kind of coalescence toward which it strives.

Keats was clearly conscious of such failure and aware, too, of its relationship to his habits and method of composition. At the opening of his epistle "To Charles Cowden Clarke," he explains to his friend, by way of apology, that

> I have never penn'd a line to thee:
> Because my thoughts were never free, and clear,
> And little fit to please a classic ear.

> (22-24)

In essaying the task of composition, he has been like the swan, aimlessly following the current of the stream that ever widens before it:

---

[4] For the text of this sonnet and "On Receiving a Laurel Crown from Leigh Hunt" (not in Bush) I have used C. D. Thorpe's *John Keats: Complete Poems and Selected Letters* (New York, 1935).

Just like that bird am I in loss of time,
Whene'er I venture on the stream of rhyme;
With shatter'd boat, oar snapt, and canvass rent,
I slowly sail, scarce knowing my intent;
Still scooping up the water with my fingers,
In which a trembling diamond never lingers.

(15-20)

Since the poetical voyage, as he conceived it, should have no predetermined course, he could only hope that, while allowing his medium, the rush of sensation, to bear him forward, he could from time to time arrest and transform its flow of images into the brighter, harder shapes and symbols of a crystallizing intention. Of course it was just the transmutation from water into diamond, from sensation into thought, that remained not simply difficult to account for but to achieve. There was, to take just one example, his ludicrous and humiliating failure with the sonnet "On Receiving a Laurel Crown from Leigh Hunt":

Minutes are flying swiftly, and as yet
    Nothing unearthly has enticed my brain
    Into a Delphic labyrinth—I would fain
Catch an immortal thought to pay the debt
I owe to the kind Poet who has set
    Upon my ambitious head a glorious gain.

Here again the strategy is to pursue the coil of sensation into the cave or labyrinth—the various analogues of those "Places of nestling green for Poets made" celebrated in one of his epigraphs for the 1817 volume[5]—with the hope of capturing something "unearthly," the type of "immortal thought." However the sonnet expresses only the painful consciousness of a strategy that remains unfulfilled. It is not so much a tribute of thanks as the analysis of a failure.

[5] See D'Avanzo's suggestive discussion of the image of the bower in *Keats's Metaphors for the Poetic Imagination* (Durham, N.C., 1967), pp. 164-72.

A note of guilt and despondency underlies much of the verse in the 1817 volume. It derives from the concerns of a poet unable to harmonize his poetic means and ends, one who is aware of his own inability to realize, except in the most wistful way, a valid and substantial relationship between them. At the opening of the epistle "To My Brother George," for example, Keats presents himself, with conscious irony, as one who must "strive to *think* divinely" (8) by lying in the grass and gazing at the stars. He is a poet who must seek his inspiration in the world of nature and its thousand particular occurrences, all the while fearing or suspecting that something more is required,

> That the still murmur of the honey bee
> Would never teach a rural song to me.
>
> (13-14)

Hence the recurring moods of depression from which he can escape only fitfully, at periods when he can write:

> At times, 'tis true, I've felt relief from pain
> When some bright *thought* has darted through my brain.
>
> (113-14)

Such moments are not only fugitive but troublingly mysterious and unaccountable, like those instants when the poet is suddenly granted

> many a verse from so strange influence
> That we must ever wonder how, and whence
> It came.
>
> ("Sleep and Poetry," 69-71)[6]

[6] Woodhouse copied out these lines on one of the preliminary pages of his copy of Keats's *Poems* and marked them in the printed text, noting they were "truly applicable to many of the author's verses." See my monograph, "Richard Woodhouse's Interleaved and Annotated Copy of Keats's *Poems* (1817)," *Literary Monographs*, vol. 1, ed. Eric Rothstein and Thomas K. Dunseath (Madison, Wis., 1967), pp. 140, 153.

There are, to be sure, periods when, as he tells George, he is able to put aside all misgivings,

> times, when those that love the bay,
> Fly from all sorrowing far, far away;
> A sudden glow comes on them, nought they see
> In water, earth, or air, but poesy,
>
> (19-22)

times when he is able to realize the fulfillment of his "mighty abstract Idea . . . of Beauty in all things." Yet even here such moments of imaginative exhilaration are vaguely disquieting, as earth and its reality seem to dissolve in a sense of almost mystical ecstasy. Moreover the visions granted him—some knights "in playful quarrel" (28) or an assemblage of fair ladies (37-38)—are fanciful and nebulous and tangential to more serious concerns. Such imaginative adventures are alluring; but Keats continually feels it necessary to recall himself to the task of speaking directly to the patriot or the sage in "happy thoughts sententious" (78), to smother his delight in visionary joys in order, paradoxically, to be "happier" because "dearer to society" (112). What we find in a work like the epistle to George is a poet whose reliance on the poetic process as a way of apprehending the timeless and the beautiful is at odds with a desire for clarity of purpose, definition, and point.

II

As has frequently been recognized, the two longest poems, "I Stood Tip-toe" and "Sleep and Poetry," occupy places of particular importance within the 1817 collection. Both resemble in many points of manner and technique the earlier epistles (it is possible for different reasons to think of either one or the other as Keats's epistle to Hunt). "I Stood Tip-toe" begins as an accumulation of disparate and minute observations of nature which gradually achieve the cohesiveness and depth of landscape, its alleys conducting the eye of the observer inward toward the cells and sheltering recesses conducive to the creation of verse. "Sleep and Poetry" both begins with and employs throughout the old device of cataloguing images from nature and art, for, as the poet tells us,

> Things such as these are ever harbingers
> To *trains* of peaceful images.
>
> (339-40)

The natural images the poem begins by itemizing only serve to lead on to and introduce the idea of sleep, the "Wreather," the "Silent entangler" (14-15), which is itself, by way of analogy, only a transition to something yet "higher beyond thought" (19)—the conception of poetry which Keats attempts to formulate now more than ever within the flow and movement of the creative process.

Despite such familiar aspects, each poem breaks important new ground in Keats's development. Each explores, in a way he had not previously undertaken, a mode of poetic expression that was to command his attention repeatedly throughout the remainder of his career. In "I Stood Tip-toe" (originally entitled "Endymion") we see him for the first time seriously pondering the origin and nature of *mythology* and (implicitly, at least) the question of its adaptability to the present demands and purposes of verse. In the central section of "Sleep and Poetry" we find him developing his evident attraction for and absorption in visionary experience in a way that for the first time clearly suggests an evolution toward *allegory*. The two works are further interrelated in one significant respect. Each makes, in its own way, claims for the validity of either faculty—the mythological or the allegorical—as major aspects of the kind of thought or intuition appropriate to verse. At the same time, however, the major assertions each work makes are in the end so subtly qualified as to leave one wondering whether its ultimate effect is more affirmative or skeptical and questioning.

It was natural that Keats should be attracted by the theory of mythology, for the subject (especially as dealt with recently

81

by both Wordsworth and Hunt)[7] was one that provided an explanation for the origin of verse. Poetry, as Keats proceeds to develop the idea in "I Stood Tip-toe," originates in mythology, for the images and stories of myth are poetry in its most primitive state—the product of that imaginative vitalization (basically personification) of natural forms and situations all men are in certain moods led to experience. Both spring from that coalescence between the perceiving mind of the primal poet and the objects of his perception. Deep in the forest, any man may catch a glimpse of fauns or dryads; and similarly any wanderer by moonlight may imagine or discover higher, ethereal intimations,

> Shapes from the invisible world, unearthly singing
> From out the middle air.
>
> (186-87)

In many respects the notion was closely related to the whole conception of intensity and the etherealizing power of the imagination that had already begun to take shape in his mind.

The larger issue raised in "I Stood Tip-toe," however, has to do not with the origin of poetry ("What first inspired a bard of old to sing?" [163]) so much as with the question of its authenticity:

> *Where had he been*, from whose warm head out-flew
> That sweetest of all songs?
>
> (181-82)

An answer is immediately implied through Keats's growing fascination with the particular legend of Endymion:

> Ah! surely he had burst our mortal bars;
> Into some wond'rous region he had gone,
> To search for thee, divine Endymion!
>
> (190-92)

It is tempting to accept the lines, as some have done, as the expression of Keats's firm commitment to some theory of

[7] See Bush's general note on the poem, p. 310 of his edition.

visionary transcendence. Yet the more one weighs the tone and mood of the passage ("Ah! *surely* he had burst. . . ."), the more he is led to wonder whether its force is that of true conviction or mere wishfulness. Nor is the particular note of ambivalence we sense untypical of the poem as a whole. At times the visionary trance seems actually to bring the poet "Shapes from the invisible world, unearthly singing"; at others, its effects are more obscure and questionable, as when it

> *Charms* us at once away from all our troubles:
> So that we *feel* uplifted from the world,
> Walking upon the white clouds wreath'd and curl'd.
>
> (138-40)

Indeed Keats must have been to some degree aware that the various myths he enumerates—not just that of Endymion and Diana but of Cupid and Psyche (141-50), Pan and Syrinx (157-62), and Narcissus and Echo (163-80)—might lend themselves to radically different conclusions to the questions uppermost in his mind. During the following months he was to discover that even his decision to devote himself to one of them alone was no guarantee he could harmonize its various implications or foresee the ultimate significance it was to acquire for him. Rather than any genuine resolution, "I Stood Tip-toe" expresses a pressure of conflicting attitudes toward the nature and validity of visionary experience together with a predilection for mythology, and the Endymion legend in particular, as a means of dramatizing and clarifying his own deeper impulses and beliefs. The poem ends not with a declaration but a further question of both generic and keen personal importance: "Was there a Poet born?" (241). It was one he could answer only in time and by means of a further, more ambitious attempt.

Keats's preoccupation with the nature of imaginative experience is evidenced again in "Sleep and Poetry," the most important work he composed before the major undertaking of *Endymion*. Beginning with the poet's longing

>   for ten years, that I may overwhelm
>   Myself in poesy; so I may do the deed
>   That my own soul has to itself decreed,

the crucial passage (96-162) describes the poet's imagined progress through various domains.

>   First the realm I'll pass
>   Of Flora, and old Pan: sleep in the grass,
>   Feed upon apples red, and strawberries,
>   And choose each pleasure that my fancy sees.
>
>   (101-104)

At length, however, he is summoned from these delights by a challenge:

>   And can I ever bid these joys farewell?
>   Yes, I must pass them for a nobler life,
>   Where I may find the agonies, the strife
>   Of human hearts.
>
>   (122-25)

This later, nobler stage of development is emblemized by the charioteer who descends in his car to summon up and pursue a host of "Shapes of delight, of mystery, and fear" (138), only to disappear into the light of heaven.

The entire progression clearly returns us to the poet's newly aroused interest in mythology. For the realm of Flora and Pan is fundamentally the primal world of mythological discovery where the poet can pick and choose amid a profusion of fresh images and enjoyments, where he learns to woo nymphs from their "shady places," and where, first with one and then another, he proceeds to read "A lovely tale of human life" (110), or rather a succession of tales that are ever-varied and ever-changing. Later on the charioteer, like the first poet in "I Stood Tip-toe," "talks / To the trees and mountains" (136-37), bringing them to life as mythological presences, the shapes of human joy and sorrow who form the pageant

84

of which he writes with such intentness. What separates the two stages as ideals of poetic creation is partly the passive acceptance of variety and pleasure as against the more strenuous effort to understand the shapes and their "mystery" within the context of human suffering—the "burden of the Mystery," as Keats was afterwards to call it, the realization that "the World is full of Misery and Heartbreak, Pain, Sickness and oppression" (I, 281). It is the difference between contentment with an abundance of self-sufficient images, with life as "The reading of an ever-changing tale" (91), and the struggle for the visionary means to assimilate such different forms and values within a coherent view of human existence. Thus the charioteer pursues a multitude of shapes who "murmur, laugh, and smile, and weep" (142), some "thousands in a thousand different ways" (148). Yet he seems to write of them knowingly and as a whole and in a way that Keats, as poet, longs to understand:

> O that I might know
> All that he writes with such a hurrying glow.
>
> (153-54)

The description of the realm of "Flora, and old Pan" and the vision of the charioteer and his car represent Keats's most ambitious attempt to convey the joys of mythological discovery but within the terms of a spiritual progression that strongly suggests allegory.

There have been a number of attempts to give the progression allegorical significance. Richard Woodhouse, perhaps the first to do so, took it as an allegory of Keats's intended stylistic development, dramatizing his desire to perfect himself gradually in all the various poetic genres, beginning with such simpler forms as pastoral and working up to a mastery of the grander and more complex demands of epic, an interpretation seconded independently and in our own day by M. H. Abrams.[8] Other critics, notably Ernest de Selin-

[8] See Woodhouse's annotations for the passage and the discussion of

court, have sought to interpret the passage in ethical terms
by relating it to those stages in human development described
in Wordsworth's "Tintern Abbey" and by Keats himself,
over a year later, in his famous letter to Reynolds concerning
the change from the "infant or thoughtless Chamber" to the
"Chamber of Maiden-Thought" (1, 280-81).[9] Far from being
contradictory, the two interpretations in many respects support each other, unless we press one or the other of them to
an extreme. It remains, for example, an open question
whether we are to look on the sojourn in the realm of "Flora,
and old Pan" as an integral and necessary stage in Keats's
growth or rather, as de Selincourt would have it, as an instance of the poet's "love of luxuriating in trivial fancies in
no way connected with his essential poetic development"
(p. 407). Characteristically, both sets of possibilities remain
open at this point in his career.

No sooner is the vision perceived than it fades into the
"muddy stream" of "real things" (157-58). The parabolic
design of vision and loss, of rapture and disillusion, was one
that Keats was to carry further in *Endymion* and that was to
prove basic to the structure of the greatest of the odes of the
spring of 1819. Yet the vision in "Sleep and Poetry" does not
fade entirely but remains in the poet's memory as a kind of
image of compelling significance, granting him the encouragement necessary to pursue his larger undertaking:

> but I will strive
> Against all doubtings, and will keep alive
> The *thought* of that same chariot, and the strange
> Journey it went.
>
> (159-62)

---

them in "Woodhouse's Interleaved and Annotated Copy of Keats's
Poems," pp. 124-25, 153-54. See also *The Norton Anthology of
English Literature*, ed. M. H. Abrams, rev. ed. (New York, 1968), II,
505-506nn.

[9] Ernest de Selincourt, *The Poems of John Keats*, 5th ed. (London,
1926), pp. 406-408.

The point is that, despite its fading, the vision of the journey has come to assume the value of an intellectual or moral ideal. The value is one Keats is led to reassert in the poem's most ringingly affirmative passage, where he juxtaposes the truths of the imagination and poetry against those of rational thought:

> What though I am not wealthy in the dower
> Of spanning wisdom; though I do not know
> The shiftings of the mighty winds that blow
> Hither and thither all the changing thoughts
> Of man: though no great minist'ring reason sorts
> Out the dark mysteries of human souls
> To clear conceiving: yet there ever rolls
> A vast idea before me, and I glean
> Therefrom my liberty; thence too I've seen
> The end and aim of Poesy. 'Tis clear
> As any thing most true.

(284-94)

If the successive images of verse are continually altering in pattern and implication, there is no sure stability to be found in the intellectual world amid the thousand changing thoughts of man. Keats, nevertheless, is moved to accord those intimations peculiar to poetry—like the vision of the charioteer and his car—the value of a formative *idea*, an idea sufficient for the present to define, if not the final truths, at least "The *end* and *aim* of Poesy." Amid "all doubtings," he remains faithful to his "vast idea" of poetry as a form of meaningful exploration and to his sense of an ultimate goal before him of sufficient clarity to justify his whole endeavor.

The conviction, however, is no sooner uttered than it is immediately questioned in the way that characterizes the larger method and progression of the poem. Has he spoken like a madman, the type of the Daedalian overreacher? Was his vision really one to "human senses fitted"? How can he hope, even after many days and much turmoil, to fathom the great ocean of poetry with its innumerable *widenesses*

(309), the sense of infinitely expanding vistas that had struck him in both his sonnets on Chapman's Homer and "On the Sea"? Was his notion of a goal and purpose distinct enough or his means for achieving them adequately clear?

In "I Stood Tip-toe" and "Sleep and Poetry" one finds Keats seeking to defend poetry, in a steadily deepening way, as a valid and significant form of human intuition. Yet one also finds him increasingly aware of the difficulties and questions underlying the very intuitiveness of his approach and of the real dangers before him. Perhaps he could find in the origins of mythology, the prototype of the earliest verse, a precedent sufficient to account for that spontaneous emergence of natural forms under the pressure of the imagination into images of human relevance and truth. Nevertheless the total sum of myths was virtually limitless, and any one of them could be developed in an infinite variety of ways. The real question was whether he could adapt a fable in such a manner as to extend and harmonize its implications, to use it as a means of effectively clarifying his own visionary concerns. The task was to develop myth so as to make it represent a view of experience that would be both meaningful and at the same time true to the real complexity of his own sense of things. Such a poetic undertaking could not help but prove allegorical, at least in the larger sense of the term suggested by his later declaration that "a Man's life of any worth is a continual allegory. . . . Shakspeare led a life of Allegory; his works are the comments on it" (II, 67).

The bulk of Keats's early verse provides the context vital to an understanding of *Endymion*. It shows us a poet increasingly involved with and dependent on the poetic and associative processes as a means both of writing and thinking. It shows us, too, a poet increasingly aware of the problems of such dependence—not just the larger question of the whole validity of visionary experience but also the more practical one of giving it a certain permanence, definition, and form. In "I Stood Tip-toe" and "Sleep and Poetry" we find him turning to mythology and allegory, or rather to the possibilities for a fresh assimilation between them, as a means of dramatizing and exploring such concerns. Nevertheless it remained to be seen whether his choice of the Endymion legend, together with his continued and determined reliance on the creativity of his own evolving consciousness, would provide the necessary grounds for realizing a work of unity and meaning as he hoped. Certainly he would never know without trying; and he was determined to make the attempt.

CHAPTER FOUR

———◄———

THE ALLEGORY OF
ENDYMION

Endymion presents particular challenges to the critic. The poem is by far the longest Keats wrote and has, among his longer pieces, the notable advantage of completeness. He devoted almost a year of his brief career to it and learned much from its composition. It seems to merit the fullest critical attention. Yet the poem is labyrinthine and over-grown, a little wilderness amid whose tangles one can wander happily but at the risk of becoming lost. Keats was himself aware both of the fascinations and the dangers of the longer work. "I have heard Hunt say and may be asked," he wrote George at about the time he began *Endymion*, "why endeavour after a long Poem? To which I should answer—Do not the Lovers of Poetry like to have a little Region to wander in where they may pick and choose, and in which the images are so numerous that many are forgotten and found new in a second Reading: which may be food for a week's stroll in the Summer?" (I, 170). A long poem could provide the reader with room to move about in, "full of Symbols for his spiritual eye, of softness for his spiritual touch, of space for his wandering of distinctness for his Luxury," as he later put it (I, 232). Nevertheless certain further guidelines and objectives were, if only by implication, necessary. "Besides," he went on to George, "a long Poem is a test of Invention which I take to be the Polar Star of Poetry, as Fancy is the Sails, and Imagination the Rudder" (I, 170). Not long earlier he had pictured himself as drifting on the stream of rhyme "With shatter'd boat, oar snapt, and canvass rent." It remained to be seen what navigational skill he could bring to the task of piloting the ship of poetry on a substantial "voyage of conception."

Such different needs—the desire for imaginative flexibility and amplitude together with the concern for some emerging pattern of realization—were ones Keats sought to reconcile within the broader outlines of romance. (When it appeared, his poem was subtitled "A Poetic Romance.") They go far toward explaining the considerable disagreement that has, over the years, separated critics who have sought to define more exactly the category of romance to which the poem belongs. One need only return to such older critics of the poem as Sir Sidney Colvin, Robert Bridges, and Ernest de Selincourt to recall that for many years it was traditional to read the work as a deliberate allegory, conceived more or less upon Platonic lines, of the poet's longing for and eventual union with the spirit of ideal beauty. While differing with respect to minor points of interpretation, these critics resolved the action of the poem into a series of gradually ascending stages of human development, beginning with the love of sensuous beauty, leading in time to humanitarian service and active sympathy for fellow man, and ending with the recognition that these, rightly perceived, are one with the ideal. The argument of the poem was both sustained and coherent in development, essentially a dramatic working-out, culminating in the union of Cynthia and the Indian Maiden, of the conviction Keats expressed the very month he put an end to his first draft: "I am certain of nothing but of the holiness of the Heart's affections and the truth of Imagination—What the imagination seizes as Beauty must be truth" (1, 184).[1]

[1] See Sir Sidney Colvin, *John Keats* (London, 1920), pp. 171-205; Ernest de Selincourt, *The Poems of John Keats*, 5th ed. (London, 1926), pp. xl-xli, 428, 443-45; and Robert Bridges, *Collected Essays Papers &c.*, iv (London, 1929), "A Critical Introduction to Keats," 85-93. The groundwork for the interpretation was actually laid, as Colvin acknowledged, by F. M. Owen in *John Keats: A Study* (London, 1880). In after years the interpretation was given a specifically Neoplatonic bent by Claude Finney (*The Evolution of Keats's Poetry* [Cambridge, Mass., 1936], 1, 291-319) and integrated more fully with-

More recently the allegorical interpretation of the poem
has come increasingly under attack. Critics like Newell Ford
and E. C. Pettet have drawn attention to a notable discrep-
ancy between Keats's supposed allegorical intention and the
discursiveness and incoherence of his narrative, together with
the strongly erotic character of much of the episode and
imagery. These inconsistencies were, of course, evident to
older critics, who explained them as the result of a gap between conception and execution understandable in a young
poet distracted and at times misled by a powerfully sensuous
nature. Such reasoning, however, is for Ford and Pettet mere
rationalization evolved by critics unwilling or unable to
confront the frank expression of Keats's longing for an "everlasting erotism,"[2] or, more simply, the sexual fantasies of a
maturing young man. With the possible exception of a few
passages, the poem is for them an instance of romance in the

---

in the larger pattern of the poet's intellectual development by Clarence
Thorpe (*The Mind of John Keats* [New York, 1926], pp. 57-62 and
passim).

2 The phrase is used by Ford ("*Endymion*—A Neo-Platonic Allegory?" *ELH*, XIV [1947], 69) to describe the central theme of the
poem. For Ford's other work and for Pettet, see Ch. 2, nn. 32, 33.
Amy Lowell was among the first to attack the allegorical interpretation (*John Keats* [Boston, 1925], I, 318 and passim). Most later criticism, like Bernard Blackstone's lengthy discussion of the poem (*The
Consecrated Urn* [London, 1959], pp. 116-203) as "magical, alchemical, occultist," has been content to ignore it. Robert Harrison's interesting "Symbolism of the Cyclical Myth in *Endymion*," *Texas Studies
in Literature and Language*, I (1960), 538-54, reveals the contradictions
facing any conventional archetypal interpretation. By contrast, North-
rop Frye's facile reading of the poem on "four levels" (*A Study of
English Romanticism* [New York, 1968], pp. 125-65) forces it to fit a
preconceived archetypal pattern that ignores virtually all the inconsistencies and contradictions older critics had at least confessed. Charles
I. Patterson's recent full-length study of the poem in *The Daemonic in
the Poetry of John Keats* (Urbana, Ill., 1970), pp. 22-100, concurs in
rejecting the traditional allegorical approach. A summary of conflicting
views, together with a qualified defense of the older position, will be
found in Jacob D. Wigod's "The Meaning of *Endymion*," *PMLA*,
LXVIII (1953), 779-90.

simplest sense—a frank love poem powerfully energized by Keats's adolescent desires. It would be difficult to imagine two interpretations more at odds. Is the work a fable intended to convey certain settled conclusions as to the nature of beauty, truth, and poetic experience? Or is it rather a chain of daydreams and reveries, best interpreted as a psychiatrist interprets the free associations of a patient and useful primarily for what it reveals concerning the quality of Keats's unconscious life?

It would be wrong to imply that critics of the poem have necessarily embraced one view or the other, the traditional and allegorical or the erotic. Nevertheless the two approaches have to date proved most influential and have polarized debate around certain questions of crucial importance. In weighing the merits of such different arguments, one must begin by admitting that Keats never confided, even to friends with whom he was intimate, that he wrote the poem with any allegorical plan in mind. He wrote to George of having to "make 4000 Lines of one bare circumstance and fill them with Poetry" (1, 170), and, divided equally between four books, the mark was one he approximated with extraordinary accuracy. Nor do his habits of composition suggest an allegorical scheme. Bailey, with whom Keats spent the month of September 1817 when he was at work on his third book, reported that Keats "sat down to his task,—which was about 50 lines a day,—with his paper before him, & wrote with as much regularity, & apparently with as much ease, as he wrote his letters."[3] If Keats intended his poem to be read as allegory in any strict sense, the key to its meaning was a well-kept secret among his friends throughout his lifetime and after his death.

Yet for all this it remains impossible to read the whole of Keats's narrative, regardless of how aimless and confusing much of it seems, as a mere play of erotic fantasy. Endymion's

[3] *The Keats Circle: Letters and Papers and More Letters and Poems of the Keats Circle*, ed. Hyder Edward Rollins, 2nd ed. (Cambridge, Mass., 1965), II, 270.

speech on happiness, the central argument of Book One, outlines an ascending order of imaginative values, beginning with a love of natural objects, leading on to sympathy and friendship, and culminating in human and divine love, a hierarchy of intensities that is both developed and put to trial in the books to come. Later in the poem Endymion's sympathy for Alpheus and Arethusa, Glaucus's pity for the drowned lovers and their joint service in restoring Circe's victims to life, and the ultimate revelation that Cynthia and the Indian Maiden are one are too clearly turning points within the narrative to be dismissed as random bits of episode. Even those critics most opposed to reading the poem as allegory are forced, in one way or another, to grant such episodes a calculated significance.[4] There was, moreover, the example set by Shelley, a fellow protégé of Hunt's whose progress Keats followed and measured himself against throughout his career and whose *Alastor or the Spirit of Solitude* had appeared only a year earlier.[5] The latter work, a poem of quest containing passages as erotic as any in *Endymion*, had taken as its theme both the ennobling heroism and the fatal self-absorption of visionary pursuit as set off by the contradictory dialectics of its preface. The dilemma Shelley depicted was one Keats found himself engrossed by: the plight of the artist who envisions to himself an image that "unites all of wonderful, or wise, or beautiful, which the

[4] Ford's account of the last two books as a development of the theme of infidelity in love (*The Prefigurative Imagination of John Keats* [Stanford, Calif., 1951], pp. 67, 74, and passim) is itself the makings of an allegorical interpretation, could it be fully worked out. Pettet finds the themes of infidelity and benevolence primary in Book Three, while he confesses (p. 191) to the temptation to read the last book allegorically, could it be taken by itself alone.

[5] In "The Genesis, Growth, and Meaning of *Endymion*," *Studies in Philology*, xxx (1933), 618-53, Leonard Brown has argued persuasively that the poem evolved in Keats's mind partly in reaction to certain aspects of *Alastor*. In particular he suggested Shelley's Arab Maiden as a source for the Indian Maiden in Book Four of *Endymion*.

poet, the philosopher, or the lover could depicture"[6] but that can be pursued only at the expense of an enervating introspection that isolates and kills. What was particularly impressive was the combination of openness and subtlety with which Shelley developed various aspects of the paradox into a parable of complex thematic significance. More broadly, however, one cannot ignore the whole larger tradition on which Keats drew for the major handling of his narrative: the main line of Elizabethan pastoral-didactic verse that runs from Spenser to Milton and includes such writers as George Sandys, the translator and interpreter of Ovid.[7] It is a tradition of mythological verse in which one discovers, along with a prodigality and confusion of detail, and instinctive drift toward allegory, in Colvin's words (p. 171) an "habitual wedding of allegory and romance."

It is, in fact, allegory in its broadest and most general sense that characterizes *Endymion*. There is no reason for believing Keats began his poem with a plan for its development or its ultimate significance clearly in view. Quite the opposite is, in all likelihood, the case. Yet, at the same time, there is every reason to believe that he looked upon the composition as a necessary "test, a trial," as he himself put it, not merely of his "Powers of Imagination" (I, 169) but of his deepest instincts and beliefs. The poem must crystallize, if only for himself, the most important of his poetic convictions. Above all it must confront the whole question of visionary experience that had emerged throughout the early verse, concentrated in his fascination with the legend of Endymion. For the latter is obviously no simple love story. In its involvement with dreams and visions, its contrast between mortality

[6] "Preface" to *Alastor or the Spirit of Solitude, The Complete Poetical Works of Percy Bysshe Shelley*, ed. Thomas Hutchinson (London, 1934), p. 14. Later citations of Shelley are to this edition.

[7] See Joan Grundy, "Keats and the Elizabethans," in *John Keats: A Reassessment*, ed. Kenneth Muir (Liverpool, 1958), pp. 1-19. For the influence of Sandys on *Endymion*, see de Selincourt pp. 391, 505, and passim, and the notes to *Endymion* in Bush's edition.

and immortality, and its culmination in transcendence, the Endymion myth is unmistakably connected with the visionary concerns of the earlier poetry. As one who has "burst our mortal bars" to ascend into "some wond'rous region," Endymion offered an unmistakable analogue for the poet who gains "Wings to find out an immortality" of poetic inspiration and fulfillment. The legend provided Keats a means for dramatizing his fundamental conviction of "the truth of imagination." At the same time it possessed the flexibility to permit him to elaborate and test the reality of that belief as he proceeded.

Yet what form, more exactly, would the elaboration take? Beyond the necessity of treating the "one bare circumstance" of his fable, Keats was bound only by the otherworldly bias of the legend—its ending in transcendence of mortality—and by the expectation of some joyous, triumphant conclusion like the marriage celebrations he had touched on briefly at the end of "I Stood Tip-toe." Otherwise his plan for proceeding was pliable, even disconcertingly vague. Nevertheless his determination to adhere to his own methods of composition carried with it the necessity of trusting to his powers of invention, his ability to improvise the kind of episode that would keep his poem moving forward dramatically. As for its further significance, that would have to come organically, "as naturally as the Leaves to a tree" (I, 238) or not at all. The poem must communicate knowledge and conviction but, in Arnold's phrase, "insensibly, and in the second place, not the first," and through what would be essentially an act of self-discovery both for poet and reader. Much later, when his mind was "pick'd up and sorted to a pip," he was to look back on the author of *Endymion* as one "whose mind was like a pack of scattered cards" (II, 323). Nevertheless the experience of writing the poem, however "slip-shod" it might later seem to him, was one he could not entirely regret. As he wrote his publisher, James Hessey, in one of the most candid and noble paragraphs of self-criticism any poet has written:

96

I will write independantly.—I have written independently *without Judgment*—I may write independently *& with judgment* hereafter.—The Genius of Poetry must work out its own salvation in a man: It cannot be matured by law & precept, but by sensation & watchfulness in itself—That which is creative must create itself—In Endymion, I leaped headlong into the Sea, and thereby have become better acquainted with the Soundings, the quicksands, & the rocks, than if I had stayed upon the green shore, and piped a silly pipe, and took tea & comfortable advice.

(1, 374; Keats's italics)

As he instinctively realized, the poem represented a headlong plunge into the sea, into the reaches of his own unconsciousness and creativity, the region from which, as in his sonnet "On the Sea," some voice or harmony would have in its own way to come. In working out the destiny of his hero he was in fact working out his own.

II

It was only natural that, faced with the necessity of making a beginning, he should start his poem with what was most fundamental: his commitment to his notion of the creative process. Following its initial declaration, the opening paragraph of *Endymion* proceeds to an enumeration of particular "thing[s] of beauty"—the sun, moon, trees, sheep, flowers, rills, and forest brakes. However its real concern is with the process by which these forms are converted, partly through the agency of sleep and dreams, into "essences" that are wellnigh spiritual. The progression proceeds from the images of the natural world to their inclusion in works of imagination ("All lovely tales that we have heard or read") only to engross them all collectively within an image of supernal energy and delight—"An endless fountain of immortal drink, / Pouring unto us from the heaven's brink." The process is the now

familiar one by which the images of nature are spiritualized
in imagination and put into "etherial existence" for man's enduring enjoyment. It is a process that both exalts and liber-
ates man in imagination and at the same time "binds" him
ever more closely to the earth—the particular tension that
Keats was to become steadily more preoccupied with as he
proceeded.

The same progression dominates the poem's finest lyric,
the "Hymn to Pan," early in Book One. In the first four
stanzas the god is celebrated as the presiding deity of the
world of natural process, only to emerge in the final stanza
as a symbol for something more:

> Be still the unimaginable lodge
> For solitary thinkings; such as dodge
> Conception to the very bourne of heaven,
> Then leave the naked brain: be still the leaven,
> That spreading in this dull and clodded earth
> Gives it a touch ethereal—a new birth:
> Be still a symbol of immensity;
> A firmament reflected in a sea;
> An element filling the space between;
> An unknown—but no more.
>
> (i.293-302)

Ultimately Pan is something more than just a god of hunts-
men, a god of the harvest. He is the symbol of a form of
thinking. Yet he represents at most a tendency, a kind of
thought that is only latent, as "a touch ethereal," throughout
the universe of natural life. He remains inscrutable, something "unimaginable," precisely because he is too diverse and
inexhaustible in his implications ever to be perfectly defined
or brought to full "conception." He remains the symbol of a
source of speculation that can have no limit, that can never
be finally grasped or formulated. He endures as a symbol of
the ultimate mystery of life but considered positively, as a
source of endless investigation and discovery.

The principal argument of Book One, the lines Keats

Claude, *The Sacrifice to Apollo* (*Landscape with the Father of Psyche Sacrificing at the Milesian Temple of Apollo*). The National Trust (Fairhaven Collection), Anglesey Abbey, Cambridgeshire, England; P: Courtauld Institute of Art, London.

likened in effect to "a kind of Pleasure Thermometer," has
already been discussed at length within the context of his
early notion of the creative process.[8] However, it is important
to observe that within the dramatic structure of his poem
Keats does not allow his hero's expression of faith in the
validity of the imagination and its intensifying power to go
unchallenged. Endymion may cling to his intimations of
divinity as "A hope beyond the shadow of a dream" (i.857),
as something more than mere "atomies / That buzz about
our slumbers, like brain-flies, / Leaving us fancy-sick" (i.851-
53). Nevertheless from our first glimpse of him in the poem
he seems pale and wan, alienated from the healthful pursuits
of his fellow Latmians by his strange fits of abstraction. Indeed it is not long before Keats himself addresses him as
"Brain-sick shepherd-prince" (ii.43). More important, Endymion's affirmations of the truth of his visionary experiences
are directly opposed by the counterarguments of his sister,
Peona, who warns him against deceiving fantasies:

> The Morphean fount
> Of that fine element that visions, dreams,
> And fitful whims of sleep are made of, streams
> Into its airy channels with so subtle,
> So thin a breathing, not the spider's shuttle,
> Circled a million times within the space
> Of a swallow's nest-door, could delay a trace,
> A tinting of its quality: how light
> Must dreams themselves be; seeing they're more slight
> Than the mere nothing that engenders them!
> Then wherefore sully the entrusted gem
> Of high and noble life with thoughts so sick?
> Why pierce high-fronted honour to the quick
> For nothing but a dream?
>
> (i.747-60)

Her argument is a plea for Endymion to return to the world
of action from the life of solitary contemplation that has

[8] See pp. 48-49 above.

absorbed him. But more than this, her speech uses several of Keats's favorite metaphors for imaginative creation only to deny their validity. The whole process of associative interweaving and etherealization is too subtle and attenuating to permit any genuine connection with reality to exist.

Thus from an early point in the poem Endymion's faith in the truth of his visionary pursuit is challenged by the warnings of his sister. Two attitudes toward his quest for happiness have emerged, one affirmative, the other skeptical. No doubt this complication was useful and even necessary to Keats for dramatic reasons, a part of the test his hero would have to undergo; but there is no reason to assume the conflict was entirely unconnected with important questions of his own. Keats was clearly committed to dramatizing his hero's struggles and ultimate reward by union with his goddess and the achievement of immortality: the conclusion was one largely determined by the fable he had chosen. Indeed we are reminded of this basic expectation from time to time along the way. At the beginning of Book Two, Endymion is informed that, like his namesake in "I Stood Tip-toe," he

> must wander far
> In other regions, past the scanty bar
> To mortal steps.
>
> (ii.123-25)

Again at the end of Book Three, after many disappointments, he is mysteriously reassured of his coming reward and of his love's intent to "snatch" him "into endless heaven" (iii.1026-27). Yet the deeper poetic elaboration of this intention is neither steady nor consistent. For one thing, as Endymion's dream-journeys toward his immortal love become more ecstatic, the end of the cycle—the fading of the dream, the return to earth, and the sense of loss and despondency—grows in intensity. The major action of the poem does not follow the pattern of gradual ascent but resembles more the parabolic structure we have seen emerge for the first time in the central vision of "Sleep and Poetry," a pattern of longing, momentary fulfillment, then loss, despondency, and doubt.

In dealing with the love interludes that provide the chief narrative involvement of the earlier books, it is necessary to examine the erotic character of the poem in closer detail. As I have indicated, it is for a number of reasons impossible to agree with critics who read *Endymion* as no more than a simple tale of sexual passion, the gratification of its author's suppressed desires. For time and again critics have failed to see that Keats's use of erotic imagery is integrally related to the visionary concerns of his poem, that it habitually calls into play instincts and feelings that, while connected with the sexual impulse, run deeper. Beginning with "I Stood Tip-toe," he had been drawn to the Endymion legend as a search for "endless bliss," an "immortality of passion." Yet in tracing the love-adventures of his hero, he was necessarily led to work out the implications of the quest at a deeper psychological level than any he had yet explored. At the height of his rapturous embrace with Cynthia in Book Two, Endymion exclaims:

> O known Unknown! from whom my being sips
> Such darling essence, wherefore may I not
> Be ever in these arms?
>
> (ii.739-41)

She is a "second self," his "breath of life," who promises him that

> I will tell the stories of the sky,
> And breathe thee whispers of its minstrelsy.
> My happy love will overwing all bounds!
> O let me melt into thee; let the sounds
> Of our close voices marry at their birth;
> Let us entwine hoveringly—O dearth
> Of human words! roughness of mortal speech!
> Lispings empyrean will I sometime teach
> Thine honied tongue—lute-breathings, which I gasp
> To have thee understand, now while I clasp
> Thee thus.   (ii.812-22)

To read such passages as mere sexual description is to fail to see that something more than sensual passion is involved. The images of mouth and lips, of kissing, sipping, speech, possess a more than physical significance. Endymion draws emotional vitality and life from the unknown form he embraces who seems almost a part of his own unconscious being, the source of feelings that cannot be readily expressed in words. The imagery, that is to say, suggests not so much the physical passion of real lovers as the communion of the poet with the vital springs of his imaginative life. The larger context of the love-embrace suggests an ecstasy of imaginative fulfillment conveyed metaphorically through the details of bodily passion.

To interpret the love theme in *Endymion* as a part of Keats's broader visionary concern is not to explain away the erotic elements in the poem (or in Keats's nature) but to restore them to their proper perspective. For one thing, the sexual drive in any individual is never self-contained but overlaps with and is inseparable from a broad range of imaginative preoccupations. In the brief, awkwardly apologetic preface Keats published with the poem he wrote: "The imagination of a boy is healthy, and the mature imagination of a man is healthy; but there is a space of life between, in which the soul is in a ferment, the character undecided, the way of life uncertain, the ambition thick-sighted." The passage, in the kind of immaturity and indecisiveness it admits, possesses unmistakable sexual overtones; nevertheless, it is the imagination in its larger sense of which he writes.

In Book One Keats had boldly outlined the scale of various degrees of imaginative involvement leading to the "chief intensity" of love. Yet it was primarily through the longing of Endymion for Cynthia and his pursuit of the goddess that he possessed the means of dramatizing the psychological reality of visionary experience and thus of translating the terms of an abstract progression into action that is vital, fluid, and emotionally meaningful. In one sense Cynthia exists as a symbol, a mere abstraction. Yet she is a value that is variously defined and given significance by a powerful sensuality of imagination, a sensuality that itself develops and changes in implication as the poem proceeds. Even from the first our attention is not drawn to the love interludes for their own sake but for their part in the whole cycle of Endymion's visionary experience—of which the union with Cynthia is the culminating moment, but nevertheless only a part. As in the earlier poetry the process begins with a gradual withdrawal from the natural world; Endymion retreats through mossy caves and bowers until, feeling "endued / With power to dream deliciously" (ii.707-708), he falls asleep. Following the exclusion of the outer world, the dream begins through which a state of intense imaginative awareness is conveyed that underlies, at some far deeper level, the rational, conceptual functions of the mind:

> Yet it was but a dream: yet such a dream
> That never tongue, although it overteem
> With mellow utterance, like a cavern spring,
> Could figure out and to conception bring
> All I beheld and felt.

(i.574-78)

The dream is not characterized merely by images of sensual gratification but by synesthesia and effortless movement, by warmth and the sudden flowering of foliage, and by the vital, flowing quality that we associate with certain states of intense imaginative experience. It is a world of fluent harmony, the expression of a primitive experience and knowledge that forever seeks yet defies precise articulation or the power of human intelligence to arrest and define.

Endymion's love for Cynthia is the expression of Keats's romance with his muse. It represents the poet's need to explore, through the metaphor of carnal knowledge, his own relation to the hidden springs of inspiration on which the life of his art depends. Nevertheless it is necessary to see that, virtually from the outset of the poem, Endymion's desire for Cynthia is neither a simple nor an unqualified attraction.

103

The emphasis on the goddess's inviolable chastity is evident, while the note of dire warning and taboo that extends even to the Indian Maiden in the final book (iv.751-58) is both explicit and implicit throughout the earlier love sections of the poem. Beyond the alluring warmth and security of Cynthia's embrace there extends a phantasmagoric world of meteors and falling stars, of chilling airs and awesome dens and caverns; and the "dizzy sky," the hints of madness, and the threat of a precipitous fall (ii.185ff.) reintroduce the theme of the Daedalian overreacher Keats had touched on in "Sleep and Poetry." As the successful lover, Endymion is united with the source of all sweetness and joy; but he is also, like an infant, *"lapp'd* and *lull'd* along the *dangerous* sky" (i.646). Moreover the pleasures he experiences are too intense to be long enjoyed. At or near their climax a countermovement toward earth begins, the fabric of the dream collapses, and Endymion is left in mere slumber, in "stupid sleep" (i.678). The power of the dream destroys, by force of contrast, all the natural beauty of the Latmian glades and meadows, leaving Endymion with a waking vision that, in its surrealistic horror, Keats never surpassed:

> deepest shades
> Were deepest dungeons; heaths and sunny glades
> Were full of pestilent light; our taintless rills
> Seem'd sooty, and o'er-spread with upturn'd gills
> Of dying fish; the vermeil rose had blown
> In frightful scarlet, and its thorns out-grown
> Like spiked aloe.
>
> (i.692-98)

Despite the apparent logic of the "Pleasure Thermometer," the destructive and inhibiting aspects of Endymion's passion do not diminish as the poem advances; they increase.

Such shifts and changes in the presentation of Endymion's quest reflect more than Keats's need to complicate and extend the interest of his narrative. They express, rather, genuine ambiguities and qualifications that came to mind only as he proceeded and as he grasped the deeper significance his treatment of the myth had begun to assume. No doubt he had from the first foreseen certain obstacles and difficulties in his hero's way. Endymion's isolation and neglect of his proper role as leader of his people are manifest. Similarly the fundamental message of the Alpheus and Arethusa episode and of that of Glaucus in Book Three seems unmistakable: in his pursuit of visionary beauty Endymion was not to be permitted to forget the need for sympathy and active service on behalf of fellow man. Yet in the implications they present such episodes resist reduction to any easy "allegoric" reading. One can take as an example the Bower of Adonis in Book Two, which traditional critics of the poem have never been comfortable in discussing. With its accumulated store of cream and ripened fruit, the Bower represents a perfectly self-contained world of sensuous and imaginative luxury, idealized beyond all threat of interruption, where the sleeper dreams of his coming joys with Venus. Indeed the episode may directly prefigure, as proponents of the erotic interpretation have argued, the very apotheosis Keats intended for his hero.[9] Yet the Bower, in its dream-like isolation from the world of process and change, seems strangely etherized and shrouded in the quiet of a deathwatch. Although grown to a man, the sleeping Adonis resembles, as much as anything, the infant in the womb or cradle whose every need is gratified. The episode may portray an ideal of imaginative realization; but it is at the same time enveloped in an air of sickliness and self-indulgence.

Such questions of nuance, and, more important, of interpretation, multiply throughout the second half of the poem. The story of Glaucus occupies almost the whole of Book Three and is the only sustained narrative interlude in *Endymion*; yet its relation to the thematic center of the poem is

[9] So Ford argues in *The Prefigurative Imagination of John Keats*, pp. 52-54, as does Pettet in *On the Poetry of Keats*, p. 171.

far from simple. On the most basic level its relevance to the themes of sympathy and humanitarian service is clear. However, the episode seems to bear upon the nature and the goal of Endymion's quest in a deeper way. More specifically, how is one to interpret Glaucus's misadventure in pursuit of his nymph Scylla? Does his failure merely serve to heighten the triumph and superior powers of his liberator, Endymion? Or does the episode possess a further significance? Does it serve as something of a warning to Keats's hero, a premonition that the search for fulfillment in imaginative experience can end in deception and enslavement rather than in happiness and truth? Does the episode stand in sharp contrast to, or does it subtly qualify, the ambition and significance of Endymion's own pursuit? The more one studies the episode, the more difficult it becomes to narrow its significance to any single implication in the thread of Keats's "allegory."

Like Endymion, Glaucus has longed for passionate joys beyond his reach and taken the plunge "for life or death" into a denser element.

> Why was I not contented? Wherefore reach
> At things which, but for thee, O Latmian!
> Had been my dreary death? Fool! I began
> To feel distemper'd longings: to desire
> The utmost privilege that ocean's sire
> Could grant in benediction: to be free
> Of all his kingdom. Long in misery
> I wasted, ere in one extremest fit
> I plung'd for life or death. To interknit
> One's senses with so dense a breathing stuff
> Might seem a work of pain; so not enough
> Can I admire how crystal-smooth it felt,
> And buoyant round my limbs. At first I dwelt
> Whole days and days in sheer astonishment;
> Forgetful utterly of self-intent;
> Moving but with the mighty ebb and flow.
> Then, like a new fledg'd bird that first doth shew

His spreaded feathers to the morrow chill,
I tried in fear the pinions of my will.
'Twas freedom!

(iii.372-91)

His plunge into the ocean brings to mind the way Keats himself "leaped headlong into the Sea" (1, 374) in committing
himself to the act of self-discovery his poem represented. The
description also recalls, in its new-found liberation, the same
initial sense of release and exhilaration that animates the
dream voyages of Keats's hero. Like Endymion, Glaucus soon
becomes enamored of an otherworldly creature, the nymph
Scylla, who becomes the object of his desire and whom he
pursues, much as Alpheus pursues Arethusa, until, in a moment of confusion, he falls prey to the charms of the enchantress Circe. The division in his affections has no counterpart in the earlier account of Endymion's quest, although it
prefigures the hero's dilemma when, at the outset of Book
Four, he suddenly finds himself in love with both the Indian
Maiden and his immortal goddess.

It is possible to regard Circe, like Acrasia (Keats's obvious
model), as an embodiment of false sensual attraction and
Glaucus's infatuation for her as a betrayal of his loyalty to
Scylla that must not go unpunished. Yet once again such a
pat rendering of Keats's allegory does little justice to our
sense of the complexity the Glaucus episode introduces into
the poem. The rose-canopied bower where Circe promises
him the supreme enjoyment of "a long love dream" (iii.440)
seems to reflect ironically on both the Bower of Adonis and
certain aspects of the love-making between Endymion and
Cynthia. Glaucus is enraptured:

> Who could resist? Who in this universe?
> She did so breathe ambrosia; so immerse
> My fine existence in a golden clime.
> She took me like a child of suckling time,
> And cradled me in roses.

(iii.453-57)

We remember that only a little earlier Endymion, clasped in his goddess's embrace, had "swoon'd / Drunken from pleasure's nipple" (ii.868-69). Glaucus, however, has confused Scylla with Circe, the Bower of Adonis with the Bower of Bliss, and one morning he awakes to find his "specious heaven" transformed to "real hell" (iii.476). Amid bursts of cruel, ironic laughter the enchantress, revealed in her true ugliness, proceeds to parody the whole conception of the love-nest and to mock the lassitude and self-indulgence of her victim:

> Ha! ha! Sir Dainty! there must be a nurse
> Made of rose leaves and thistledown, express,
> To cradle thee my sweet, and lull thee: yes,
> I am too flinty-hard for thy nice touch:
> My tenderest squeeze is but a giant's clutch.
> So, fairy-thing, it shall have lullabies
> Unheard of yet: and it shall still its cries
> Upon some breast more lily-feminine.
>
> (iii.570-77)

Glaucus has discovered not Cynthia but La Belle Dame. His infatuation and its end in powerlessness and withered age represents a caricature of the whole notion of the romantic quest which inevitably raises certain questions concerning Endymion's own pursuit. One senses again that the larger meaning of the poem, the real "allegory" of *Endymion*, lies in the way such episodes as those of Alpheus and Arethusa, Endymion's love-encounters with his goddess, the Bower of Adonis, and Glaucus's confusion between Scylla and Circe play off against and qualify each other. Together they reflect the gradual emergence of Keats's deeper attitude toward visionary experience rather than the elaboration of any settled plan.

Our suspicion that Endymion's dilemma has fully become Keats's own increases with Book Four. The induction to this book is the shortest and weakest of the four and introduces a note of despondency that virtually every commentator has in

one way or another observed. Keats has now thoroughly tired
of the poem and is already looking forward to *Hyperion* as a
work that will accomplish what he knows *Endymion* cannot.
More significant is the appearance of the Indian Maiden, an
event that is sudden and altogether unprepared for. At the
very time when he should be struggling upward on the final
lap of his journey toward the "chief intensity," Endymion is
unexpectedly confronted with the choice between two quite
different and opposing ideals of love—the one transcendent,
ecstatic, and immortal; the other warm, earthly, and filled
with the passion of the human heart. The dilemma, touched
on by Shelley in *Alastor,* is one that from the first had fascinated Keats. Yet the struggle, crystallizing ambiguities
latent in the earlier part of the narrative, now begins to
achieve the proportions of a crisis demanding a new and more
profound kind of resolution than any he could have possibly foreseen. As Book Four progresses, the conflict between
the two ideals for possession of Endymion's soul becomes
steadily more intense and divisive, up until the abrupt conclusion. When, for example, Endymion and the Indian
Maiden mount two winged steeds and soar into the region
of the skies—the obvious dramatization of Endymion's urge
to reconcile his earthly and his heavenly loves—the moon
appears from behind a cloud.

> While to his lady meek the Carian turn'd,
> To mark if her dark eyes had yet discern'd
> This beauty in its birth—Despair! despair!
> He saw her body fading gaunt and spare
> In the cold moonshine. Straight he seiz'd her wrist;
> It melted from his grasp: her hand he kiss'd,
> And, horror! kiss'd his own—he was alone.
> Her steed a little higher soar'd, and then
> Dropt hawkwise to the earth.
>
> (iv.504-12)

Beautiful as it first appears, the moon assumes an openly
destructive role, withering in its chill light the warm beauty

by Endymion's side. The baleful part of Cynthia's influence is now fully evident. Attempting to kiss the Indian Maiden, Endymion kisses his own hand, an act of autoeroticism that clearly suggests the solipsistic dangers of the visionary ideal and its ability to dissolve the ties of real human love. From his lofty perch Endymion is plunged into the Cave of Quietude, a kind of Keatsian Center of Indifference. Here he regains his presence of mind but only to reassess, a few lines later, the significance of his quest in a new and startling way:

> I have clung
> To nothing, lov'd a nothing, nothing seen
> Or felt but a great dream! O I have been
> Presumptuous against love, against the sky,
> Against all elements, against the tie
> Of mortals each to each, against the blooms
> Of flowers, rush of rivers, and the tombs
> Of heroes gone!
>
> (iv.636-43)

The very intensity of Endymion's otherworldly longing has fatally overtaxed the sustaining, elemental power of those bands of natural association and human affection that prompt man's higher intimations even while they bind him more securely to the earth. Gaining conviction, he proceeds to reject the whole reality and worth of his heavenly pursuit:

> Caverns lone, farewel!
> And air of visions, and the monstrous swell
> Of visionary seas! No, never more
> Shall airy voices cheat me to the shore
> Of tangled wonder, breathless and aghast.
>
> (iv.651-55)

With such words he has, as it were, come round to agreeing with his sister's judgment, and the whole value and meaning of his pilgrimage is brought into question.

For critics of the older school such speeches are only the final darkness before the onrushing dawn, Endymion's last moment of doubt before the revelation that the conflicting attractions that confront him are in fact but different aspects of a single ideal. Such a reading, whatever its validity as an ex post facto judgment, betrays the deeper meaning of the poem considered as a process of creative self-discovery. For it ignores the tone of real conviction and dramatic urgency that characterizes the struggle in Book Four and, by contrast, the brief and remarkably spiritless conclusion. The final resolution arrives in the last hundred lines with the bewildering speed of anticlimax. Cynthia's light, once so hostile and destructive, irradiates the features of the Indian Maiden with the force of a maternal blessing. There is no time for rejoicing or acclaim or the marriage festivities Keats had contemplated celebrating in "I Stood Tip-toe." The two lovers simply bless Peona, then flee away into the night. Endymion's dilemma is thus disposed of, but it is never really resolved. The point of the identification Keats brings about in the closing lines is intellectually unmistakable; but as Douglas Bush has written, it "is only a bit of 'Platonic' algebra, not an equation felt on the pulses."[10]

Reasons can be cited, virtually without end, to explain the manifestly disappointing and unsatisfactory state of the conclusion—Keats's boredom and fatigue with the ordeal the completion of the poem had become, his eagerness to pass on to other projects, his lack of concern for or want of experience in creating an effective ending. Such explanations must, however, be subordinated to the poem's underlying honesty, an honesty that marks so much of Keats's writing and that springs from genuine commitment to the act of composition itself. The point can best be made by turning to a curious passage not far from the end of Book Four. Momentarily abandoning the turbulence and uncertainty of the action, Keats intervenes as narrator to address some words of apology to his hero which are, however, intended chiefly for the reader:

[10] *John Keats: Selected Poems and Letters* (Boston, 1959), p. 315.

Endymion! unhappy! it nigh grieves
Me to behold thee thus in last extreme:
Ensky'd ere this, but truly that I deem
Truth the best music in a first-born song.

(iv.770-73)

Obviously it is Keats himself who is most of all unhappy,
embarrassed by the tangled involvements of his narrative and
aware that his poem should by now have achieved its resolution. Yet the difficulty he faces is surely not that of literally
carrying out the conclusion required by his fable. Endymion
would have been "Ensky'd ere this" were it not, Keats tells
us, that a kind of truth forbids, and the reason deserves to be
taken with full seriousness.

The "truth" seems to be not only that Keats had become
genuinely involved in the allegory of his poem but that, as
Glen O. Allen has argued, the emphasis of the allegory had
changed significantly in the course of composition and that
the "enskying" of his hero had lost much of its climactic
importance.[11] Endymion is not apotheosized in Cynthia's
visionary heaven. There is no ascension to the skies. The two
lovers merely slip quietly away together through the woods.
The conclusion his poem demanded, Keats realized, was not
his hero's elevation to the "chief intensity" but rather some
balance between light and shade, desire and restraint, mortality and immortality that he could only intimate in the

---

[11] "The Fall of Endymion: A Study in Keats's Intellectual Growth,"
Keats-Shelley Journal, VI (1957), 37-57. See also John Middleton
Murry's discussion of the poem in *Keats* (London, 1955), pp. 166ff.,
which begins with a consideration of the passage last quoted. I am
particularly indebted to Allen's essay and agree with his contention that
during the composition of *Endymion* Keats's attitude toward visionary
experience underwent a significant change, a change that is both vital
to an understanding of his poem and reflected in it. However, I do not
accept his premise that Keats began *Endymion* having fully accepted
the "Neoplatonic view that poetic inspiration carries the poet into
higher reality" (p. 41). Nor do I believe that the poem, while a
turning-point, marks the abandonment of Keats's faith in the poetic
imagination, as Allen seems to argue (pp. 39, 50).

union of Cynthia and the Indian Maiden. Yet the need for such a larger reconciliation was one he had only gradually become aware of and did not lend itself to the old climactic design and structure of his legend. Nor was it one that, for deeper reasons, he could dramatize in any genuinely satisfying or "truthful" way. This is not to argue that toward the end of his poem Keats suddenly lost faith in visionary experience. It is to say, rather, that the obstacles to Endymion's success, as Keats elaborated them, had so qualified the nature of his goal as to become themselves part of a new and more complex solution than any he had, however dimly, foreseen.

Such a hypothesis can be verified by examining within the course of the poem itself certain shifts of emphasis that reveal a remarkable change and maturing in Keats's aesthetic assumptions. The theoretical keystone of the structure of the work is the central passage in Book One, Endymion's speech on happiness which Keats likened to a "Pleasure Thermometer." Yet it is impossible to ignore the growing emphasis on disappointment and unhappiness as an integral part of human experience both as the poem proceeds and as a theme reflected increasingly in Keats's letters of the autumn of 1817, when he was at work on his last book.[12] As early as Book Two the lovers' ecstasy is broken by Cynthia's cry, "Endymion: woe! woe! is grief contain'd / In the very deeps of pleasure, my sole life?" (ii.823-24). In the roundelay of the Indian Maiden in Book Four the perception of sorrow is for the first time admitted as an unavoidable and creative element in the experience of beauty. In his letter to Bailey of November 22, 1817, written when he was halfway through his final

[12] See his remarks to Bailey in late October that "Health and Spirits can only belong unalloyed to the selfish Man—the Man who thinks much of his fellows can never be in Spirits" (1, 175); his comments, again to Bailey, in early November on "Griefs and Cares" (1, 182); and, on November 22, his remarks to Reynolds on "Heart-vexations" (1, 188) and to Bailey on "Worldly Happiness": "I scarcely remember counting upon any Happiness—I look not for it if it be not in the present hour" (1, 186). Keats's letters up to and including his early work on *Endymion* do not demonstrate a comparable maturity.

book, Keats cited *both* Book One and "O Sorrow" as demonstrations of his "favorite Speculation" as to the truth of the imagination. Yet he must himself have been aware of important differences between them, and if we return to look more carefully at the famous passage in his letter, we can see his concern to bring the two parts of his poem more fully into accord. "I am certain of nothing," he wrote, "but of the holiness of the Heart's affections and the truth of Imagination—What the imagination seizes as Beauty must be truth —whether it existed before or not—for I have the *same* Idea of *all* our Passions *as of Love* they are *all* in their sublime, creative of essential Beauty" (1, 184; my italics). Keats, in other words, had already begun to move toward that deeper conception of beauty springing from intense awareness of the whole of human life in all its mingled joy and sorrow that was to become a major theme of *Hyperion*. This is not to say that the "Ode to Sorrow" is much more than a weak and sentimental approximation to that ideal, but, insofar as it attempts to reconcile sorrow within a deeper apprehension of beauty, the shift it marks in the direction of Keats's allegory is clear. One might say, perhaps, that by the end of the poem the pleasure principle expounded in the first book had at least been qualified by a recognition of the need for a broader and deeper participation in the whole of human experience. In the same way the earlier idea of Endymion's quest as a search for "oneness" or ecstatic self-annihilation in sympathetic feeling has in the end become partly modified (through the working out of Keats's fable) by an awareness much closer to a simultaneous apprehension of joy and sorrow, mortality and immortality, desire and human limitation.

Endymion, then, is a work whose scope and meaning to a large extent evolved during the months Keats worked on it and which is, therefore, not fully coherent as an allegory for the reason that it embodies new truths and insights Keats discovered only in the course of composition which could not be perfectly expressed within its old design. This is not to say, of course, that the poem is any less meaningful; it is to argue, rather, that its real significance lies as much in the questions it raises as in those it solves. Foremost among these was the whole problem for Keats of the adequacy of his habits and method of composition. In *Endymion* he had begun with a set of vague affirmations and a number of equally vague doubts and misgivings concerning the nature of visionary experience. His method for progressing had been to trust his own powers of improvisation, to let the poem find its own way, create its own involvements, and derive its own solutions. A clear, premeditated plan, even had he been able to conceive of one, was alien to the spirit and larger purpose of his undertaking. It was enough to "send / My herald thought into a wilderness," as he wrote at the outset of Book One, "and quickly dress / My uncertain path with green, that I may speed / Easily onward" (i.58-62). His progress with the work had taken him from the long, increasingly complicated dream-involvements of the earlier books to the apparent digression of the Glaucus episode and to his innovation of the Indian Maiden as a necessary rival and counterpart of Cynthia in Book Four. But in the end he had finished with a work lacking real definition or coherence, having had to extricate himself through the patent device of a *dea ex machina* conclusion. Somewhat like his hero, he had become trapped in the convolutions of the poem without the ability to transcend it.

The irony was hardly lost on him. "J.S. is perfectly right in regard to the slip-shod Endymion," he wrote Hessey. "That it is so is no fault of mine.—No!—though it may sound a little paradoxical. It is as good as I had power to make it—*by myself*" (1, 374). He would continue to write in the way he knew he must—"independently." He would continue faithful to the principles of "sensation & watchfulness," to his belief that "that which is creative must create itself." He must, however, learn to write "*with judgment*," with greater deliberation and purpose. The realization lies behind his first, somewhat puzzling, reference to *Hyperion* in a letter in which he declares a major contrast he intends between the two works.

In *Hyperion,* he wrote Haydon several months before *Endymion* was published, "the march of passion and endeavour will be undeviating—and one great contrast between them will be—that the Hero of the written tale being mortal *is led on,* like Buonaparte, *by circumstance;* whereas the Apollo in Hyperion *being a fore-seeing God will shape his actions like one*" (I, 207). The comment reflects more light on his own poetic intentions than it does on the character of either hero. The question was, could he maintain his allegiance to Pan, his symbol for that generative mystery from which all that was truly valuable in poetry sprang, and at the same time cultivate the prescience and control of Apollo? He would continue to write in the only way he could, from within himself; but he must acquire the clearness and finality of utterance he knew he must achieve for greatness.

CHAPTER FIVE

THE *EPISTLE TO*
JOHN HAMILTON
REYNOLDS

THE period immediately following the revision of *Endymion*
for the press was one of dislocation poetically. Keats was relieved to have the major task completed and out of the way,
leaving him once more free for new endeavors. At the same
time, beyond a sense of general dissatisfaction with the work,
he was left with the pressing intellectual and aesthetic
questions it had raised which he knew he would have to
face in order to make progress. The best evidence of this
unsettled state of things is his verse epistle to John Hamilton
Reynolds. The verses make up the greater part of a letter he
sent his friend on March 25, 1818, about a month before
Endymion went to press, and recount the effects of a powerful and strangely moving depression he has been suffering.
In the past there has been considerable reluctance to view the
poem as much more than the reflection of a passing mood.[1]
For one thing it is an occasional piece that begins as a playful
attempt to provide some humorous distraction for Reynolds,
who was ill at the time, starting off with a jocularity Keats is
only briefly able to maintain. The poem as a whole seems

[1] Criticism of the poem has been, relatively speaking, small. I have
found especially useful Albert Gérard's "Romance and Reality: Continuity and Growth in Keats's View of Art," *Keats-Shelley Journal*, xi
(1962), 17-29, incorporated as a part of ch. 10 of his *English Romantic
Poetry*; Walter Evert's discussion in *Aesthetic and Myth in the Poetry
of Keats* (Princeton, 1964), pp. 194-211; and Mary Visick's " 'Tease us
out of thought': Keats's *Epistle to Reynolds* and the Odes," *Keats-
Shelley Journal*, xv (1966), 87-98. My discussion is in varying ways
indebted to all these as well as to Bate.

strangely disjointed and even, at times, incoherent, especially when compared with the poet's more polished work. Indeed it is somewhat unfair, as Bate reminds us, that these hasty and impromptu verses Keats never intended to meet the public eye have been printed alongside his other poetic work "and then approached with formal expectations that are wildly irrelevant."[2] Yet it is precisely the kind of disturbance they succeed in revealing that tells us a great deal about Keats and that, in the study of his development, makes the poem of greater interest than the new romance in which he sought refuge—the longer, more finished, but languid *Isabella*. The *Epistle to Reynolds* goes far toward explaining the sense of mist and darkness, the feeling of the "burden of the Mystery," that was beginning to oppress him while forcing him, at the same time, to extend his vision into the "dark Passages" that were opening on all sides.

In many respects the lines to Reynolds mark a return to the manner of the earlier verse epistles and the longer pieces of the 1817 volume. The poem begins with the very situation that had in the past proved so fruitful for composition: a sleepless evening passed amid a flow of images and associations. One recalls, for example, the origin of "Sleep and Poetry" in a sleepless night spent "upon a couch at ease" (353) in Hunt's study. Once again there is the device Keats had used so often in the past of working into the poem by elaborating a chain of images and associations that he hoped might lead on to a major theme. Again we find the poet ready to spin "that wonted thread / Of shapes, and shadows, and remembrances" (2-3) into the woof of poetry. Yet the opening of the lines to Reynolds reads almost like a caricature of Keats's earlier technique, for the images that now come forward are all perversely incongruous or anachronistic:

> Things all disjointed come from north and south,—
> Two witch's eyes above a cherub's mouth,
> Voltaire with casque and shield and habergeon,

[2] *John Keats* (Cambridge, Mass., 1963), p. 307.

And Alexander with his nightcap on;
Old Socrates a-tying his cravat,
And Hazlitt playing with Miss Edgeworth's cat.

(5-10)

The passage seems at first only a bit of admirable fooling intended for Reynolds's diversion until Keats's tone darkens and we realize that what he is describing is a more serious and unaccountable disruption of the usual associative processes of composition. There are few, he proceeds to lament, whose reveries and dreams are not sometimes spoiled by "hellish" apparitions. It is not merely that the images themselves are ludicrously inconsistent with each other; but they neither suggest nor lead on to anything more. They are, in fact, totally inconsistent with that ideal process that, by way of contrast, he proceeds to describe in terms of

> flowers bursting out with lusty pride,
> And young Æolian harps personified;
> Some, Titian colours touch'd into real life,—

(17-19)

that flowering of art into the fullness of reality that is the end of all aesthetic creation. It is this criterion of "aliveness," of higher verisimilitude, that Keats has most in view and that suddenly prompts him, by way of providing an example, to "touch into life" the scene of pagan sacrifice so remarkably prefigurative of stanza four of the "Ode on a Grecian Urn," a scene full of flashing light, color, movement, and music caught in a moment of ceremony and communal worship:

> The sacrifice goes on; the pontiff knife
> Gleams in the sun, the milk-white heifer lows,
> The pipes go shrilly, the libation flows:
> A white sail shows above the green-head cliff,
> Moves round the point, and throws her anchor stiff;
> The mariners join hymn with those on land.

(20-25)

As various commentators have pointed out, there is no painting known by Titian that contains a scene similar to the one Keats describes; and it is commonly assumed that, through some slip of memory, he confused with the Venetian the work of another painter, perhaps the *Sacrifice to Apollo* of Claude Lorrain, whose *Enchanted Castle* Keats is shortly to recall at length.³ Most probably Keats's description draws upon a general recollection of a number of different prints and canvases. Yet the mention of Hazlitt a few lines earlier strongly suggests there is a deeper logic at work in his allusion to Titian within this particular context and that he had in view, at the same time, central differences between the two painters. In his essay "On Gusto" in *The Round Table*, a collection with which Keats was familiar, Hazlitt had praised Titian for the very ability the poet is attempting to depict. Hazlitt had written of Titian's power to "interpret one sense by another" so as to bring to "the look and texture of flesh" the sense of "feeling in itself,"⁴ the power, in short, to bring a scene or a face "swelling into reality" (to use Keats's phrase) by endowing the elements of nature with an intensity of human passion and feeling. A few months earlier, in the Negative Capability letter written near the very end of 1817, Keats had, as we have seen, defined this ability with specific reference to the work of a painter quite different from either Titian or Claude—Benjamin West. Familiar as it may be, the passage must be quoted in full:

³ See Sir Sidney Colvin, *John Keats* (London, 1920), p. 264, whom most commentators have followed. The *Sacrifice to Apollo*, however, does not depict the mariners who join the hymn; and most recently James Dickie (*Bulletin of the John Rylands Library*, LII [1969], 96-114) and Alan Osler (*TLS*, April 16, 1971) have suggested Keats was remembering as well other specific paintings by Titian or Claude. In *Keats and the Mirror of Art* (Oxford, 1967), Ian Jack takes the scene the poet describes as a composite and thinks "it is certainly most unlikely that Keats is here describing any particular painting" (p. 221).

⁴ *The Complete Works of William Hazlitt*, ed. P. P. Howe (London, 1930), IV, 77. References to this edition are hereafter included within the text of this chapter.

I spent Friday evening with Wells & went the next morning to see *Death on the Pale horse*. It is a wonderful picture, when West's age is considered; But there is nothing to be intense upon; no women one feels mad to kiss; no face swelling into reality. the excellence of every Art is its intensity, capable of making all disagreeables evaporate, from their being in close relationship with Beauty & Truth— Examine King Lear & you will find this examplified throughout; but in this picture we have unpleasantness without any momentous depth of speculation excited, in which to bury its repulsiveness.

(1, 192; Keats's italics)

As Bate has shown, Keats's conception of "intensity" owes a great deal to Hazlitt's "gusto,"[5] although one must add that the two are far from identical. Indeed the *Epistle to Reynolds* represents Keats's working through in a far deeper way some of the notions that had first been suggested to him by the older critic and his own consideration of West's painting.

Keats's method in the lines to Reynolds is progression by way of contrasts and oppositions. He turns from Titian and the idealized scene of ritual he has just touched into life to a particular painting that has come to mind, the work of a quite different master—Claude Lorrain. The imaginative scene he has created, in its relation to the two painters, has slowly crystallized the major preoccupation of his poem: the degree of idealization—both in a good and bad sense—that art can achieve in its transcendence of actuality. The theme, of course, is one intimately connected with his growing interest in the sublime, both as a general and long-established ideal of art and in its relation to his own more particular sense of the process of aesthetic sublimation by which the materials of art are purged of "disagreeables," fused in imagination, and "put into etherial existence for the relish of one's fellows" (1, 301). It is natural, then, that he should turn to one of the great neoclassic exemplars of the sublime, not of

[5] *John Keats*, p. 244.

those aspects associated with scenes of terror and destruction (the conditions he is to touch on at the end) but rather with peace, security, happiness, and a sense of repose.[6] The painting, *The Enchanted Castle*, is one that best epitomizes "the grand quiescence of Claude." Yet Keats's attitude toward the aspect of sublimity, however attractive, that Claude represents is, as we shall see, hardly one of unqualified admiration. Here again our best guide for tracing the chain of association that leads Keats from Titian to Claude and *The Enchanted Castle* is Hazlitt who, in his essay "On Gusto," turns from praising the earlier painter to a more detailed analysis of the peculiar charm of the later:

> Claude's landscapes, perfect as they are, want gusto. This is not easy to explain. They are perfect abstractions of the visible images of things. . . . He saw the atmosphere, but he did not feel it. He painted the trunk of a tree or a rock in the foreground as smooth—with as complete an abstraction of the gross, tangible impression, as any other part of the picture. His trees are perfectly beautiful, but quite immovable; they have a look of enchantment. In short, his landscapes are unequalled imitations of nature, *released from its subjection to the elements*, as if all objects were become a delightful fairy vision, and the eye had *rarefied and refined away the other senses.*
>
> (IV, 79; my italics)

Turning to Keats's long description for Reynolds of the exact impression he holds of Claude's painting, one can see that it is this very quality of enchantment, of abstraction from gross reality, that he singles out as most characteristic. Whereas, however, Hazlitt sees the effect Claude achieves by his mastery as serene and charming, Keats represents the mood as partly frozen, unnatural, even perverse. Claude's trees, which Hazlitt describes as "perfectly beautiful, but quite immov-

---

[6] See the contrast drawn between Salvator and Claude in "The Sublime in Painting," ch. 9 of Samuel Monk's *The Sublime* (New York, 1935).

able" with "a look of enchantment," for Keats seem held under a harsh, restraining spell so that they "shake / From some old magic like Urganda's sword" (28-29). Hazlitt had written that Claude's landscapes "are perfect abstractions of the visible images of things. . . . He saw the atmosphere, but he did not feel it." Keats's impression of *The Enchanted Castle*, on the other hand, while once again following the general tenor of Hazlitt's remarks, is more ambivalent and complex:

> You know it well enough, where it doth seem
> A mossy place, a Merlin's Hall, a dream;
> You know the clear lake, and the little isles,
> The mountains blue, and cold near neighbour rills,
> All which elsewhere are but half animate;
> There do they look alive to love and hate,
> To smiles and frowns; they seem a lifted mound
> Above some giant, pulsing underground.
>
> (33-40)

At first glance the painting seems perfectly dreamlike in its self-containment and abstraction. Yet this unifying mood is not everywhere maintained. Parts of the landscape seem unnaturally, even morbidly, alive with feeling. The image of some giant pulsing underground in particular creates a sense of titanic forces of upheaval ready at any moment to break into open eruption to destroy the surface placidity. The mood of sublimity the painting creates, in other words, only imperfectly transcends a vast underlying disorder it can only partly repress or conceal.

Other aspects peculiar to Keats's view of *The Enchanted Castle* can be best defined by briefly returning to Hazlitt's remarks. For example, Hazlitt marvels at Claude's ability to transform the elements of nature into "a delightful fairy vision." So Keats develops the idea of enchantment, but with a quite different emphasis:

> The doors all look as if they oped themselves,
> The windows as if latched by fays and elves,

And from them comes a silver flash of light,
As from the westward of a summer's night;
Or like a beauteous woman's large blue eyes
Gone mad thro' olden songs and poesies.

(49-54)

The note of elvish mischief seems incongruous with the
larger theme of calm and sublimity, while the flashing eyes
of the woman, like the Abyssinian maid's vision of "flashing
eyes" and "floating hair" in Coleridge's "Kubla Khan" (a
poem that, in its preoccupation with the balance art struggles
to achieve between energy and control, resembles Keats's)
introduces a hint of danger and madness. Even the "sweet
music" that issues from the castle to greet the "golden galley
all in silken trim" (56) as it serenely approaches its port for
some reason brings fear to the herdsman who hears it. Hints
of dark magic in its more bizarre aspects also color Keats's
description of the castle itself. He had noted, of course, that
the castle in Claude's painting is very much a conglomerate
affair, combining, as Colvin points out,[7] ancient Roman
features with medieval battlements and later Palladian elements in the manner of many old structures that have been
built onto through the centuries. Though somewhat fanciful,
the fusion of styles is not inharmonious in Claude's painting
but creates an effect that is calm, mysterious, and imposing.
Keats's imaginary account of its architects and history, however, reduces the structure to the level of the macabre and
fantastic:

Part of the building was a chosen See,
Built by a banish'd Santon of Chaldee;
The other part, two thousand years from him,
Was built by Cuthbert de Saint Aldebrim;
Then there's a little wing, far from the sun,
Built by a Lapland witch turn'd maudlin nun;
And many other juts of aged stone
Founded with many a mason-devil's groan.

(41-48)

[7] *John Keats*, p. 264.

The same sense of anachronism that characterized the train of disjointed images passing before Keats's eyes at the very outset of the poem in all their ludicrous incongruity now extends itself to his awareness of Claude's painting. There is the same failure of the associative process, now visualized as an aspect of the painting itself, to achieve a harmonious and unified effect.

Critics have at this point generally accepted the failure as Keats's own, an instance of the moodiness and morbidity of which he openly complains to Reynolds at the end. The disordered state of imagination he has described to his friend at the outset has now obtruded itself upon his appreciation of the painting and perversely distorted the values of Claude's landscape.[8] Yet the implications of the poem go a good deal beyond this. Keats obviously recognizes that the creations of art necessarily depend for their success upon a large degree of sympathy and responsiveness. As the poem goes on to make clear, however, the ability to respond can be impaired not merely by a captious state of mind but by a condition of awareness that, in its fullness or complexity, exceeds the powers of any particular work of art to harmonize or satisfy. More specifically, in its effort to expel all "disagreeables," to "swell into reality" and idealize a particular aspect of beauty or truth, the work of art can fatally remove itself from that wealth of human knowledge and experience that provides the substratum of all aesthetic apprehension. As in his remarks some months earlier on West's *Death on the Pale Horse*, what preoccupies Keats in his reflections on *The Enchanted Castle* is a failure in the attempt to achieve the sublime.[9] Yet the problem he now returns to is one he had barely touched on earlier, a problem related to his whole conception of "intensity." The failure as he had analyzed it in West's painting was a lack of anything "to be intense upon," a dearth of material for the imagina-

[8] See, e.g., Evert, *Aesthetic and Myth*, pp. 200-201.
[9] Bate points out (*John Keats*, p. 243) that West's painting had been praised as a successful effort at the sublime.

tion to "swell into reality." The problem that confronts him now, however, is a deeper one, for it has to do with the very nature of "intensity" itself: its continual tendency to refine away too much that is fundamental to our general awareness of life, its drift into one-sidedness and subjectivity. Such, at least, is the larger aspect of the problem that, turning away from his immediate consideration of Claude's painting, Keats seeks to sum up for Reynolds in what is the most abstract and in many ways difficult section of his poem:

> O that our dreamings all, of sleep or wake,
> Would all their colours from the sunset take:
> From something of material sublime,
> Rather than shadow our own soul's day-time
> In the dark void of night. For in the world
> We jostle. . . .
>
> (67-72)

A key phrase (a consciously ironic one) for elucidating Keats's meaning is "material sublime," expressing as it does the desire of the imagination to possess at once the best of both worlds, the ethereal and the concrete. Here again perhaps our best gloss on the passage as a whole is provided by some general remarks of Hazlitt's on the nature of painting, written, though they were, after the poet's death:

> A fine gallery of pictures is a sort of illustration of Berkeley's Theory of Matter and Spirit. It is like a palace of thought—another universe, built of air, of shadows, of colours. Every thing seems "palpable to feeling as to sight." Substances turn to shadows by the painter's arch-chemic touch; shadows harden into substances. "The eye is made the fool of the other senses, or else worth all the rest." The material is in some sense embodied in the immaterial, or, at least, we see all things in a sort of intellectual mirror. The world of art is an enchanting deception.
>
> (x, 19)

Once again the dissimilarity-in-similarity between Keats's lines and Hazlitt's remarks is revealing. What for Hazlitt is an ideal translation of the material into the spiritual is the very aspect of the creative process most troubling to Keats. We long in our reveries, whether those of mere dreaming or those that engross us in our contemplation of the world of art, for the colors of the sunset—some substantial element of the real world that lies outside. Yet instead of such colors we must remain content with fleeting, doubtful moments of inner illumination that fade away into shadows and uncertainty. Hazlitt recognizes and accepts an element of illusion as a part of aesthetic creation: "The world of art is an enchanting deception" tinted into reality by the painter's "arch-chemic touch." Yet it is clear that Keats is unwilling to accept the easy logic of such an equation and that what Hazlitt delights in as enchantment can assume for him the horror of a subjective *enfer*.

For a moment he draws back from some of the metaphysical questions he customarily sought to avoid confronting head-on, then plunges a little further into the problem:

> . . . but my flag is not unfurl'd
> On the admiral-staff,—and to philosophise
> I dare not yet! Oh, never will the prize,
> High reason, and the lore of good and ill,
> Be my award! Things cannot to the will
> Be settled, but they tease us out of thought;
> Or is it that imagination brought
> Beyond its proper bound, yet still confin'd,
> Lost in a sort of Purgatory blind,
> Cannot refer to any standard law
> Of either earth or heaven? It is a flaw
> In happiness, to see beyond our bourn,—
> It forces us in summer skies to mourn,
> It spoils the singing of the nightingale. (72-85)

In his remarks a few months earlier prompted by his consideration of West's *Death on the Pale Horse* he had gone on to postulate as an ideal for the artist the state of Negative Capability, that is "when man is capable of being in uncertainties, Mysteries, doubts, without any irritable reaching after fact & reason." More particularly, he had imagined that the great work of art would, like *Lear*, achieve what West's painting had failed to accomplish, that it would bury all "unpleasantness," all "repulsiveness," all disagreeable and insistent questioning, by engrossing the imagination in a "momentous depth of speculation" (i, 192-93). However it is precisely the failure of this stratagem that now forms the burden of his complaint to Reynolds. Resisting the lure of speculation, the will remains unappeasable in its desire for certainty. Moreover Keats has come to realize that the state of speculation itself can be as vexing in its irresolution as it can be momentous in its implications. The phrase "tease us out of thought," which he was to use again within a subtly different context in the "Ode on a Grecian Urn," here suggests the tantalizing ability of the speculative life to raise, only to defer answering, our final questions. Seen in a different light, that very immunity of the imagination to ordinary kinds of interrogation that had in the past seemed of positive value might suggest corresponding limitations and defects. The "Penetralium of mystery," rich with suggestiveness and undiscovered meaning, could become the poet's "Purgatory blind." The latter phrase, apt like so many of his personal coinages, sums up the dilemma he seeks to convey. Though liberated, the poetic imagination can relate itself to no single "standard law" of either earth or heaven, the material world or the sublime. Lacking the ability to reconcile the two domains, it must experience them as a "hateful siege of contraries"[10] that together spoil whatever consolations either taken singly might afford. Thus we can mourn at the beauty of summer skies or at the singing of the nightingale. The poet is trapped in limbo, somewhere between the uncertain heaven figured by the visionary imag-

[10] See Keats's use of this phrase from *Paradise Lost*, ix.121f., in a letter some months later (*Letters*, i, 369).

ination and the real hell of actual existence when stripped of all romantic possibilities.

It is, of course, to the hell life becomes when viewed in an uncompromisingly realistic and antiromantic light that Keats turns in the final section of the poem. The Darwinian vision of life as an unrelenting struggle for survival waged throughout nature is terrifying and quite unlike anything in his earlier verse. The scene as it unfolds, however, does not stand in isolation but relates itself organically to earlier sections of the poem. The setting in the early evening by the seaside briefly recalls in its pastoral tranquility the mood of Claude's painting. Once again, however, Keats's eye probes beneath the surface to discern signs of sacrifice, oppression, and underlying disorder—not the bloodless and beautifully ceremonial picture of sacrifice that had earlier come alive in his imagination but one of nature "red in tooth and claw." The sublimity and refinement of the painter's ideal world are sensed in contrast to the naked brutality of primeval nature, and the two contexts for conceiving reality develop between them uneasy reverberations in a way now familiar to us as the prevailing method of the poem.

With its abrupt shifts and changes of perspective the *Epistle to Reynolds* reveals an undeniable instability and lack of central focus. The poem may compress only the transitory fantasies of a single evening, but the dislocation it exposes is too fundamental to be written off, as some critics would have it, as a passing case of bad nerves. Although at the very end Keats berates those "horrid moods! / Moods of one's mind" (105-106), the work is much more than a mere poem of mood. The strange distortion of Claude's scene of elysian quiet and the brief, terrifying glimpse of nature reduced to universal rapacity are both, in different ways, troubling and even perverse, but it is not sufficient to dismiss them as unaccountable aberrations from Keats's usual poetic mode, instances of that "horrid Morbidity of Temperament" (1, 142) of which he from time to time complained. There is a logic to the poem's apparent disorder, and if such scenes can justly be described as "morbid," they are so in such a way as to counterbalance and explain each other. If at the end Keats appears more naturalist than poet and sees "Too *far* into the sea" (94), it is in part because he has earlier sensed the treacherous tendency of art to encourage us "to see beyond our bourn" (83) in the opposite extreme. There is a principle of compensation at work by which the imagination struggles to rectify itself and discover a proper balance. The charge of morbidity is unjust if only because the poem itself provides the grounds for understanding how depression and unevenness of vision are to some degree unavoidable to those who struggle to reconcile a full and sympathetic participation in the world of art with a knowledge of the actuality that lies outside. As in Wordsworth's mature reappraisal of the relationship art holds to reality in his "Elegiac Stanzas" on Sir George Beaumont's painting of Peele Castle, a poem that in theme and method must have been in the back of Keats's mind,[11] the true subject is not the vagaries of an errant imagination but the way in which our whole approach to art is radically altered by a change in our perspective on the reality it mirrors. If Keats emphasizes the element of subjectivity in our awareness, he does so with an understanding of the various ways in which, during the centuries spanning Titian, Claude, and his contemporary West, a spontaneous sublimity of style has become increasingly difficult to achieve. His lament is not purely personal but in part historical and cultural.[12]

The deeper questions that lie behind the *Epistle to Reynolds* are philosophic and more particularly aesthetic and reveal how much, during the months following the completion of *Endymion*, Keats had come to question some of his

[11] So Claude Finney has argued in *The Evolution of Keats's Poetry*, 1, 391.

[12] There is no need to elaborate here a point developed throughout Bate's biography and again by Harold Bloom in "Keats and the Embarrassments of Poetic Tradition," in *From Sensibility to Romanticism: Essays Presented to Frederick A. Pottle*, ed. F. W. Hilles and Harold Bloom (New York, 1965).

Claude, *The Enchanted Castle* (also known as *Landscape with Psyche and the Palace of Amor*). Published by courtesy of C. L. Loyd; P: Courtauld Institute of Art, London.

earlier poetic assumptions, especially those concerning the
nature of the poetic process. The point now most at issue is
his deepening sense of the nature of "intensity" and the role
it plays in the creation of art. The central question, to put
it simply, is what and how does art "intensify"? Does the
imagination, in fact, concentrate and sublime a material
and substantial beauty? Or does it rather, in purging away
"disagreeables"—all that is discordant or repulsive—distill a
vision that, for any complex intelligence, must remain hopelessly tenuous and unreal? Is art a heightening and enrich-
ment, or is it rather an abstraction and evasion, of reality?
The chain of associations leading Keats, partly in company
with Hazlitt, from Titian, Claude, and the sublime in painting to the terrors of brute nature reveals the degree to which
such questions had become of vital concern. It reveals, too, a
state of irresolution it would not be too much to call a period
of crisis.[13] Although it cannot claim to rank among his major
productions, the *Epistle to Reynolds* illuminates more clearly
than any other single work the major problems with which
Keats wrestled in passing from *Endymion* to his first attempt
at *Hyperion*.

[13] See Evert's discussion, noted above, and p. 212.

CHAPTER SIX

———— ✦ ————

THE NORTHERN WALKING
TOUR

THE dislocation—emotional, aesthetic, and intellectual—the *Epistle to Reynolds* exposes continues to pervade the next major interlude of Keats's life. The same concerns and pressures the poem reveals are evident throughout the verse and letters of the walking tour with Brown in the Lake District and parts of Scotland and Ireland in the summer of 1818. Keats looked forward to the trip both as an opportunity to lay up a store of new sensations for the poems he was already contemplating for the coming autumn and winter as well as a relief from the knowledge of what he was leaving behind—the declining state of Tom's health and the loss of George and Georgiana to America. Yet the interval was also welcome as a time for reconsidering some of the major questions that had begun to emerge as to the nature of poetic beauty and truth and their relation to his larger, complex, and often painful awareness of life. Indeed the tour is chiefly notable for the effort to achieve a new emotional and aesthetic integration one can follow taking place, often unconsciously, within the short occasional pieces and the letters. Judged in terms of quality and quantity, the verse Keats produced is disappointing. The pace of traveling Brown set was formidable, and after a full day of walking there was little leisure for any kind of sustained composition. Anyway, Keats had not looked forward to the trip as a chance for writing and devoted what time he had to keeping friends and family, especially Tom, supplied with a full quota of rich and unusually descriptive letters, interspersed with verse. In the end the trip settled nothing. It was remarkable, rather, for the mounting urgency with which

Keats returned to the same problems, especially those relating to the creative process, that he had crystallized in the *Epistle to Reynolds* and for his attempt to reach some greater understanding of them.

The mood of uncertainty and inconclusiveness that dominated the trip is summed up in one of the best of the poems Keats composed and one of the very last he wrote before abandoning Brown to return to Hampstead in early August, the sonnet "Written upon the Top of Ben Nevis":

> Read me a lesson, Muse, and speak it loud
>   Upon the top of Nevis, blind in mist!
> I look into the chasms, and a shroud
>   Vaporous doth hide them,—just so much I wist
> Mankind do know of hell; I look o'erhead,
>   And there is sullen mist,—even so much
> Mankind can tell of heaven; mist is spread
>   Before the earth, beneath me,—even such,
> Even so vague is man's sight of himself!
>   Here are the craggy stones beneath my feet,—
> Thus much I know that, a poor witless elf,
>   I tread on them,—that all my eye doth meet
> Is mist and crag, not only on this height,
> But in the world of thought and mental might!

The verses look back both to the earlier sonnet "To Homer" ("Standing aloof in giant ignorance") and, as Bate has pointed out,[1] to the letter of May to Reynolds on the "Chamber of Maiden Thought" and the dark passages opening on all sides. "We see not the ballance of good and evil," Keats had written. "We are in a Mist" (1, 281). Yet in these earlier instances the metaphor of mist and darkness had held the promise of a deepening vision, "a budding morrow in midnight," "a triple sight in blindness keen." The lines on Ben Nevis are, by comparison, oppressive, even purgatorial, in tone. They do not allude to the creative potential hidden in those "uncertainties, Mysteries, doubts" that constitute

[1] *John Keats* (Cambridge, Mass., 1963), p. 361.

"the burden of the Mystery" (I, 193, 281). They describe, rather, the painful state of "Purgatory blind," the stance of one wrapped in obscurity between earth and heaven and lacking any clear norm of reason, "any standard law," to serve as guide. Keats had bundled all three volumes of Dante's *Commedia* in Cary's translation into his knapsack, and his reading of the earlier portions of the work had obviously helped to bring home a sense of his predicament—a sense of moving ever deeper into the unknown.[2]

Once we seek, however, to push beyond such a general sense of Keats's position, it becomes necessary to examine more closely the poems and letters of the tour as a whole. The letters from this period of his life are exceptionally revealing and, read as a group (as they rarely are), confirm the pattern we have seen emerging in his habits of aesthetic thinking, a pattern more than ever vital to an understanding of the shorter poems as they appear. Among the latter it is a group of poems, more intimately written, more troubled and obscure in meaning, that has the most to tell us. These are the poems having to do with Keats's visit to the Burns country and his efforts to commemorate the spirit of the older poet.

Within the larger allegory of Keats's life, the letters and poems of the walking tour with Brown enjoy a special place and unity. To understand this fact, however, it is necessary to begin at the beginning. As we have seen, Keats left for the trip with an ideal of the creative process clearly in mind, however much he may have come to question it in certain ways. As he expressed it in his first letter of the tour, written to Tom: "I shall learn poetry here and shall henceforth write more than ever, for the abstract endeavor of being able to add a mite to that mass of beauty which is harvested from these grand materials, by the finest spirits, and put into etherial existence for the relish of one's fellows" (I, 301). The same letter provides a more concrete illustration of his

[2] See Robert Gittings, "Keats's Debt to Dante," *The Mask of Keats: A Study of Problems* (Cambridge, Mass., 1965), esp. pp. 7, 15-17.

134

meaning. He had begun his "journal" of the trip by attempting to sketch for Tom his first impression of the beauty of Lake Windermere and the surrounding mountains. "I cannot describe them," he wrote; "they surpass my expectation." Shortly thereafter, however, he succeeded in giving Tom a fuller description of the scene which contains the germ of one of his finest sonnets, "Bright Star":

> There are many disfigurements to this Lake—not in the way of land or water. No; the two views we have had of it are of the most noble tenderness—they can never fade away—they make one forget the divisions of life; age, youth, poverty and riches; and refine one's sensual vision into a sort of north star which can never cease to be open lidded and stedfast over the wonders of the great Power. The disfigurement I mean is the miasma of London.
>
> (I, 299)

There is a dreamlike quality about the scene, a suspension in time and space. Yet there is also a strong idea of process evidenced by the central verb "refine." The material elements within the poet's "sensual vision" are condensed and transmuted until they approximate, or rather are sensed as concentrated in, the higher, ethereal nature of the star. The "disagreeables," not only the "disfigurements" inflicted by tourists of which Keats was always so aware ("O Isle spoilt by the Milatary," he had written a year earlier from the Isle of Wight), but those divisions—"age, youth, poverty and riches"—that might detract from the sense of timelessness vanish or are dissipated. Yet the star is no cold idealization, no mere fixity. It both presides over and takes its being from the workings of "the great Power," an endless potential for creation, an ideal of beauty latent amid the elements of human perception. Unlike the famous sonnet Keats afterwards composed, the description in the letter opens no division between the world of sensuous experience and the higher being of the star. In its intensity of vision the scene represents an ideal of creativity, a perfect accommodation between the perceiving mind and the objects of its perception which, in its fullness of realization, recalls the axioms for poetry he had sent Taylor earlier in the year. "I live in the eye," he added, near the end of his letter to Tom, "and my imagination, surpassed, is at rest" (1, 301).

Set down in his first letter as a sketch of Windermere and its presiding star, the ideal of creativity with which Keats began the tour was one he nevertheless found increasingly difficult to maintain as he proceeded. The dramatic mountain scenery brought steadily into view his whole deeper involvement with the nature of the sublime and the necessity, one he would soon have to deal with in quite practical ways, of accommodating the grander impressions of nature to the terms and processes of art. The concern for an appropriate context or formula, the old problem, even, of how to make a beginning, is discernible beneath the banter of the opening of his first letter to his fellow poet Reynolds: "I'll not run over the Ground we have passed. that would be merely as bad as telling a dream—unless perhaps I do it in the manner of the Laputan printing press—that is I put down Mountains, Rivers Lakes, dells, glens, Rocks, and Clouds, With beautiful enchanting, gothic picturesque fine, delightful, enchancting, Grand, sublime—a few Blisters &c" (1, 322). The statement is a humorous parody of the old habits of cataloguing and reliance on association Reynolds would by now understand. The mechanism of the Laputan printing press conveniently dispenses with the need for a genuine assimilation of nature and poetic style and treatment, for a means for extending the reality of mountain scenery toward such an effect as the sublime, not overlooking the blisters, the disagreeable realities of traveling.

The same larger issue, actually the whole problem of decorum, reemerges some weeks later in Keats's description in mid-July of their impression of Loch Lomond in a passage that deserves to be compared with his earlier description of Windermere:

Steam Boats on Loch Lomond and Barouches on its sides
take a little from the Pleasure of such romantic chaps as
Brown and I—The Banks of the Clyde are extremely
beautiful—the north End of Loch Lomond grand in
excess—the entrance at the lower end to the narrow part
from a little distance is precious good—the Evening was
beautiful nothing could surpass our fortune in the
weather—yet was I worldly enough to wish for a fleet of
chivalry Barges with Trumpets and Banners just to die
away before me into that blue place among the mountains.

(I, 334)

There is much here of the painter's concern for composition.
Indeed Keats actually accompanied the prose description
with a pen drawing, blocking out the major areas of color for
Tom while leaving him to fill out the sketch in his imagination. Nevertheless one is aware again of certain incongruities
of vision. As in the *Epistle to Reynolds* one is confronted by
three different aspects of the scene, which not only fail to
harmonize, but compete for attention. First there are the
elements of ugliness and deformity—the steamboats and
barouches—that distract the poet from his enjoyment of the
prospect and that he would gladly eliminate, without, in
fact, being able to do so. Transcending these is the larger
beauty of the scene, the grander natural forms Keats outlined
for Tom in his rough pen drawing. Lastly there is the drift,
in the background of the description, toward a remote idealization—the "chivalry Barges with Trumpets and Banners"
Keats half wishes, half imagines to see fading away into the
distance. The description, like that of Windermere really a
tentative kind of composition, approximates the depth and
perspective of a painting. Yet the inconsistency of its parts
prevents any harmonious play of the eye through the setting
as a whole. The steamboats in the foreground seem as anachronistic as the chivalry barges in the distance, each representing the opposite poles of unyielding literalness and roman-

tic dilation. The two extremes appear partly to compensate for each other. While the setting strives for a resolution of visual accuracy and imagination, however, it achieves only an incongruity emphasized by the deliberate irony of Keats's phrasing: "Such romantic chaps," "grand in excess," "worldly enough to wish."

The descriptions of Windermere and Loch Lomond testify to Keats's rapt enjoyment of northern scenery. Yet they show him also at a deeper, partly unconscious, level seeking to formulate his impressions of its beauty in a way that would conform with his sense of the creative process and his conception of the imagination as it operates upon the experience of the senses. In this respect the two prose passages are really practice sketches, studies toward a definition of the sublime in landscape. To compare the earlier description with that of three weeks later is, however, to observe how increasingly more difficult the task of mediating between fidelity to concrete detail and the continually idealizing demands of the imagination was becoming. The difficulty came in attempting actually to realize his ideal of a "material sublime," a sense of the wonderful proceeding from a full and continuous relation to reality. In practice his conception of the etherealizing power of the imagination was proving increasingly vulnerable to the old, recurring problems: the persistent intrusiveness of inappropriate details, the tenuousness and instability of the marvelous, and the sense of paradox and irony that too often resulted.

II

Together the two passages from the letters do little more than confirm the same problems of aesthetic perception revealed in the *Epistle to Reynolds*. Keats was forced on to a further depth of realization only by a new event. This was his visit to the Burns memorials and his unsuccessful attempt to celebrate the genius of the older poet in several sonnets, the first written in the churchyard, the second at the poet's cottage. Not long before setting out on the tour Keats had written Bailey: "Scenery is fine—but human nature is finer— The Sward is richer for the tread of a real, nervous, english foot—the eagles nest is finer for the Mountaineer has look'd into it—Are these facts or prejudices?" (1, 242). The term "prejudice" was one that was to preoccupy him increasingly as the tour proceeded. However in his struggle to come to terms with the genius of Burns Keats was obliged to go beyond a consideration of the kinds of distortion that can unsettle our apprehension of the beauty of the natural world as we perceive it directly or through the medium of art. He was now obliged to consider the necessary "disinterestedness" of the imagination in its larger grasp of human character and in a way that prefigures his conception of the heroic ideal of the poet that was to emerge from *Hyperion*.

Keats eagerly looked forward to his visit to the Burns country and its memorials as the opportunity both to apprehend more deeply and to celebrate the standard of poetic greatness Burns had come to represent for him. As with Chatterton, but more profoundly, Keats admired and identified himself with Burns, with the older poet's gusto, humor, and independence, and above all with his courage and determination to succeed against the obstacles humble birth or a hostile society could place in his way. The degree of his involvement with Burns made the task of composing a fitting tribute at once more necessary and more difficult. Both sonnets are, as Keats immediately realized, failures; but like most of his failures they reveal much that is significant. Of the two, it is the first, written in the churchyard, that is by far more powerful:

On Visiting the Tomb of Burns
The town, the churchyard, and the setting sun,
  The clouds, the trees, the rounded hills all seem,
  Though beautiful, cold—strange—as in a dream,
I dreamed long ago, now new begun.
The short-liv'd, paly Summer is but won

From Winter's ague, for one hour's gleam;
  Though sapphire-warm, their stars do never beam:
All is cold Beauty; pain is never done:
For who has mind to relish, Minos-wise,
  The Real of Beauty, free from that dead hue
    Sickly imagination and sick pride
  Cast wan upon it? Burns! with honour due
    I oft have honour'd thee. Great shadow, hide
Thy face; I sin against thy native skies.

Although intended as a tribute to Burns, the sonnet is
remarkable chiefly for its mood of strange dissociation from
the setting, for Keats's inability to establish any unified or
sympathetic rapport with the scene he contemplates. Like
Coleridge in "Dejection: An Ode," he can only "see, not
feel," the sapphire-warmth of the stars, the potential for
beauty latent in the actual moment. Instead of entering into
the scene before it, the imagination seems curiously locked in
a world of its own. Indeed the sonnet creates the impression
not so much of a single landscape as of two, one a landscape
remembered or envisioned, the other an underlying image
of the actual, which do not reinforce each other but together
produce, as Aileen Ward has put it, a troubling sense of
déjà vu.[3] Beyond the problem of accounting for this phenomenon and the pain it occasions, the sonnet raises particular questions of interpretation. What is the sickliness of
imagination and pride which in the closing line approximates a sense of "sin" close to moral self-condemnation?
What does Keats mean by "cold beauty" and how is the term
related to "the Real of Beauty" he afterwards proclaims.

[3] *John Keats: The Making of a Poet* (New York, 1963), p. 197. The
discussions of the sonnet I have found most valuable are Murry's
classic essay " 'The Feel of *Not* to Feel It,' " *Keats* (London, 1955),
pp. 199-209; J. C. Maxwell's "Keats's Sonnet on the Tomb of Burns,"
Keats-Shelley Journal, IV (1955), 77-80, which proceeds from a discussion of textual problems; and George Yost's "A Source and Interpretation of Keats's Minos," *Journal of English and Germanic Philology*, LVII
(1958), 220-29.

THE NORTHERN WALKING TOUR

The strange intensity the poem develops with its images of frozen power, an intensity of a kind relatively new and unfamiliar in his work, gives these questions a particular immediacy.

The logical starting-point for fuller understanding of the poem is Keats's own comment upon it: "This Sonnet I have written in a strange mood, half asleep," he wrote to Tom. "I know not how it is, the Clouds, the sky, the Houses, all seem anti Grecian & anti Charlemagnish—I will endeavour to get rid of my prejudices, & tell you fairly about the Scotch" (I, 309). The form of "prejudice" to which Keats alludes is fairly apparent. It relates to the familiar difficulty of compelling the imagination to continue faithful to the real nature of its materials rather than evolving a context merely congenial to its own desires or predispositions. One recalls the "chivalry Barges with Trumpets and Banners" disappearing in the background of the description of Loch Lomond. In a similar way Keats's sonnet and his comment on it reflect an inability to assimilate the northern beauty of Burns's country in itself, the need to approach it by way of standards alien to it, whether classical and southern or medieval and chivalric. That such distortion of the landscape could lead further, to a dangerous, almost willful misrepresentation of the character of the poet himself, is revealed in some comments on Burns written a few days later, partly to humor Tom. "Poor unfortunate fellow," he wrote on July 7, "his disposition was southern—how sad it is when a luxurious imagination is obliged in self defence to deaden its delicacy in vulgarity, and riot in thing[s] attainable that it may not have leisure to go mad after thing[s] which are not" (I, 319-20). Yet the self-indulgence of such romanticizing, the error of conceiving Burns as a forlorn spirit, hungering in imagination for the pleasures of the warm south, was shortly brought home to him on actually approaching the poet's birthplace. "We were talking on different and indifferent things," he wrote Reynolds on July 13, "when on a sudden we turned a corner upon the immediate County of Air—the Sight was as rich as possible—I had no Conception that the native place of Burns was so beautiful—the Idea I had was more desolate, his rigs of Barley seemed always to me but a few strips of Green on a cold hill—O prejudice! it was rich as Devon" (1, 323). The climax of the sonnet written at Burns's tomb anticipates what was to be a steady growth of realization as the trip proceeded. The "sin" against Burns's "native skies" lay in obscuring their true character, in the failure of the imagination to conform itself to the real nature of its objects.

However the "Sickly imagination" against which Keats complains represented more than a sin against the landscape. Ultimately it was an affront to the spirit of Burns himself. "Poor unfortunate fellow." The characterization comes dangerously close to sentimentalizing the poet whom Hazlitt, earlier in the year and perhaps in Keats's hearing, had described as possessing "the same magnanimity, directness, and unaffected character" as Shakespeare. "He was not a *sickly* sentimentalist, a namby-pamby poet, a mincing metre balladmonger, any more than Shakspeare," Hazlitt declared. "He was as much of a man—not a twentieth part as much of a poet as Shakspeare. With but little of his imagination or inventive power, he had the same life of mind: within the narrow circle of personal feeling or domestic incidents, the pulse of his poetry flows as healthily and vigorously. He had an eye to see; a heart to feel:—no more."[4] All three of the lyrics Keats composed in the north that take Burns as their focus are poems of landscape. At a deeper level, however, they are attempts to come to terms with the spirit of Burns himself. Yet, as with the prose descriptions in the letters, there were such different, conflicting contexts to work within. There was, to begin with, the cloud of sentimentality besetting Burns's accomplishment—the tendency to overdramatize the moving, painful circumstances of the life. At the

[4] "On Burns, and the Old English Ballads," *Lectures on the English Poets, The Complete Works of William Hazlitt*, ed. P. P. Howe (London, 1930), v, 128 (my italics).

same time there was, as Keats observed, the element of "vulgarity" surrounding the man—the mixture of coarseness, dissipation, and licentiousness of which Arnold was later to complain. Transcending these was the poet's larger humanity and achievement which Hazlitt, together with all the great Romantics, had sought to discriminate. The problem was to achieve a proper synthesis. "My head is sometimes in such a whirl in considering the million likings and antipathies of our Moments," he wrote Reynolds the same day he recounted his visit to the cottage, "that I can get into no settled strain in my Letters—My Wig! Burns and *sentimentality* coming across you and frank Floodgate in the office" (I, 324). We miss the point of Keats's pilgrimage to the Burns memorials unless we see it in large part as an attempt to distill from a conflicting set of attitudes a just and fuller sense of that poet's enduring greatness.

Chagrined and disappointed, Keats must bid the "great shadow" of Burns, like a Dantean guide and master, hide its face in shame at the inability and confusion of its pupil. Nevertheless the sestet of the sonnet in the churchyard moves beyond the frustrations of the immediate occasion to define a further aspect of the problem. Later in the year Keats was to attack Hunt's "disgusting" (because self-centered and obtrusive) taste, which "distorts one's mind—make[s] one's thoughts bizarre—perplexes one in the standard of Beauty" (II, 11). Self-accused of some of these same faults, he asks the question how one can ever, at least in practical terms, define a just and adequate "standard of Beauty." If the "Real of Beauty" lies in a fidelity to human experience vitalized by a power of imaginative insight, how is it possible, lacking the absolutely clear and disinterested judgment of a Minos, to discern their perfect composition? Within the working of the aesthetic process, is it ever really possible to separate the beauty of the mortal world which the imagination enters into and intensifies from the bias the mind inevitably projects or "casts" upon its objects in its effort to clarify and distill? The conclusion to the first of the Burns sonnets poses such questions more strongly than anything Keats had yet written.

"All is cold Beauty; pain is never done." The deeper problem confronting Keats in the sonnets to Burns was the need to refine the true beauty of the older poet's achievement without sentimentalizing or obscuring the actual pain and hardship of his career—or rather to see both the pain and beauty in intimate relationship to each other. The difficulties of aesthetic visualization, so evident throughout the tour, had begun to assume a moral dimension. More and more he was being forced to redefine the quality of "disinterestedness" less as mere openness to experience and more as an active and ethical ideal. The lines, "The short-liv'd, paly Summer is but won / From Winter's ague, for one hour's gleam," recall an observation he had made to Bailey the preceding fall, "that there are no Men thouroughly wicked—so as never to be self spiritualized into a kind of sublime Misery—but alas! *'t is but for an Hour*—he is the only Man 'who has kept watch on Man's Mortality' who has philantrophy enough to overcome the disposition [to] an indolent enjoyment of intellect—who is brave enough to volunteer for uncomfortable hours" (1, 173). If, as he had declared, all the human passions, not merely love, "are in their sublime creative of essential beauty," there was a beauty latent in the suffering of Burns. Yet the effort to abstract that beauty, to discern the enduring value at the heart of Burns's mortality, was requiring both a greater selflessness and power of transforming vision than any yet demanded of him.

One can follow, virtually step by step, Keats's failure to realize such an ideal in a single letter, that of July 11 and 13 to Reynolds, in which he recounts his visit to Burns's cottage and the composition of a second sonnet written there. The keynote for the visit is set by his hopeful expectation on setting out: "One of the pleasantest means of annulling self is approaching such a shrine as the Cottage of Burns—

we need not think of his misery—that is all gone—bad luck
to it—I shall look upon it hereafter with unmixed pleasure
as I do upon my Stratford on Avon day with Bailey" (I,
323). The casualness of the remarks does not gainsay an
underlying seriousness of intention. Like the middle age of
Shakespeare, as Keats was afterwards to see it, Burns's days
might be "all clouded over" (II, 116). Nevertheless there
was a way of reading such a life more deeply—"allegorically"
—so as to see its apparent unhappiness as only part of a
larger pattern and a type of greatness triumphant at the
center of its "Mystery." There was a visionary power sufficient to dispel all "disagreeables," to distill "unmixed
pleasure" through the apprehension of a higher beauty and
truth. Yet on Keats's arrival at the cottage any capability
for such creation disappeared amid a sense of distraction and
unhappiness too overwhelming to be resolved. The anecdotes
in homage delivered by the garrulous, endlessly tippling
caretaker only revealed the narrowness and hypocrisy of the
Scots world by which Burns was surrounded. "O the flum-
mery of a birth place!" Keats wrote. "Cant! Cant! Cant! . . .
his gab hindered my *sublimity*" (I, 324-25). The repugnant
aspects of the setting were too insistently oppressive to be
"evaporated" or resolved. He could only stare blindly
through the windows into Burns's meadows, and drink the
toddy offered him. The token effort he composed, "This
mortal body of a thousand days," was too disappointing even
to include within his letter. He had hoped by keeping watch
on man's mortality to celebrate the immortality of fame.
But his powers of imaginative transformation had failed him.
"O for a Remedy against such wrongs within the pale of the
World," he had written Bailey the preceding fall. "The
thought that we are mortal makes us groan" (I, 179).

The continuation of the letter to Reynolds distills a vision
quite different from any Keats had anticipated on setting
out:

[Burns's] Misery is a dead weight upon the nimbleness of
one's quill—I tried to forget it—to drink Toddy without

any Care—to write a merry Sonnet—it wont do—he talked
with Bitches—he drank with Blackguards, he was miserable—We can see horribly clear in the works of such a
man his whole life, as if we were God's spies.

(I, 325)

Rather than transcending the sordidness and misery of
existence, the Burns who here emerges into view has been
engulfed by them. The echo of *Lear* is the more ironic when
we remember that it was the work that, in Keats's remarks
on West's painting in the Negative Capability letter, had
testified to a process of imaginative transformation that here
has failed. The vision of Burns's misery is unrelieved by any
reconciling allegory. "We can see horribly clear." The glance
is the same as the glimpse at the end of the *Epistle to Reynolds* "into the core / Of an eternal fierce destruction" too
horrifying to contemplate. Only now the confrontation with
Burns was forcing him to struggle to assimilate the discord-
ancies of experience less in their effect on the productions
of art and more as basic elements conditioning the value and
meaning of human existence. The problems of aesthetic perception and the larger issues of human life were beginning to
merge inextricably.

III

The climax of the tour, the encounter with Burns, was
unsettling to Keats both practically—in terms of what he had
hoped to accomplish—and for its further impact on his
whole notion of the nature of poetic creation. The degree of
that unsettlement is revealed in a poem that comes as an
ironic coda to the whole experience. "I had determined to
write a Sonnet in the Cottage," he wrote Bailey on July 22.
"I did but lauk it was so wretched I destroyed it—howev^r in
a few days afterwards I wrote some lines cousin-german to
the Circumstance which I will transcribe or rather cross
scribe in the front of this" (I, 343-44). The lines, in slow
marching septenaries, are those "Written in the Highlands

after a Visit to Burns's Country." At first glance they appear to be one final attempt to commemorate Burns as a poet "who was great through mortal days and died of fame unshorn" (12).[5] The relationship between the work and the two sonnets that precede it is not, however, a simple one; for the longer poem, both in positive and negative respects, adopts a quite different tack toward the now difficult and strained connection between the imagination and actuality. Indeed there is something perverse about the way the "Lines" exacerbate even while they exploit the frustrations of the earlier failures. For Keats now begins by pursuing a solution that virtually from the outset is recognized as inadequate, deliberately indulging the imagination in its desire to evade its problems through inner withdrawal, only in the end to reveal the disastrousness of such an escape. There was a certain justice to the preparatory warning he gave Bailey at the outset of his letter: "I carry all matters to an extreme—so that when I have any little vexation it grows in five Minutes into a theme for Sophocles" (1, 340).

The lines written in the highlands return to the same strange, dreamlike mood of dissociation from the landscape that had preoccupied Keats in his sonnet in the churchyard. Yet they develop the value and implications of that mood in a very different way. The failure Keats dramatizes in the sonnet, its painful effect of "cold beauty," was the result of an awareness of a gap between reality and imaginative perception, of an inability of the imagination to enter fully into a setting still permeated by a sense of the older poet's struggle and accomplishment. In the later lines, however, the very dissociation he had earlier deplored now ironically becomes a positive resource, the wellspring of "a deeper joy than all," "of more divine a smart" (7-8). The joy the lines describe arises from the self-obliviousness "When weary feet forget themselves" (9) upon the road to a poetic shrine. Yet the joy is entirely different from that "unmixed pleasure" or

[5] The text is that of the *Letters* (1, 344-45) corrected in one or two places by Keats's draft and later transcripts and with normalized spelling and punctuation.

that ideal "annulling [of] self" Keats had anticipated in his letter to Reynolds on visiting the cottage. For the pleasure comes not through any new assimilation or understanding of Burns or his greatness but rather through a total concentration on an imaginative realm within from which all awareness of external circumstance is deliberately excluded and where the fancy is free to conjure heroic shapes and shadows of its own creating:

> Light heather-bells may tremble then, but they are far
>   away;
> Wood-lark may sing from sandy fern,—the sun may
>   hear his lay;
> Runnels may kiss the grass on shelves and shallows
>   clear,
> But their low voices are not heard though come on
>   travels drear;
> Blood-red the sun may set behind black mountain
>   peaks;
> Blue tides may sluice and drench their time in caves
>   and weedy creeks;
> Eagles may seem to sleep wing-wide upon the air;
> Ring-doves may fly convuls'd across to some high-
>   cedar'd lair;
> But the forgotten eye is still fast wedded to the
>   ground—
> As palmer's that with weariness mid-desert shrine
>   hath found.
>
> (13-22)

The verses pulse with a strange, almost hypnotic power. They explore, however, a conception of intensity quite opposite to that Keats had formerly espoused. Heretofore he had conceived that power as a heightening and reinforcement, not as a denial of reality. By this time, however, he had come to see that, through such devices as chiaroscuro, the imagination could gain a dramatic effectiveness as readily by withdrawing from actuality, by exploiting a deliberate contrast rather than correspondence with the real. The paradox was one he was to develop into the continuous juxtaposition of appearance and reality and the brilliant range of effects he was to achieve in such a later work as *The Eve of St. Agnes*. What he was beginning on one level to explore was a further range of complexity in the field of Romantic aesthetics.

Within the context of the tour as a whole and its broader ideals, however, the kind of intensity Keats achieves in the "Lines Written in the Highlands" seems perversely anachronistic. Nevertheless the effect is one he indulges only up to a point and with the intention of revealing evident dangers. Head bent upon the ground in solitary contemplation, the palmer paces forward, drawing us into his world as he advances,

> Filling the air, as on we move, with portraiture intense,
> More warm than those heroic tints that fill a painter's
>   sense,
> When shapes of old come striding by and visages
>   of old,
> Locks shining black, hair scanty grey, and passions
>   manifold.
>
> (35-38)

Such a state of absorption is in one way appealing, more "intense," because the ideal of heroism it depicts is self-contained and removed from any taint of the complexities of "the sweet and bitter world," the real domain of human experience. Here again, as in the *Epistle to Reynolds*, painting serves Keats as an analogy for the possible isolation art may achieve in its condition of sublimity. In form and passionate attitude the epic shapes appear compellingly suggestive; but at the same time their relationship to the theme of pilgrimage, the Scottish countryside, or Burns himself is at best only implicit. They seem featureless and idealized to the point of inhumanity. It is with the realization of such dehumanization that the poem reaches its culmination:

> O horrible! to lose the sight of well
> remember'd face,
> Of brother's eyes, of sister's brow, constant
> to every place.
>
> (33-34)

The lines suggest how great the shock of losing George and Georgiana had proved for Keats. Yet they also serve to interrelate biography and aesthetics. Later that autumn, deeply engrossed in his epic *Hyperion* while missing his brother and sister-in-law more than ever, Keats wrote to them to declare how "my Solitude is sublime." "No sooner am I alone than shapes of epic greatness are stationed around me, and serve my Spirit the office which is equivalent to a king's body guard," he wrote. "The roaring of the wind is my wife and the Stars through the window pane are my Children," he explained. "The mighty abstract Idea I have of Beauty in all things stifles the more divided and minute domestic happiness—an amiable wife and sweet Children I contemplate as a part of that Beauty" (1, 403). No doubt his absorption in his art, the concentration necessary to achieve the elevation required of a work like *Hyperion*, went far toward justifying a degree of self-preoccupation, selfishness even. Nevertheless it remained to be seen whether and how he could transcend the "more divided and minute" aspects of existence without having to "stifle" or suppress a necessary part of his own humanity. Clearly his view of art as an abstraction of experience was beginning by its very evolution to suggest definite qualifications and limits.

Ultimately the desire for intensity, the quest for grandeur and sublimity, would need to be founded on a deeper knowledge and fidelity to the roots of all experience buried in the human heart and its attachments. Although imperfectly expressed, the realization informs Keats's picture of the palmer's trance-like state and his withdrawal to a world of ideal images:

> At such a time the soul's a child, in
> childhood is the brain;
> Forgotten is the worldly heart—alone,
> it beats in vain.
>
> (23-24)

The most obscure and difficult in the poem, the lines are best understood if we realize that Keats was here already working toward that expansion of the "infant or thoughtless Chamber" of his letter of May to Reynolds into his conception of the world as a school for teaching children to read that was to form the basis of his later view of life as a "vale of Soul-making." "I will call the *human heart* the *horn Book* used in that School—and I will call the *Child able to read, the Soul* made from that *School* and its *hornbook*," he declared. "Not merely is the Heart a Hornbook," he added, "It is the Minds Bible, it is the Minds experience, it is the teat from which the Mind or intelligence sucks its identity" (II, 102-103; Keats's italics). If, in his expansion of the Negative Capability formulation, he envisioned poetry as an escape from or transcendence of the limits of identity, it was all the more necessary to see it as the discovery or creation of identity at a level that was more profound.

Once cut off from the human heart and its sustaining passions and affections, the products of the imagination, however alluring or refined in themselves, lose their human value and identity. The "Lines Written in the Highlands" take us a step beyond Keats's letter of May 3 where he had written Reynolds that "when we come to human Life and the affections it is impossible how a parallel of breast and head can be drawn" (I, 277) by establishing a vital link between them. The poem dramatizes the tendency of the imagination to idealize beyond the limits of human endurance, to sublimate its materials beyond their grounding in the affections, in such a way as to lend a special urgency to Keats's hope "That man may never lose his mind on mountains bleak and bare" (46). At the climax of the "Lines" there is a moment of catatonic terror which opens a "gulph," a "terrible division," as he had before expressed it, between the real world and the imagined.[6]

> No, no, that horror cannot be, for at the cable's
>   length
> Man feels the gentle anchor pull and gladdens in
>   its strength:
> One hour, half-idiot, he stands by mossy
>   waterfall,
> But in the very next he reads his soul's
>   memorial:
> He reads it on the mountain's height, where
>   chance he may sit down
> Upon rough marble diadem—that hill's
>   eternal crown.
>
>   (39-44)

In the end the anchor of the human sympathies exerts its strength and the poet and his poem regain their equilibrium. Up to a point it was only by forcibly dramatizing, even at the risk of some exaggeration, the strains he was under that he could work out his deepening understanding of the nature of "intensity," its connection with "identity," and the vital interrelationship between heart and head. The method of using such works as the *Epistle to Reynolds* and the "Lines Written in the Highlands" to explore imbalances and dangers in his sense of the creative process, as well as various means of compensation, was proving instructive, however troubling or neurotic the results might appear. Early the following spring, writing out his sonnet "Why did I laugh tonight" for George and Georgiana, he told them: "I wrote with my Mind—and perhaps I must confess a little bit of my heart." "I went to bed, and enjoyed an uninterrupted sleep," he added. "Sane I went to bed and sane I arose" (II, 81-82).

[6] See "God of the Meridian," written in January 1818.

IV

"I should not have consented to myself these four Months tramping in the highlands," Keats wrote Bailey in the same letter in which he transcribed his septenaries, "but that I thought it would give me more experience, rub off more Prejudice, use [me] to more hardship, identify finer scenes load me with grander Mountains, and strengthen more my reach in Poetry, than would stopping at home among Books even though I should reach Homer" (1, 342). In the end the expectation was amply justified and in more ways than he could have possibly foreseen. The trip, to be sure, provided him with much of the scenery for the poem he was already meditating. However, it did more than this. It forced him to bridge the gap between the grander forms of landscape and an ideal of the heroic in human nature in a way necessary for an epic attempt beyond the merely perfunctory or banal. Such an attempt would need to be founded on something more than a mastery of epic style and manner, the ability to maneuver stock figures against a background of scenery. It would have to spring from a genuine vision into human life and its destiny—its larger "Mystery." More particularly it would have to proceed from a fuller understanding of the power of the imagination, its authority and limits, to idealize and transform.

From the outset of the tour he had become increasingly aware of a gap between his ideal of the creative process and the real inequalities of vision to which it was in actual practice subject. But it was only in his confrontation with Burns —when he was forced to shift the weight of his concentration from landscape to human character—that he realized how obstinate and obtrusive were the difficulties that stood in the way of the fulfillment of his plan. The experience of the tour was more instructive than disillusioning, however, for if it confirmed the perception of weaknesses he had already felt, it also suggested new strengths. His sense of landscape and of the heroic in human life was beginning to combine

within a deeper kind of understanding one could only call
"heart knowledge."[7] The vast, permanent forms of nature
were mute memorials to the anguish of humanity's enduring
struggle, a tragic knowledge the imagination could, through
selflessness and patient study of the heart, still hope to master
and transcend. The centrality of these relationships had
already, as he knew, been movingly expressed by the greatest
poet of the northern landscape and its somber beauty:

> Exchange the shepherd's frock of native grey
> For robes with regal purple tinged; convert
> The crook into a sceptre; give the pomp
> Of circumstance; and here the tragic Muse
> Shall find apt subjects for her highest art.
> Amid the groves, under the shadowy hills,
> The generations are prepared; the pangs,
> The internal pangs, are ready; the dread strife
> Of poor humanity's afflicted will
> Struggling in vain with ruthless destiny.
>
> (*The Excursion*, vi.548-57)[8]

"How is it," Keats exclaimed on catching his first glimpse of
Burns's native town of Ayr with a view of the sea and the
black mountains around it, "they did not beckon Burns to
some grand attempt at Epic?" (I, 331). Setting and a sense of
the heroic character were beginning to assume the shape of
epic drama in his mind.

---

[7] Some comments in two notes only recently recovered by Helen
Haworth from Keats's copy of Lamb's *Specimens* are pertinent here.
Keats records that someone had observed to him that "he could not
understand any greatness or sublimity at all in mountains seas and
the elements but only in the heart of Man." "Yet there must be a
human reality in the grandeurs of the world's face," Keats writes; "the
human heart and the mountainous world are both great to us."
("Keats's Copy of Lamb's *Specimens of English Dramatic Poets*,"
BNYPL, LXXIV [1970], 424).

[8] References to the poem are to *The Poetical Works of William
Wordsworth*, ed. Ernest de Selincourt and Helen Darbishire (Oxford,
1959), vol. v, and are included by book and line number within the
text.

CHAPTER SEVEN

THE FIRST *HYPERION*

I N many respects the first, epic version of *Hyperion* is the most difficult of all Keats's major works. The poem has all the usual difficulties of fragments (one thinks of those of Coleridge and Shelley), complicated by the fact that it involves us, sooner or later, with Keats's equally fragmentary attempt in *The Fall of Hyperion* to recast the poem as a vision or dream. The two versions are part of a single effort (Keats seems to have referred to them indifferently as "my Hyperion") and, as most critics have realized, are essential to the interpretation of each other. Beginning with the early autumn of 1818 and continuing as late as the early winter of 1819, the whole effort, which clearly embodied Keats's highest hopes, draws upon the richest period of his creative life, and ever since Arnold critics have been tempted to speculate almost endlessly as to the causes of his inability to complete it. One can judge the poem's failure only in the light of the magnitude of the assimilation Keats hoped to achieve. It may, indeed, be useful to consider, in a brief, preliminary way, some of the different goals he hoped to combine. Among other aims, his treatment of the fable of the fallen Titans and the emergence of a new race of gods represents his attempt (1) to define the poet and his function with relation to some of the major intellectual, political, and historical movements of the age; (2) to sketch a hierarchy of poetic values relevant to his time and to place himself in positive relation to it by adumbrating an ideal of poethood; (3) to dramatize certain competing ideas of the poetic character and method; and (4) to formulate in poetic terms the higher ideal of beauty toward which he had for some time been moving. In scope and purpose the work was by far the most ambitious he was ever to attempt. All these themes are, of course, profoundly interrelated, and it is difficult to know how or where to begin. To emphasize any one aspect of the poem to the neglect of others is to lose balance and perspective in a work where point of view is all-important.[1]

To begin with what seems most fundamental, one can say that Keats conceived of the work above all as an attempt to dramatize the truth of "heart knowledge" through a return to mythology—this time to an epic theme more sweeping in its implications than any he had taken up, the classical story of the Fall. As far back as "Sleep and Poetry," he had set his sights on the epic as the mode best suited to his ultimate goal of coming to terms with "the agonies, the strife / Of human hearts." "I wish you knew all that I think about *Genius* and *the Heart*," he wrote Bailey in November 1817, as a prologue to what follows in the "Adam's dream" letter, "and yet I think you are thoroughly acquainted with my innermost breast in that respect or you could not have known me thus long and still hold me worthy to be your dear friend" (I, 184; my italics). Certainly by this time the two words, both of prime importance to his poetic vocabulary, had achieved a reciprocal relationship. (Keats extends the values of the older, neoclassic term "genius" in a way that brings it closer to our modern sense of "insight.") It is, most of all, in the great letter of May 3, 1818, to Reynolds, the letter that remains the best gloss we have on his intentions in *Hyperion*, that the two terms are developed in such a way as to shed important light on his choice of subject and

[1] Throughout this chapter I am especially indebted to Kenneth Muir's "The Meaning of *Hyperion*," *Essays in Criticism*, II (1952), 54-75, reprinted in *John Keats: A Reassessment*, ed. Kenneth Muir (Liverpool, 1958), pp. 102-22. Muir has discussed the relationship between the poem and Keats's political thinking and his ideas of the poetic character more perceptively than any critic to date. In his various discussions, but especially in his important essay, "Keats and His Ideas," *English Romantic Poets: Modern Essays in Criticism*, ed. M. H. Abrams (New York, 1960), pp. 326-39, Douglas Bush has dealt revealingly with the work's aesthetic implications.

chances for succeeding with it as he had begun to think about them. Very broadly, the situation into which *Hyperion* plunges—the fall of the Titans from Saturnian bliss to misery—is no more than the epic rendering of that fundamental change Keats describes to Reynolds as the change from "the infant or thoughtless Chamber" to a realization that the world is actually "full of Misery and Heartbreak, Pain, Sickness and oppression" (I, 280-81).

From the time he first decided to attempt a treatment of the epic fable, actually before the completion of *Endymion*, Keats found himself steadily drawn to it both for its universality and for its more specific contemporary relevance. Its theme was the one most central to the sober realization Wordsworth above all had summed up for the generation of poets that followed him in such lines as the ones Hazlitt never tired of quoting from the greatest of his lyrics, the "Intimations Ode":

> What though the radiance which was once so bright
> Be now for ever taken from my sight,
>   Though nothing can bring back the hour
> Of splendour in the grass, of glory in the flower.

The sense of loss, endemic to the times, was one that could be described or elaborated in a variety of ways, most often through the feeling of a broad decline in power and ability from the past. Partly it was the change from a golden age of innocence and simple faith and the kinds of powerful creativity they fostered to a modern awareness of the "burden of the Mystery" and, with the awakening of "the thinking principle," of the need for a new, more strenuous, difficult, and intellectual apprehension of existence. It was the loss of control over the great, simple forms and modes of belief— those of mythology, for example—for an understanding fractured by reason, science, and the growth of historical awareness. It was the change from an era of godlike assurance (or complacency) to the evidences of postrevolutionary

disillusionment and despair that Keats could see in much
of the art and political thinking of his time.

The change was partly cultural and historic. Nevertheless,
coming back to the permanent aspects of the myth, he had
come to conclude that the state it described was also individual and universal. It represented a state of consciousness,
a kind of maturity even, that was broadly characteristic of
the human condition, especially for poets. "One of the great
reasons that the english have produced the finest writers in
the world," he was afterwards to declare, "is, that the English
world has ill-treated them during their lives and foster'd
them after their deaths. . . . [Boiardo] had a Castle in the
Appenine. He was a noble Poet of Romance; not a miserable
and mighty Poet of the human Heart" (ii, 115). In one
form or another the realization of "the Mystery" had come
to seem to him virtually inevitable for any artist regardless
of time or period (except for lesser talents too self-preoccu-
pied or ineffectual to face it) and fundamental to any kind
of greatness. "The middle age of Shakspeare," he went on
in his remarks on Boiardo, "was all c[l]ouded over; his days
were not more happy than Hamlet's." Given this truth, it
followed that "genius" in a writer lay in his ability to explore
the human predicament and to evolve the kinds of resolution
the arts have traditionally afforded.

The gift of genius was not, in other words, a merely
natural or primitive phenomenon, the unrivaled good fortune of the first great poets to arrive on the scene, who had
said all there was to say. It was, rather, a kind of insight that
was progressive and evolving. Needless to say, by this time he
had acquired a strong sense of the oppressive weight of poetic
tradition, the difficulty of saying something new, of pushing
further. The whole issue was far from simple. Indeed his
metaphor of life as a "Mansion of Many Apartments" is
really the outgrowth of a long internal argument, a characteristic "proing and coning," in which he juxtaposes Milton
against Wordsworth in order to work through again the
old debate of "ancients versus moderns." The meditation,

actually a delicate weighing of the advantages and liabilities of the modern poet, provides not only the necessary rationale for the new poetic undertaking but important clues as to his larger theme and treatment. "You seem . . . to have been going through with a more painful and acute zest the same labyrinth that I have," he wrote Reynolds.

> I have come to the same conclusion thus far. My Branch-ings out therefrom have been numerous: one of them is the consideration of Wordsworth's genius and as a help, in the manner of gold being the meridian Line of worldly wealth,—how he differs from Milton.—And here I have nothing but surmises, from an uncertainty whether Mil-tons apparently less anxiety for Humanity proceeds from his seeing further or no than Wordsworth: And whether Wordsworth has in truth epic passion, and martyrs himself to the human heart, the main region of his song.
>
> (I, 278-79)

For the moment the larger issue might remain unsettled. Nevertheless the passage is revealing for the possibilities it leaves open. Foremost among these is that Wordsworth's genius, the likelihood of his "seeing further," stems from a more active concern for humanity and a larger understand-ing of "the human *heart*." (Keats's change of "mind" to "heart" in the famous phrase from the *Prospectus* to *The Excursion*, "the Mind of Man— / My haunt, and the main region of my song," is a significant substitution.) Indeed the passage, by questioning the depth of Wordsworth's vision, reveals that Keats had already begun to perceive ways of going further. The language in which he ponders whether Wordsworth has in fact achieved true "epic passion" points directly forward to the climax of *Hyperion* and its signifi-cance. For the birth throes of Apollo, his "dying into life," represents that *martyrdom* to the human heart and its knowl-edge that Keats could already foresee as the necessary cul-mination of his poem.

The debate was in reality three-cornered, meaningful

finally only as it helped illuminate his own opportunities at the present time. Following a brief digression, therefore, he returned to Wordsworth, this time by direct comparison with himself. "I will return to Wordsworth," he writes, "whether or no he has an extended vision or a circumscribed grandeur—whether he is an eagle in his nest, or on the wing —And to be more explicit and to show you how tall I stand by the giant, I will put down a simile of human life as far as I now perceive it; that is, to the point to which I say we both have arrived at" (1, 280). The simile that follows serves as a resolution to the whole debate that has preceded it, for it both defines an enduring "Mystery" as the center of life and justifies conviction in the steady growth and evolution of an ideal of poetic "genius" adequate to illuminate and explore what remains unknown.

We are now in that state—We feel the "burden of the Mystery," To this point was Wordsworth come, as far as I can conceive when he wrote "Tintern Abbey" and it seems to me that his Genius is explorative of those dark Passages. Now if we live, and go on thinking, we too shall explore them. he is a Genius and superior [to] us, in so far as he can, more than we, make discoveries, and shed a light in them—Here I must think Wordsworth is deeper than Milton—though I think it has depended more upon the general and gregarious advance of intellect, than individual greatness of Mind.

(1, 281; Keats's italics)

For the time being, at least, Keats would have to disagree with Hazlitt's contention that "the depths and soundings of the human heart were as well understood three thousand years ago, as they are at present"[2] if that meant there was no progress in the kind of understanding communicated by the arts. Keats was too great a poet not to grasp the immensity

2 "Why the Arts Are Not Progressive?—A Fragment," *The Round Table, The Complete Works of William Hazlitt*, ed. P. P. Howe (London, 1930), IV, 162. Later references to Hazlitt in this chapter are to the Howe edition and are included in the text.

of achievement *Paradise Lost* represented or the way it over-shadowed virtually all the poetry that followed it. Neverthe-less, however unfair it might be in some respects, there was a certain justice to his further observation that Milton's "Phi-losophy, human and divine, may be tolerably understood by one not much advanced in years." Whatever else it might be, *Paradise Lost* was not the representation of life as a "Mys-tery" in the way all the great Romantic poets had at various times experienced it. Milton had played a major role in the movement that had freed Europe from "a great superstition," those "certain points and resting places in reasoning" that in time had hardened into an order assumed to be "etherial and authentically divine." In the end, however, he had only reconstituted many of the same points into a system of his own that was in some respects as constricting as that it had replaced. There was a difference between a sense of form and order that was tentative and evolutionary and one that was basically fixed and authoritarian.

Ultimately Keats was too much a child of the Enlighten-ment not to believe in the ideal of progress, in the necessity of each generation's reinterpreting the inherited *mythos* of the past in the light of its own experience. "In regard to his genius alone," he had written Reynolds of Wordsworth, "we find what he says true as far as we have experienced *and we can judge no further but by larger experience*" (I, 279; my italics). If the great central truths of human life had already been expressed, there was still a steadily accumulating store of fresh experience to bring to them; "for axioms in philos-ophy are not axioms until they are proved upon our pulses" (I, 279). Culture was not simply the dead weight of an inherited tradition; it was a continuous process of refinement and fresh discovery. Hence, despite his realization of Milton's greater poetic talents, Keats can conclude that "he did not think into the human heart, as Wordsworth has done. Yet," he went on, "Milton as a Philosopher, had sure as great powers as Wordsworth—What is then to be inferr'd? O many things—It proves there is really a grand march of intellect—, It proves that a mighty providence subdues the mightiest Minds to the service of the time being, whether it be in human Knowledge or Religion" (ɪ, 282). His own more subjective ideal of "genius" and its relation to a deepening vision into the heart of life's mystery was in fact dependent on a larger belief in human progress generally, the idea of a "grand march." "All civiled countries become gradually more enlighten'd," he wrote some time later, "and there should be a continual change for the better" (ɪɪ, 193).

The criterion of "genius" that he had for some time been in the process of defining both as an abstract ideal and a matter of individual talents derived its strength and authority from larger cosmic forces that were, perhaps, turbulent and unsteady but nevertheless gradually advancing in a way that was both exhilarating and at the same time humbling to contemplate. The conception, moreover, was now proving materially useful in determining the theme and epic treatment of his fable and in suggesting the way he could transcend Wordsworth by seeing and thinking further, as he knew he must. As far back as the "Adam's dream" letter of the preceding November, in which he had opened the whole subject of "Genius and the Heart" by comparing "Men of Genius" to "certain ethereal Chemicals" that operate without "any individuality, any determined Character," he had emphasized the poet's need for "Humility and capability of submission" (ɪ, 184). If, as he had gone on to argue later, there really was "a spiritual yeast," a "ferment of existence," genuine poetic vitality could spring only from a heightened responsiveness to the special qualities of the age, from a willingness to suppress all personal ambition in order to identify with larger hopes, disappointments, and achievements. Indeed it was possible to make this "capability of submission" (actually the moral equivalent of Negative Capability) the central virtue in a work of epic conflict whose point would be the inexorable force of cultural and historical development—how, whether they will or no, "a mighty providence subdues the mightiest Minds to the service of the time being."

It was just here that he was equipped by his own poetic talents, as far as he could see, in a way superior to Wordsworth. Later in the year, in October, the very month when he was hard at work on *Hyperion*, he drew for Woodhouse, apropos "the whole pro and con, about genius," a dramatic distinction between his own ideal of the "poetical Character" and "the wordsworthian or egotistical sublime; which is a thing per se and stands alone" (I, 386-87). More forcibly articulated, the distinction was really the outgrowth of the contrast he had drawn the preceding autumn for Bailey between "Men of Genius" and "Men of Power." The contrast was to prove useful in a number of ways; but for the moment its relevance to his fable and its dynastic involvements and hierarchy of gods and Titans was unmistakable. In great part the argument of *Hyperion* is the superiority of "Men of Genius" over "Men of Power."[3] But equally important was Keats's intention to dramatize the difficult and sometimes subtle relationship between them.

The contrast was one that needed further working out. For one thing it was impossible, except perhaps for theoretically minded and insistent friends like Woodhouse, to view the two types in total opposition to each other. One could begin as a poet of one kind and end as a poet of the other, as was probably the case with Wordsworth himself, if one considered his career as a whole, not merely what he had become. "Genius" and "Power," or whatever set of terms one preferred, were really different aspects, perhaps alternating stages, of a larger cycle of poetic creativity. The earlier, more fundamental kind of creativeness, that which struck him as the most genial to the spirit of poetry, found its source in "gusto" and the love of pure sensation, in an entire respon-

[3] Muir (*John Keats: A Reassessment*, p. 107) prefers to describe it as the victory of the "men of achievement" over the "men of power," taking the former phrase from the Negative Capability letter where it is used not to define a dichotomy but to describe Shakespeare.

siveness to the whole of experience. The second, later kind, more characteristic of the poetry of his own day, derived its power from a concentration on its own abstractions, from the permanence and identity it brought to experience, but which in time only rendered it inadequate to deal with the complexity of existence as an ever-changing and evolving whole. Using the myth of the Fall of the older race of Titans, he could dramatize the steady decline of vitality that he sensed in Wordsworth and in much of the poetry of the latter day. At the same time, at the climax of the poem and through the development of the character of Apollo and the younger race of gods, he hoped to express the rebirth of a more primary kind of poetic energy appropriate to his own day but one proceeding from a full awareness of the modern consciousness and from a willing self-surrender to a knowledge of the course of history and the immense pain such understanding must impose.

II

By the Spring of 1818 the major thematic concerns of *Hyperion* were already uppermost in Keats's mind. But how was he to proceed with his intention to combine them in a new epic treatment of the Fall? Ever since the later seventeenth century the task of writing any long poem in English, not to mention epic, had been rendered formidable if not insuperable by the overriding example of *Paradise Lost,* a poem that in its mastery of structure, symbol, and the whole *mythos* of the classical world as well as that of Christianity had developed a form and a coherence beyond which, for sheer effectiveness, it seemed impossible to proceed. Beginning with Dryden and Pope, one expedient regularly employed by poets faced with the problem had been that of imitating or adapting various aspects of Milton's epic or its machinery to their own purposes. In this the Romantic poets were hardly exceptions, although one can argue almost endlessly the degree to which some of the longer visionary poems of Blake and Shelley are really versions—or inversions—of Milton's cosmology and to what extent they embody original forms of myth-making. Keats's decision to take Milton as his acknowledged master, to model his style more openly on that of *Paradise Lost* than any major poet had yet attempted is understandable, for it provided important initial advantages. Primarily the decision provided for the poem a recognizable idiom and decorum of established viability that with readers of any intelligence would command immediate authority and respect. Of course the task of fulfilling with any kind of originality expectations so aroused was full of dangers. Nor could he have foreseen the steady drain upon his energies the need to subdue his own creative impulses to the style and sensibility of his model—"a beautiful and grand Curiosity" (II, 212), as he later referred to it—would, as time passed, increasingly demand. From the outset, however, the most urgent question was whether he could appropriate the story of the Fall and invest it with a significance of his own.

With the decision as to style out of the way and with the modest stability it afforded, Keats was left free to concentrate on the thematic development of his epic material, for it was here that he was intent on demonstrating his originality. Naturally it was impossible to ignore the method and progression of *Paradise Lost*. Nevertheless it was from the contemporary scene that he hoped to draw the real significance of his treatment. In this connection nothing was to prove more useful than his growing insight (partly with the help of Hazlitt) into Wordsworth and more especially *The Excursion*. In point of style *Hyperion* displays the most remarkable assimilation of the manner of *Paradise Lost* of any poem in English after Milton. However, on the level of ideas it represents a thorough working through, virtually step by step, of the same difficult ground Wordsworth had traveled over in *The Excursion*. Indeed it is only by studying the latter work, as it were through the eyes of Keats himself, that we can fully grasp his intentions for *Hyperion*. Milton and Wordsworth, the two polar figures that dominate the letter of May to Reynolds with its crucial implications, were to remain, if in quite different ways, the commanding influences throughout his work upon the poem.

Early in 1818, while thinking about the "works of genius" of his own time, Keats had written Haydon and afterwards his brothers that "if there were three things superior in the modern world," they were *The Excursion*, Haydon's pictures, and Hazlitt's "depth of Taste" (1, 203-205). While the tribute to Haydon was perhaps deliberately flattering, there can be no doubt of Keats's admiration for Wordsworth's narrative. At the same time, as he realized, some further discriminations were essential. For one thing, Hazlitt's view of Wordsworth, in particular his two essays on *The Excursion* in *The Round Table* and his remarks in his lecture "On the Living Poets," all of which Keats came to know intimately and which had a profound influence on his own attitudes, were strongly qualified, at times openly hostile to the older poet. Hazlitt's approach to Wordsworth was revealing because it proceeded from the central premise that the great school of poets at whose head Wordsworth had stood in the generation just preceding Keats's own, the Lake School, had found "its origin in the French revolution, or rather in those sentiments and opinions which produced that revolution" (v, 161). In fact Hazlitt was inclined to trace the success and failure of the school, and of Wordsworth in particular, as a pattern of progressive rise and decline corresponding to its ability to react in a consistent and positive way to the mighty ferment of the times and its alternate hopes and despairs. By retreating in disappointment from the real field of battle to the security of his lakes, Wordsworth had, as Hazlitt saw it, established a record that was neither consistent nor courageous and one inevitably doomed to defeat any hopes for larger achievement.

Hazlitt's assessment of the limits and decline of Wordsworth's power was valuable to Keats not simply as practical criticism but for its relevance to the developing thematic concern of his poem. The judgment served to confirm his own impression of Wordsworth, based on limited personal acquaintance, as a leading spirit of a former age who had, through inflexibility, pride, and disillusionment, cut himself off from the vital currents of his day to withdraw morosely into solemn objurgations on a world that no longer corresponded to his expectations. There was, after all, a difference between the author of the patriotic sonnets of 1802 and the poet who in 1818 "went rather huff'd out of Town," having "left a bad impression where-ever he visited," Keats reported to his brothers, "by his egotism, Vanity and bigotry" (1, 265, 237). Keats was not alone in feeling the pervasiveness of such gloom and intransigence. Early in 1818, in the same month that Hazlitt had commenced his lectures, Shelley, whose work Keats, with a natural emulousness, could never lose sight of for very long, had published his *Revolt of Islam*, a work written to deplore the mood of tyrannical reaction that had swept over Europe in the aftermath of the French Revolution and, even more, the hopelessness that had overcome many former adherents of progress and liberty, who now abandoned themselves to what Shelley in his "Preface" termed "an age of despair." "Hence gloom and misanthropy," Shelley went on to write with obvious relevance to both Wordsworth and *The Excursion*, "have become the characteristics of the age in which we live, the solace of a disappointment that unconsciously finds relief only in the wilful exaggeration of its own despair. . . . Our works of fiction and poetry have been overshadowed by the same infectious gloom."[4] If, as Hazlitt had written, "fortitude of mind is the first requisite of a tragic or epic writer" (v, 152), it was to be doubted whether Wordsworth, for all his insight into the human heart, had shown the necessary courage in adversity, whether he had martyred himself to his deeper knowledge or merely evaded it.

Partly mindful of Wordsworth and his comfortable ties

[4] *The Complete Poetical Works of Percy Bysshe Shelley*, ed. Thomas Hutchinson (London, 1934), pp. 33-34.

with officialdom, Keats found his thoughts turning to politics as he got down to work on *Hyperion* in October. "As for Politics," he wrote George and Georgiana,

> they are in my opinion only sleepy because they will soon be too wide awake—Perhaps not—for the long and continued Peace of England itself has given us notions of personal safety which are likely to prevent the reestablishment of our national Honesty—There is of a truth nothing manly or sterling in any part of the Government. There are many Madmen In the Country, I have no doubt, who would like to be beheaded on tower Hill merely for the sake of eclat, there are many Men like Hunt who from a principle of taste would like to see things go on better, there are many like Sir F. Burdett who like to sit at the head of political dinners—but there are none prepared to suffer in obscurity for their Country—the motives of our wo[r]st Men are interest and of our best Vanity—We have no Milton, no Algernon Sidney—Governors in these days loose the title of Man in exchange for that of Diplomat and Minister—We breathe in a sort of Officinal Atmosphere.
>
> (1, 396)

He was back to Milton and the kind of steadiness and resolution that remains undaunted through revolutionary and counterrevolutionary times. Certainly one could not depend on smooth sailing. But if, as he believed, progress could be achieved, it would require more sacrifice and self-exertion than was presently being made. At the same time, as he went on to George and Georgiana, he could not agree with Dilke, "a Godwin perfectibil[it]y Man" who looked to the United States. Dilke, he wrote,

> pleases himself with the idea that America will be the country to take up the human intellect where england leaves off—I differ there with him greatly—A country like the united states whose greatest Men are Franklins and

Washingtons will never do that—They are great Men doubtless but how are they to be compared to those our countrey men Milton and the two Sidneys. . . . Those American's are great but they are not sublime Man—the humanity of the United States can never reach the sublime.

(I, 397-98)

It was possible to put one's trust in progress without assuming that it would be either easy or steady in coming. It was necessary to eschew the extremes of undue optimism and pessimism alike.

Coming back to Wordsworth, however, it was inescapable that, for all his limitations, he had gone further than anyone in seeking a realistic and affirmative resolution for such different strains and possibilities—and nowhere with a greater sense of the contemporary situation than in *The Excursion*. For it was here, and in particular in the character of the Solitary, that he had directly confronted the problem of the French Revolution and the very kind of despair that Shelley had found most characteristic of the age. Plunged from the bliss of happy marriage into blank despondency at the death of his wife and children, and again into utter gloom by the collapse of more disinterested hopes momentarily reborn by the revolution in France and all it had promised for humanity, the Solitary ended by withdrawing to the isolation of north country hills, "Steeped in a self-indulging spleen, that wants not / Its own voluptuousness, . . . at safe distance from 'a world / Not moving to his mind' " (ii.311-12, 314-15). The most compelling in the poem, the portrait contained something of Wordsworth himself, the beginning, even, of a mature self-reappraisal. What was particularly impressive, however, was the way in which the Solitary and his personal unhappiness were subsumed within a larger, reasoned view of human destiny. His sufferings were only incidental to the vision of an instability at the very core of human life—

Knowing the heart of man is set to be
The centre of this world, about the which
Those revolutions of disturbances
Still roll; where all the aspects of misery
Predominate; whose strong effects are such
As he must bear, being powerless to redress.

(iv.324-29)

What Wordsworth had composed was something more than just another variation on the great Renaissance theme that "Mutability is Nature's bane" (iii.458), however much he may have taken it over as his own. He had, in fact, reinterpreted that elemental truth with fresh relevance to the alternating transports of revolutionary optimism and postrevolutionary despair so characteristic of the times. Among many passages that must have struck Keats forcibly, one might cite the following:

—Man is of dust: ethereal hopes are his,
Which, when they should sustain themselves aloft,
Want due consistence; like a pillar of smoke,
That with majestic energy from earth
Rises; but, having reached the thinner air,
Melts, and dissolves, and is no longer seen.
From this infirmity of mortal kind
Sorrow proceeds, which else were not; at least,
If grief be something hallowed and ordained,
If, in proportion, it be just and meet,
Yet, through this weakness of the general heart,
Is it enabled to maintain its hold
In that excess which conscience disapproves.

(iv.140-52)

Keats had for some time realized the truth of the lines in terms of the ethereal chemistry of the poetic processes. However Wordsworth's treatment of the tenuousness of man's desire, the pattern of rising hopes and subsequent disappointment, and the inevitability of human sorrow, was now useful to him in reinterpreting his favorite analogy in a more broadly human and moral way.

Opposed to the skepticism and despondency of the Solitary were the more cheerful arguments of the Wanderer, and here one could say at least that Wordsworth had attempted to develop an alternative that stood for something more than merely stoical endurance. Whatever else his limitations, the Wanderer was a character one could admire for his ability to sympathize deeply with his fellow beings, for his insight into and compassion for those "made desperate by 'too quick a sense / Of constant infelicity'" (vi. 532-33). Realizing "The universal instinct of repose, / The longing for confirmed tranquillity, / Inward and outward" (iii.397-99) only made him more tolerant of human weakness, more ready to commiserate with "anguish unrelieved, and lack of power / An agonizing sorrow to transmute" (iv.167-68). Yet his special strength, his power to help others, derived from more than mere susceptibility. He was a being, as Wordsworth himself had emphasized, who "could *afford* to suffer / With those whom he saw suffer" (i.370-71); and this ability and the grounds for its creation had been for some time to Keats matters of chief importance, especially in deliberating the character of his hero, Apollo. In the contrasting portraits of the Solitary and the Wanderer, Wordsworth had sought to define a middle ground between unfounded optimism and pure hopelessness at the recurring liabilities of man's estate in a way Keats could hardly help admiring. "The two extremes are equally disowned" (iv.268) and must continue to be. If there were any obvious misgivings they had to do with whether, amid all the "sad embroidery" of the poem, the strength of the Wanderer and his power of vicarious suffering had emerged as forcibly as they might and, related to this, whether Wordsworth had succeeded, after all, in advancing a means for assuaging, if not transmuting, the sorrow of which he was so genuinely aware.

One inevitably came round, that is, to a more negative

view of the poem. It was not that Wordsworth's preoccupation or themes were wrong or that his characters, even, lacked a certain interest. It was the total lack of any dramatic involvement and development that became so palling. From its highpoint, the strangely touching story of Margaret set against a tract of barren landscape at the outset, the poem rapidly lost all narrative or descriptive headway, shrinking to the form of a long internal dialogue in which all the voices that spoke gradually merged into one—recognizably Wordsworth's own. "Even the dialogues introduced in the present volume are soliloquies of the same character, taking different views of the subject," Hazlitt had complained. "The recluse, the pastor, and the pedlar, are three persons in one poet" (IV, 113). One might, making special allowance for the intellectual aspects of the questions Wordsworth was attempting to confront, remain content to read the poem as an internal monologue and no more. Yet the problem went deeper. At the very time when he was urging the need for compassion and an active sympathy with fellow man, Wordsworth seemed to be struggling unsuccessfully to free himself from the toils of his own doubts and preoccupations. "An intense intellectual egotism," as Hazlitt put it, "swallows up every thing" (IV, 113). The voice or voices in the poem spoke of the general heart and the needs of common humanity, but the tone was cold and thin and, beyond an abstract concern, communicated little to the pulse and bloodstream of the reader. Although harsh, there was considerable justification for Shelley's remark that the "poem contains curious evidence of the gradual hardening of a strong but circumscribed sensibility, of the perversion of a penetrating but panic-stricken understanding."[5] The poem seemed constricted to the limits of a private catechism pursued with almost paranoiac energy in which an individual mind, tormented by the questions facing it, sought to persuade itself of solutions it could not with any conviction espouse. Within the progress of the poem the falling-off was

[5] Prose note to *Peter Bell the Third*, ed. Hutchinson, p. 359.

not only dramatic but intellectual, for the early and middle books, where the debate had been maintained with considerable power and honesty, were best. With the advent of the Pastor, the voice of the Solitary had been gradually suppressed in favor of a combination of Christian orthodoxy and folk-wisdom, and the real issues lost sight of amid the platitudes and paraphernalia of a Sunday picnic-outing.[6]

There was much, then, Keats could admire in *The Excursion*—its concern for humanity, its awareness of issues central to the times, and, up to a point, the honesty with which Wordsworth grappled with them, an honesty whose limits were revealed, as much as anything, by a notable unevenness of style. Considered, however, as any kind of formal model, the poem had serious defects. Lacking, except at the outset, any strong narrative interest, the work, in its reliance on abstract argument alone, gradually wore down the patience of the reader. Even within the relatively somber tradition of reflective-meditative verse, Wordsworth's method was too introverted and austere. These, however, were faults that a poem with a more dramatic approach to events and character could hope to avoid, as Keats was determined his epic treatment must. The major question was whether he could develop and control the implications of the vast archetypal legend he had chosen in a way that was relevant to the issues of his own generation and that dramatized his own vision of human struggle and destiny. Having chosen his epic theme, he must now command it, in a sense make it his own.

The task was no easy one, for it demanded clarifying what he wanted to say—his whole concern with genius and the heart—and then deciding how to proceed in adapting the epic fable to his intentions. Here again, however, *The Excursion* proved of major help. From the time of "I Stood Tip-toe" he had found Wordsworth's explanation of the

[6] The failure of the poem has been astutely analyzed in our own day by E. E. Bostetter in his chapter on Wordsworth in *The Romantic Ventriloquists: Wordsworth, Coleridge, Keats, Shelley, Byron* (Seattle, 1963), a study I have found consistently suggestive and stimulating.

origin of mythology in the fourth book increasingly suggestive. As he studied the poem more carefully, however, he
began to discover further clues. Within Book Four there
was perhaps his favorite passage, the lines in which Wordsworth describes how the archetypal poet

> fetched
> Even from the blazing chariot of the sun,
> A beardless Youth, who touched a golden lute,
> And filled the illumined groves with ravishment.
>
> (iv. 857-60)

"Keats said this description of Apollo," Bailey remembered
years afterwards, "should have ended at the 'golden lute,' &
have left it to the imagination to complete the picture,—
how he 'filled the illumined groves.' "[7] The image should
have been abbreviated—or expanded dramatically in a way
that Wordsworth's method would not permit. Keats was now
intent on filling out the picture, on explaining the "how" of
Apollo's golden melody.

Beyond providing a momentary inspiration, Wordsworth's
picture of Apollo was of little use in suggesting any way of
proceeding. Nevertheless other aspects of the earlier books
were more revealing.[8] While characteristically maintaining
his own independent view both of the work and of Hazlitt's
bias as a critic, Keats had studied the poem partly through
Hazlitt's eyes and had come to see that it prepared the
ground for a significant contemporary interpretation of the
story of the Fall from a mythical golden age. One of the most
interesting sections of the poem, as Hazlitt points out in the
first of his essays on *The Excursion*, is that where Words-

---

[7] *The Keats Circle*, ed. Hyder Edward Rollins, 2nd ed. (Cambridge,
Mass., 1965), II, 276 (Bailey's italics).

[8] The notes to Bush's edition provide a number of suggestive parallels between *Hyperion* and *The Excursion*. Some of these are discussed
by Thora Balslev in *Keats and Wordsworth: A Comparative Study*
(Copenhagen, 1962), but chiefly in terms of "echoes." Perhaps the
best discussion is Murry's essay, "Keats and Wordsworth," in his
Keats (London, 1955), pp. 269-91.

worth "treats of the French Revolution, and of the feelings
connected with it, in ingenuous minds, in its commencement and its progress" (IV, 117). Taking up the theme with
regard to the character of the Solitary, Hazlitt proceeds to
juxtapose several long and important passages from Books
Three and Four in such a way as to condense a major part
of Wordsworth's argument. He cites, first, the passage in
which the Solitary, roused by the fall of the Bastille, imagines
how

> From the wreck
> A golden palace rose, or seemed to rise,
> The appointed seat of equitable law
> And mild paternal sway. . . .
>
> (iii.713-16)

and how he promptly joins in the triumphant chorus singing

> Saturnian rule
> Returned,—a progeny of golden years
> Permitted to descend, and bless mankind.
>
> (iii.756-58)

From the height of such raptures the Solitary and a number
of his fellow optimists are plunged into infernal gloom by
the course of subsequent events, and Hazlitt immediately
proceeds to condense another long passage from the fourth
book in which Wordsworth returns to the subject "with the
same magnanimity and philosophical firmness," a passage
that deserves to be cited in the way Hazlitt abridged it:

> For that other loss,
> The loss of confidence in social man,
> By the unexpected transports of our age
> Carried so high, that every thought which looked
> Beyond the temporal destiny of the kind—
> To many seemed superfluous; as no cause
> For such exalted confidence could e'er
> Exist; so, none is now for such despair.

175

The two extremes are equally remote
From truth and reason; do not, then, confound
One with the other, but reject them both;
And choose the middle point, whereon to build
Sound expectations. This doth he advise
Who shared at first the illusion. At this day,
When a Tartarian darkness overspreads
The groaning nations; when the impious rule,
By will or by established ordinance,
Their own dire agents, and constrain the good
To acts which they abhor; though I bewail
This triumph, yet the pity of my heart
Prevents me not from owning that the law,
By which mankind now suffers, is most just.
For by superior energies; more strict
Affiance in each other; faith more firm
In their unhallowed principles, the bad
Have fairly earned a victory o'er the weak,
The vacillating, inconsistent good.

(iv.260-73, 296-309; IV, 118-19)

Briefly, what Keats discovered both from his own independent study of *The Excursion* and from Hazlitt's pointed critique was that the whole myth of the Fall from "Saturnian rule" to "a Tartarian darkness" had already been invested with strong contemporary overtones of a historical, political, and social kind he could hope to build on but in any case could hardly ignore. No doubt he would differ at many points in his view of the world events Wordsworth described. Nevertheless the older poet's treatment of them was suggestive in a number of ways. Indeed "the law," as Wordsworth had enunciated it, by which "superior energies" had gained their victory over "the weak, / The vacillating, inconsistent good" was already taking shape in Keats's mind as the quite different principle by which the younger race of gods were destined to dispossess their forebears—"the eternal law / That first in beauty should be first in might" (ii.228-29).

Wordsworth and Hazlitt were proving materially useful to
Keats in considering the ways in which he could first establish and then proceed to develop the implications of the
epic action of his poem. Often, of course, the suggestions
that were most valuable arose by way of contrary reactions.
No sooner had he cited the long passage from Book Four
of *The Excursion* than Hazlitt, for example, had gone on to
comment: "In the application of these memorable lines, we
should, perhaps, differ a little from Mr. Wordsworth; nor
can we indulge with him in the fond conclusion afterwards
hinted at, that one day *our* triumph, the triumph of humanity and liberty, may be complete." "All things move," he
added significantly, "not in progress, but in a ceaseless
round." Keats's own modified ideal of progress, his belief in a
slow but steady "grand march of intellect" that took into
account man's limitations and the emergence of new obstacles remaining to be faced, was distinct from either position. If Wordsworth believed in the imminence of the
millennium and Hazlitt in mere historical circularity, Keats
would have to differ from both. Yet here, Keats may well
have felt, Hazlitt was being somewhat unjust, for if there
were any passage in the poem that seemed to sum up Wordsworth's view, it was the Wanderer's lofty and impressive
recapitulation near the end of Book Seven, a passage that
must have struck Keats with particular force:

> "So fails, so languishes, grows dim, and dies,"
> The grey-haired Wanderer pensively exclaimed,
> "All that this world is proud of. From their spheres
> The stars of human glory are cast down;
> Perish the roses and the flowers of kings,
> Princes, and emperors, and the crowns and palms
> Of all the mighty, withered and consumed!
> Nor is power given to lowliest innocence
> Long to protect her own. The man himself
> Departs; and soon is spent the line of those
> Who, in the bodily image, in the mind,

In heart or soul, in station or pursuit,
Did most resemble him. Degrees and ranks,
Fraternities and orders—heaping high
New wealth upon the burthen of the old,
And placing trust in privilege confirmed
And re-confirmed—are scoffed at with a smile
Of greedy foretaste, from the secret stand
Of Desolation, aimed: to slow decline
These yield, and these to sudden overthrow:
Their virtue, service, happiness, and state
Expire; and nature's pleasant robe of green,
Humanity's appointed shroud, enwraps
Their monuments and their memory. The vast Frame
Of social nature changes evermore
Her organs and her members, with decay
Restless, and restless generation, powers
And functions dying and produced at need,—
And by this law the mighty whole subsists:
With an ascent and progress in the main;
Yet, oh! how disproportioned to the hopes
And expectations of self-flattering minds!"

                                              (vii.976-1007)

If this was an ideal of progress it could hardly be accused of being a fondly optimistic one. Indeed the view was remarkably close to that Keats himself had come to accept. Yet what mattered most was not the way in which Wordsworth's views served to corroborate his own conclusions but that his reading of *The Excursion* had helped him discover a growing wealth of implication a new study of the Fall could draw upon and which he could pursue without the need to confine himself within the limits of any narrow allegorical conception. It was primarily through the scope and drama of an epic action and by means of his depiction of the character of Apollo that he hoped to exceed the power of Wordsworth's starker narrative. If, however, there was any point on which he was determined to focus, it was on that conflict between individual hopes and expectations and the laws of a controlling providence that Wordsworth had so notably explored—the "strife / Of poor humanity's afflicted will / Struggling in vain with ruthless destiny" (vi.555-57). For Keats had come to see that this was the essence of the "Mystery" of life as well as of Wordsworth's mastery of the human heart.

III

With epic speed *Hyperion* plunges the reader *in medias res*. A great dynastic revolution has shaken Saturn from his throne, and a new race of gods, more vital and more beautiful than their predecessors, has gained ascendancy. The opening landscape and the depiction of the fallen Saturn is one of the most carefully wrought passages in all of Keats's poetry.

> Deep in the shady sadness of a vale
> Far sunken from the healthy breath of morn,
> Far from the fiery noon, and eve's one star,
> Sat gray-hair'd Saturn, quiet as a stone,
> Still as the silence round about his lair;
> Forest on forest hung about his head
> Like cloud on cloud. No stir of air was there,
> Not so much life as on a summer's day
> Robs not one light seed from the feather'd grass,
> But where the dead leaf fell, there did it rest.
> A stream went voiceless by, still deadened more
> By reason of his fallen divinity
> Spreading a shade: the Naiad 'mid her reeds
> Press'd her cold finger closer to her lips.
>
> (i.1-14)

While closing steadily upon the solitary figure of the downcast Titan, the scene possesses a primeval vastness, something of "the same overwhelming, oppressive power" Hazlitt had observed as characteristic of the northern landscape from which Keats had only shortly returned. "We are surrounded with the constant sense and superstitious awe," Hazlitt wrote near the beginning of the first of his essays on *The Excursion*, "of the collective power of matter, of the gigantic and eternal forms of nature, on which, from the beginning of time, the hand of man has made no impression" (IV, 111-12). Yet the extraordinary stillness of the setting and the images of numbness, cold, and constriction that surround the god— summed up in the image of "the Naiad 'mid her reeds" who presses "her cold finger closer to her lips"—only suggest his loss of power and vital creativity. Indeed a conception of power in its various degrees, the ability to animate and vitalize creation, is fundamental to the scene and to the question Saturn cannot answer: "Who had power / To make me desolate? whence came the strength" (i.102-103). His might is one inextricably involved with his whole sense of "strong identity, my real self" (i.114) which, now fled from him, provides the necessary clue for understanding the nature of his plight. For as he struggles to his feet in the hope of momentarily reasserting his sway—

> But cannot I create?
> Cannot I form? Cannot I fashion forth
> Another world, another universe,
> To overbear and crumble this to nought?
> Where is another chaos? Where?
>
> (i.141-45)

—we realize we are in touch with strong creative energies once omnipotent but now outworn, or at least no longer relevant to the occasion. Saturn can only look to the past, to a heaven he has lost, for the rehabilitation of his godhead. Blinded by his egoism, he is unaware of a strong irony implicit in his words,

it must—it must
Be of ripe *progress*—Saturn must be King.
(i.124-25)

Nor, in his self-preoccupation, can he see a new and tragic beauty written large in Thea's face, a "Sorrow more beautiful than Beauty's self" unrevealed before, which already prefigures the triumph of his dispossessors.

The thematic significance of Keats's portrait of Saturn at the outset of *Hyperion* has always proved in some ways puzzling. The chief clue to its meaning lies in Keats's letter of October 27 to Woodhouse in which he implies that he has "at that very instant been cogitating on the Characters of saturn and Ops," the same letter where he distinguishes between the "wordsworthian or egotistical sublime" and his own ideal of the poet who "has no Identity" (1, 387). Indeed the essence of Keats's conception of the character of the older god seems to derive, again partly through the help of Hazlitt, from his long-standing meditation on the extent and limits of Wordsworth's power as a poet. Throughout his writing Hazlitt often treats Wordsworth as if he were describing some primeval god. Thus he writes that "his mind is, as it were, coëval with the primary forms of things; his imagination holds immediately from nature, and 'owes no allegiance' but 'to the elements.'" Or again: "He may be said to create his own materials; his thoughts are his real subject. His understanding broods over that which is 'without form and void,' and 'makes it pregnant'" (IV, 112). Such passages are typical of the way Hazlitt portrays Wordsworth's godlike, elemental power. Yet Hazlitt uses the same figurative language to express his awareness of its limits. "He tolerates only what he himself creates," he writes again; "he sympathizes only with what can enter into no competition with him, with 'the bare trees and mountains bare, and grass in the green field.' He sees nothing but himself and the universe" (v, 163). It remained for Keats to draw such images and ambivalent impressions together in his picture of the godlike but no longer omnipotent Saturn.

This is not to claim that Saturn *is* Wordsworth, although there may be a certain limited truth to such an assertion. It is to argue, rather, that *Hyperion*, like most of Keats's longer poems, is on one level concerned with poetry and the various degrees of its power and that the hierarchy it describes is largely a poetic or aesthetic one. It was only natural for Keats, in working toward the criterion of tragic beauty appropriate to his own age, to begin by crystallizing a sense of the failure of the generation of poets before his own. Saturn and his fellow gods have fallen because, although they once played vital roles as symbols of that "beauteous life / Diffus'd unseen throughout eternal space" (i.317-18), they have been unable to adjust to vast new forces of sorrow and disorder. They have outlived their usefulness to a destiny they are unable to comprehend except in terms of narrow self-interest.

Throughout the action of the first two books it is the passionate desire of the Titans to discover some reason for their downfall that, as readers, we find particularly compelling. Yet the whole balance which Milton had so brilliantly defined in *Paradise Lost* between higher necessity on the one hand and free will, responsibility, and sin on the other, Keats prefers, partly for dramatic reasons, to leave ambiguous or to emphasize in different ways as he proceeds. Indeed, the more we are led to ponder the question of causation, the more we begin to sense its irrelevance to the larger issues of the poem as they unfold. The fall of Saturn and the Titans cannot be "explained" any more than one can explain the fading of "the glory and the dream" at the end of the first movement of Wordsworth's "Intimations Ode." Primarily it is the change from a golden to a silver age, the loss of the controlling, universal modes of mythic apprehension for an historical awareness, a fall from timelessness into time that Keats had for some while come to sense as fundamental to the modern consciousness. "Earth-born / And sky-engendered," the offspring of "the infant world" (i.309-10, 26), the Titans are the children of an earlier unity and innocence, presiding over "days of peace and slumberous calm,"

> Those days, all innocent of scathing war,
> When all the fair Existences of heaven
> Came open-eyed to guess what we would speak:—
> That was before our brows were taught to frown,
> Before our lips knew else but solemn sounds.
>
> (ii.335-40)

From such contentment and placidity they have been plunged into a very different state, a world of "fear, hope, and wrath; / Actions of rage and passion" (i.332-33), a perturbation unfamiliar to them and with which they are unprepared to deal. With the knowledge of grief has come a new sense of transience and impermanence. Thea's complaint, "O aching *time*! O moments big as years" (i.64), is similar to the distress voiced by Coelus, who can only urge his child, Hyperion, to struggle to "oppose to each malignant *hour* / Ethereal presence" (i.339-40). Hyperion, "phrenzied with new woes," must bend "His spirit to the sorrow of the *time*" (i.299-301).[9] The point is not that the Titans are erring or reprehensible. They are simply helpless to contend against the change in circumstances that has overtaken them, for it was Keats's intention to use them as the background for defining a higher, more active ideal of sublimity than any they, in their complacency, could represent. One recalls Keats's speculation to Reynolds as to whether Wordsworth had truly "martyred himself to the human heart" and its knowledge, whether he had proved "an eagle in his nest, or on the wing" (I, 279-80). Towering, not like "pale solitary doves," but "eagles golden-feather'd" as Oceanus describes them

---

[9] I am indebted to William G. Locke for pointing out to me how often in the poem the imagery of time is used to emphasize the former realm of innocence and timelessness from which the Titans have fallen.

(ii.225-26), the younger gods are not antipathetic to their forebears, only more vigorous and capable of facing and transcending the new complexities and oppositions the Titans cannot endure. For it was to be Keats's argument that only through the knowledge of time could time be conquered. Apollo achieves his godhead not by shrinking from the burden of the modern consciousness—the sense of sorrow, impermanence, and loss—but by being baptized into the agony of full historical awareness and its immensity of pain.

Keats's ability to dramatize the limitations of the fallen Titans is nowhere better seen than in their council in Book Two, a scene that inevitably bears comparison with the debate in Pandemonium in Book Two of *Paradise Lost* on which it is obviously modeled.[10] The different sophistries within the various arguments of Milton's devils are quickly recognized. However, one can easily miss the special subtlety of Keats's handling—the way in which each Titan's speech comments on the particular limitations in the viewpoints of his fellows and at the same time adumbrates an aspect of the perfection to be summed up in Apollo. To be sure, Oceanus's great speech is sometimes taken as the kernel of Keats's meaning, and it cannot be doubted that its vision of eternal change and gradual evolution toward ever higher states of being is closely related to the modified ideal of progress Keats had come to espouse.

[10] An excellent study of the parallels between the two works is provided in Brian Wilkie's chapter on Keats in *Romantic Poets and Epic Tradition* (Madison and Milwaukee, 1965), one of the few discussions that adds materially to Muir's essay. He comments aptly on the "riskiness" of accepting at face value any of the speeches of the Titans, like that of Oceanus (whom he compares to Belial [p. 276]), as some commentators have done. His discussion deals with the poem within the context of the change from innocence to experience, a change he examines skillfully in terms of the imagery of gold and silver and the reversal it undergoes within the poem. However, he minimizes the importance of the political and poetic themes. His rejection of "theories . . . that . . . ascribe to Keats an interest in public affairs and a powerful belief in the value of culture for which there is very little evidence in his letters" (p. 156) seems questionable.

And first, as thou wast not the first of powers,
So art thou not the last; it cannot be:
Thou art not the beginning nor the end.

. . . .

         The ripe hour came,
And with it Light, and Light, engendering
Upon its own producer, forthwith touch'd
The whole enormous matter into life.
Upon that very hour, our parentage,
The Heavens and the Earth, were manifest:
Then thou first-born, and we the giant-race,
Found ourselves ruling new and beauteous realms.
Now comes the pain of truth, to whom 'tis pain;
O folly! for to bear all naked truths,
And to envisage circumstance, all calm,
That is the top of sovereignty. Mark well!
As Heaven and Earth are fairer, fairer far
Than Chaos and blank Darkness, though once chiefs;
And as we show beyond that Heaven and Earth
In form and shape compact and beautiful,
In will, in action free, companionship,
And thousand other signs of purer life;
So on our heels a fresh perfection treads,
A power more strong in beauty, born of us
And fated to excel us, as we pass
In glory that old Darkness.
                     (ii.188-90, 194-215)

There is, indeed, a certain justification for the sea-god's claim that, while Saturn has been blinded by his sheer supremacy, he alone has "wandered to eternal truth" (ii.187). Yet to accept his speech as the point of the poem is to ignore the dramatic context in which it is delivered. For all his wisdom he has not been able to preserve his godhead or to escape a scalding in the sea, while his plea for calm of mind arises from a stoic resignation that does not approach the ideal of sublimity Keats was intent on expressing in the character of Apollo, as the ending of the fragment makes clear. Thus Oceanus's impassiveness is juxtaposed against both the overemotional but instinctive insight of Clymene and the mighty but self-destructive power of Enceladus.

It is sometimes argued that throughout the council scene one can see Keats finding his way, that Clymene's account of fleeing from the music that has made her "sick / Of joy and grief at once" (ii.288-89), for example, shows him groping toward the more mature conception of beauty to be represented by Apollo in Book Three.[11] Yet the weakness and sentimentality of her narration seem part of Keats's intention to dramatize the inability of the Titans, whether on the level of pure emotion, intellect, or power, to achieve the mastery of Apollo. Enceladus, in many ways the least appealing of the Titans, is not simply drawn; for all its fierceness his nature is not, like Moloc's, innately warlike but has become so through anguish at the loss of an innocence and calm that earlier were his chief delight. In his potentially godlike but unmastered power he recalls both the "Poets Polyphemes" Keats had taken to task for their disruptive turbulence in "Sleep and Poetry" and the proud, self-dramatizing "Hectorers" he was to excoriate at the end of the disputed lines in *The Fall of Hyperion*, both passages that critics since Woodhouse's day have read as veiled attacks on Byron.[12] Enceladus dramatizes Keats's perception in the earlier poem that "strength alone though of the Muses born / Is like a *fallen angel*" (241-42), and as he raises himself up to answer Clymene—

> while still upon his arm
> He lean'd; not rising, from supreme contempt—
>   (ii.307-308)

---

[11] See Muir's discussion, "The Meaning of *Hyperion*," pp. 105-106.
[12] See Ernest de Selincourt, *The Poems of John Keats*, 5th ed. (London, 1926), pp. 408-409, 519n.; and "Richard Woodhouse's Interleaved and Annotated Copy of Keats's *Poems* (1817)," *Literary Monographs*, vol. 1, ed. Eric Rothstein and Thomas K. Dunseath (Madison, Wis., 1967), pp. 123-24, 155.

we realize how far his moody violence falls below the ideal
of poetic majesty and "mildest sway" Keats had depicted in
the same passage in "Sleep and Poetry" as "the supreme of
power; / 'Tis might half slumb'ring on its own right arm"
(236-37). The character of Enceladus is tinged by overtones
of the same Byronic titanism Keats had come to see as one
further manifestation of the anguish and desperation of his
day.

In his reaction to the ascendancy of the new dynasty, then,
each of the fallen Titans provides a genuine but limited
insight into the coming nature of Apollo. However, the
older deities are hopelessly divided among themselves and
cannot combine or distill their separate intuitions as the
reader is implicitly invited to. The various views expressed
within the council collectively define the coming genius of
Apollo in a way that none of the Titans, ironically, can understand. The drama of the episode thus directly prefigures
the unification of sensibility to be achieved by Apollo by
revealing its groundwork in the welter of conflicting attitudes—passive resignation, sentimental pathos, or anguished
violence—that are destined to be superseded. One can add,
without pressing the point too far, that as a prelude to the
birth of Apollo as the "Father of all verse" (iii.13), the
drama of the first two books reveals Keats's awareness of that
dissociation in terms of the chief poetic attitudes of his day,
from stoicism (one of the less appealing aspects of *The
Excursion*) to the stormy desolation of a poem like *Childe
Harold*.

IV

A mystery at the center of the poem, one most critics
have found it convenient to pass over rather than confront,
is the character of Hyperion himself and the nature of his
anguish. The meaning of the agony Apollo undergoes while
he reads in Mnemosyne's eyes the "Knowledge enormous"
that transforms him at the climax of the fragment is un-

mistakable. Apollo achieves godhead and the condition of true poet through agonizing self-surrender to the tragic knowledge of human history communicated in her gaze. By comparison, Hyperion's torments as he paces the once serene arcades of his blazing palace, now menaced by monstrous apparitions, now agonized by the muscular spasms that contort him, are both more compelling and obscure. The portrait is filled with an anxiety, frustration, and exhaustion—culminating in the god's collapse "in grief and radiance faint" following his struggle to force open prematurely the portals of the dawn—that seem a reflection of some deeper level of Keats's emotional life and possess a reality that, by contrast, makes Apollo's pain appear merely cerebral. The puzzlement of critics over the nature of the Titan's distress and the larger problem of his relation to Apollo is generally conveyed through certain obvious questions. Had he continued the work, how would Keats have proceeded? Would there have been a renewal of conflict? Would Hyperion have been brought directly into confrontation with Apollo and been forcibly dispossessed? Or would he have recognized the superiority of his adversary and given way without a struggle? To which one might add, why is Hyperion, alone among the Titans, as yet unfallen? And not least, why did Keats entitle his poem *Hyperion* and not *Apollo*?

The truth is that *Hyperion* is something more than the deliberate elaboration of a set of themes through adaptation of epic legend, as every intelligent reader has more or less sensed. It is also a poem of considerable self-involvement. It represents Keats's attempt to realize the central action of his poem, the transition between two orders of deity, on the level of his own emotional and psychological life and in terms of the symbolic value each god had steadily assumed for him. It suggests, indeed, an effort that certain schools of twentieth-century psychology would describe as the struggle for reintegration of personality. Perhaps this is only to say that Keats's commitment to the work was, more than merely dramatic or intellectual, deeply personal, and that major sections of the action and characterization draw their peculiar power from different aspects of his own being. To put the matter another way, the problems and solutions he was struggling to articulate within the work were not merely theoretical ones. They were basic to the constitution of his own poetic creativity, and nowhere is the fact more clearly suggested than in his characterization of Hyperion.

As we have seen, a major goal in Keats's undertaking of *Hyperion* was his desire to dramatize the superiority of his own ideal of the poetical character—the type of poet who has "no identity . . . no self," as he told Woodhouse—over other kinds, especially the one he had come to associate with Wordsworth. Yet there are aspects of the work that suggest the practical difficulties he was experiencing in controlling the very imaginative abilities he was seeking to acclaim. It is difficult to explore this aspect of the poem—the character of Hyperion himself—without necessarily becoming more subjective in approach. Yet it is hard not to connect the feverish anxiety and restlessness of the god with many of the feelings Keats was suffering in the autumn and early winter of 1818 when he was at work on the poem. One senses that, if Apollo represents an emotional and poetic ideal Keats was struggling to achieve, Hyperion conveys the nervous intensity and distraction to which the poet was actually a prey. The circumstances in which Keats found himself on his return to Hampstead are too well known to need extensive summation. He had returned from the walking tour in ill-health to find Tom desperately unwell. *Endymion* was shortly attacked in several of the great reviews; and at about this time he met and fell in love with Fanny Brawne. The ordeal of nursing his brother through an illness all the symptoms of which he sympathized with as his own ended only with Tom's death on December 1.

The combined force of these pressures would tax the composure of any individual; but in Keats's case they were intensified by the poet's hypersensitive imagination. On September 21 he wrote Dilke:

I wish I could say Tom was any better. His identity presses upon me so all day that I am obliged to go out—and although I intended to have given some time to study alone I am obliged to write, and plunge into abstract images to ease myself of his countenance his voice and feebleness—so that I live now in a continual fever—it must be poisonous to life although I feel well. Imagine "the hateful siege of contraries"—if I think of fame of poetry it seems a crime to me, and yet I must do so or suffer—I am sorry to give you pain—I am almost resolv'd to burn this—but I really have not self possession and magninimity [*sic*] enough to manage the thing othe[r]wise.

(I, 368-69)

The next day he wrote Reynolds:

I never was in love—Yet the voice and the shape of a woman has haunted me these two days—at such a time when the relief, the feverous relief of Poetry seems a much less crime—This morning Poetry has conquered—I have relapsed into those abstractions which are my only life—I feel escaped from a new strange and threatening sorrow.—And I am thankful for it—There is an awful warmth about my heart like a load of Immortality.

Poor Tom—that woman—and Poetry were ringing changes in my senses.

(I, 370)

The anguished, haunted tone of these passages, together with certain of their phrases—"I live now in a continual fever," "poisonous to life," "a new strange and threatening sorrow" —suggest a source in Keats's own experience for his description of the restlessness and anxiety of Hyperion. Nor was his state of mind a transient one. "I feel I must again begin with my poetry—for if I am not in action mind or Body I am in pain," he wrote George and Georgiana in December, when he was still actively at work on the poem. "I live under an everlasting restraint—Never relieved except when I am com-

posing" (II, 12). "My Mind," he wrote Fanny Brawne at a
later day, "has been the most discontented and restless one
that ever was put into a body too small for it" (II, 275).
Early in 1820 he wrote a letter sympathizing with Rice's
illness and its "hypochondriac symptoms" and relating that
even when in health he had not been free from a host of
"haunting and deformed thoughts and feelings." "I may say
that for 6 Months before I was taken ill I had not passed a
tranquil day," he wrote. "Either that gloom overspred me or
I was suffering under some passionate feeling, or if I turn'd
to versify that acerbated the poison of either sensation"
(II, 260). The imagery of suffocation and constriction, the
"dreams of day and night" and the specters by which Hyperion is haunted, are something more than mere dramatic
invention. They represent, rather, one expression of the
poet's vital but hypersensitive and often unstable imaginative
life. On the level of abstract concern the change that over-
takes Hyperion might be described as the inevitable darken-
ing of the "second Chamber." More intimately, however, it
was the reflection of a sorrow and perturbation actually unsettling the current of the poet's own existence. Now more
than ever there was need, as he wrote to Dilke, for a new
"self-possession and magnanimity," the particular values he
was seeking to sum up in the nature of Apollo.

The difficulty lay in actually realizing the ideal he was
seeking intellectually to propound. "I wish I could say Tom
was any better. His identity presses upon me so all day." It
was all very well to argue that the poet, having no identity
of his own, participates in the existences of others; that he
lives as readily in the dark as in the bright side of things; that
he could achieve the disinterestedness and magnanimity to
share vicariously in human pain; that, like Wordsworth's
Wanderer, he "could *afford* to suffer / With those whom he
saw suffer." "After thinking a moment or two that you suffer
in common with all Mankind," he wrote George and Georgiana in October, "hold it not a sin to regain your cheerfulness"
(I, 391-92). Nevertheless, in the face of his brother's helpless

misery, there were times when the ideal seemed little more than an impractical abstraction. Keats complained to Woodhouse about periods when "the identity of every one in the room begins [so] to press upon me that, I am in a very little time an[ni]hilated" (I, 387); and early the next year he complained of being "surrounded with unpleasant human identities; who press upon one" (II, 77). However, having to nurse his brother through the final stages of his illness, tormented hourly by Tom's "countenance his voice and feebleness," he was finding that the very openness and susceptibility, the capacity for sympathetic identification he had so praised to Woodhouse, were beginning to exact an intolerable revenge. He was being martyred to the necessity of living out the argument of his poem within the reality of his day-to-day experience. Only there were times when the "abstractions" of his verse, in their removal from anything he could actually hope to achieve, seemed more an intellectual refuge and escape than a genuine distillation of heart knowledge. His ideal of the protean spirit, of the "camelion Poet," so attractive in theory, especially when dignified by understanding and compassion as the moral vision of Apollo, had in practice developed a dark ironic counterpart from whom he was unable to detach himself—the vital but restless and eternally anguished Satan who stands behind the figure of Hyperion.

Apollo and Hyperion are, in fact, complementary figures. They represent the lighter and darker sides, the potential strengths and actual liabilities of the broad criterion of Negative Capability Keats was seeking to articulate and refine into a moral ideal of the poet. The problem was that he himself was intimately involved within the struggle of the poem, that he was in different ways committed to both deities at once, that they were projections of conflicting sides of his own poetic nature he could not as yet resolve. The end of his poem, the birth throes of Apollo, was full of clear personal significance: it represented the purgation of the unstable, tormented existence he in many ways detested and the birth of the secure, serene type of creator he desired to become. Yet the confrontation between the two deities, the decisive triumph of the one over the other, was something Keats could not fully dramatize for the reason that he had not experienced it within the terms of his own being.

V

It is only with the opening of Book Three and our first glimpse of Apollo that we realize how tenuous and uncertain was the assimilation Keats was struggling to achieve. The picture of the young god, his tears trickling down his golden bow, is sentimental and at total variance with the heroic tone and theme of the first two books. As many critics have observed, the opening description of the god seems to revert to the freedom, at times lushness, of Keats's earlier manner. One has to read no further than the opening lines, where Keats bids farewell to the Titans and their woes, to discover why:

> O leave them, Muse! O leave them to their woes;
> For thou art weak to sing such tumults dire:
> A solitary sorrow best befits
> Thy lips, and antheming a lonely grief.

(iii.3-6)

The "solitary sorrow," the "lonely grief," was the death of Tom. On December 18, a little over a fortnight after his brother's death, Keats wrote George and Georgiana: "I went on a little with [*Hyperion*] last night—but it will take some time to get into the vein again" (II, 12). Both Bate and Gittings, among others, have argued convincingly that the point to which Keats had gotten by December 1 was the end of the first two books.[13] However it was now impossible for him "to get into the vein again." The floodgates of emotion had broken, and it was impossible to steel himself for the

[13] W. J. Bate, *John Keats* (Cambridge, Mass., 1963), p. 403; Robert Gittings, *John Keats* (London, 1968), pp. 268-69.

kind of effort that writing in what he later termed "an artful or rather artist's humour" (ii, 167) required. Under the impress of real grief he no longer possessed the strength to subdue himself to the task of resuming the artifice necessary to perpetuate the style and machinery of his epic model. It was not just that his mind was already turning to a new, more intimate, visionary mode of expressing his meaning, one capable of rendering "the true voice of feeling" (ii, 167). It was also that his conception of the apotheosis of Apollo beneath the gaze of history had come to seem too academic and abstract; and there is much to support Bate's brilliant conjecture that Keats simply decided to plunge forward and telescope the final lines, bringing the fragment to an end prematurely as a way, however unsatisfactory, of getting the conclusion off his chest and freeing himself from a poem that, in its present form, he was disinclined to continue.[14] As in the case of *Endymion*, we are dealing with a work whose groundwork in experience had outrun the limits of its conception.

Studying the inadequacy of the first version of *Hyperion* in the light of the second, as we must, we can see that a major difficulty is that in one sense its significance is *too* clear. Apollo is deified by Mnemosyne, the mother of the muses, the goddess of memory, and the repository of the knowledge of universal mutability and impermanence, the "eternal truth" Oceanus had earlier perceived. Yet the

> Names, deeds, gray legends, dire events, rebellions,
> Majesties, sovran voices, agonies,
> Creations and destroyings

(iii.114-16)

that pour into the "wide hollows" of Apollo's brain and deify him are too much a catalogue of intellectual abstractions and never convey the emotional reality of the tragic awareness Keats was attempting to express. "Memory," he had written Reynolds earlier, "should not be called knowledge" (i, 231).

[14] *John Keats*, p. 406.

In the birth throes of Apollo he was seeking to depict the full emotional realization of that "Knowledge enormous" Oceanus stoically accepts and the other Titans overemotionally react to or imperfectly perceive. Nevertheless the scene in which Apollo, staring into Mnemosyne's eyes, is suddenly convulsed borders on anticlimax:

> Thus the God,
> While his enkindled eyes, with level glance
> Beneath his white soft temples, stedfast kept
> Trembling with light upon Mnemosyne.
> Soon wild commotions shook him, and made flush
> All the immortal fairness of his limbs;
> Most like the struggle at the gate of death;
> Or liker still to one who should take leave
> Of pale immortal death, and with a pang
> As hot as death's is chill, with fierce convulse
> Die into life.
>
> (iii.120-30)

As Bate has written, "The episode sways dangerously on the brink of the grotesque."[15] We seem to be witnessing an act of mental telepathy rather than experiencing the effect Keats intended—a sense, in Wordsworth's phrase, of "truth . . . carried alive into the heart by passion."[16]

Under different circumstances Keats might have successfully revised the episode or, for that matter, completed the entire work within an epic framework. Nevertheless his revision of the fragment in *The Fall of Hyperion: A Dream* reveals abundant reasons for his abandoning the poem in its earlier form, reasons that transcend mere problems of style and involve important changes in conception. At the root of Keats's struggle to complete the whole *Hyperion* project was the nature and extent of his dependence on *Paradise Lost*.

[15] *Ibid.*, p. 404.
[16] "Preface" to the second edition of *Lyrical Ballads, The Poetical Works of William Wordsworth*, ed. Ernest de Selincourt (Oxford, 1952), II, 386.

The first two books of *Hyperion* present a unique and moving recreation of Milton's hell. However in the third, when the older poet's consolations were gathering before him—the promise of a new creation, a drama leading to the Fall of man but ending, nevertheless, in divine compassion and abundant grace—Keats could turn only to his own later redaction of "Adam's dream" in the birth of Apollo through the wisdom hidden in Mnemosyne's eyes. Keats could not accept Milton's reasoned view of divine providence. But the vague trust in evolutionary progress that forms the underpinning of the epic fragment he abandoned seems frail and unsatisfying. Despite its correlation with an important strain of speculation in the letters, the formulation was too theoretic and removed from the mainstream of his own experience. Nor was it sufficiently strong to survive the strain and grief of Tom's decline and death. When, after an interval of months, Keats returned to the work in the effort to revise it, he did so from the prospect of a far more original and profound assimilation of *Paradise Lost* and with a vastly altered vision of world destiny and its significance.

Nevertheless, it would be badly wrong to minimize the extent of what Keats was seeking to accomplish in the first *Hyperion* or the depth and honesty of thinking it reveals. Here it is important to recognize the significance of the fragment's ending in a *partitudo interrupta*, that the text of the poem printed in the 1820 volume ends without the climactic half-line preserved amid Richard Woodhouse's transcripts: "Glory dawn'd: he was a god!"[17] Keats clearly recognized that he had not achieved the assimilation he was struggling to represent in the birth of Apollo. However one can still admire the purpose and intelligence of his conception. For what he had begun to confront in his drama of the fallen and divided Titans was one aspect of the ailment endemic to all poetry since Milton's day that has been de-

[17] See John Middleton Murry, *Keats and Shakespeare* (London, 1925), p. 82 and n.

scribed by Eliot as "dissociation of sensibility."[18] What he was seeking to resolve in the birth of his hero was a desire for Shakespearean energy and responsiveness, the dramatic ideals of Negative Capability, with the longing for a poetry of knowledge, authority, and deliberate statement. If Keats failed, he did so in directly facing a task that no other English poet of the nineteenth century was able to accomplish.

[18] See Eliot's essay on "The Metaphysical Poets" in *Selected Essays* (New York, 1932). Eliot writes that "in one or two passages of Shelley's *Triumph of Life*, in the second *Hyperion*, there are traces of a struggle toward unification of sensibility" (p. 248). It can be claimed Keats directly confronted the dissociation itself in the earlier version.

CHAPTER EIGHT

ROMANCE AS WISH-FULFILLMENT:
THE EVE OF ST. AGNES

FOLLOWING the temporary collapse of his ability to continue *Hyperion*—the kind of poem on which he found it difficult to concentrate under any circumstances—Keats fell back for relief on a work of a totally different kind, one that has always seemed to many of its admirers closer to his particular vein of romanticism. *The Eve of St. Agnes* was composed in January and February of 1819, and the contrast between the two poems could hardly be more complete. *St. Agnes* marks Keats's momentary abandonment of Milton for Spenser, of the spirit of heroic endeavor for imaginative escape, of epic for a return to romance. Yet having said this one must immediately add, with a glance back at a poem like *Isabella*, written early the preceding year, that *St. Agnes* is romance of a sort totally different from any he had yet attempted. It is not just that the poem reveals a new, breathtaking advance in technical mastery. More important, the apparent simplicity of Keats's tale conceals a new sophistication, an extraordinary awareness of the *devices* of romance, and a fascination with both their possibilities and limitations. Behind the work one can sense the conflicting strains under which *Hyperion* broke down—the death of Tom at the beginning of December and the dawning, almost simultaneously, of the poet's love for Fanny Brawne—reflected in the powerful contrasts that dominate the poem, the play of light against darkness, warmth against cold, gratification against denial, life against death. Unlike *Hyperion*, however, which seeks to create a serious intellectual and dramatic means for transcending such oppositions, *St. Agnes* grants

them greater sensuous and emotional intensity within a world
of dreams and make-believe whose retreats and sublimations
are only the more alluring for their transparency.

Many of the issues that arise in approaching *St. Agnes*
revolve around the fundamental question of its tone. For
Keats's contemporaries and the Victorians, most of whom in
one way or another came under its spell, there was no mistak-
ing the poem's "meaning." It was for them the essence of
romance, a gorgeous bit of tapestry, full of color, tenderness,
passion, and high feeling. Leigh Hunt thought it "the most
delightful and complete specimen of [Keats's] genius" among
the longer pieces, a poem standing midway between efforts
like *Isabella*, at times more sensitive but feebler, and "the
less generally characteristic majesty of the fragment of
Hyperion."[1] Modern criticism, with its distaste for such
banalities, has by contrast dealt with the poem somberly
and with a certain grim intellectual seriousness.[2] Yet *St.*

---

[1] Leigh Hunt, *Imagination and Fancy*, 2nd ed. (London, 1845),
p. 314.

[2] The two most influential discussions have been Earl Wasserman's
chapter on the poem in *The Finer Tone: Keats' Major Poems* (Baltimore, 1953), pp. 97-137; and Jack Stillinger's essay, "The Hoodwinking of Madeline: Scepticism in 'The Eve of St. Agnes,'" *Studies in
Philology*, LVIII (1961), 533-55. Wasserman broke sharply with earlier
interpreters by reading the poem (in a way that would have staggered
the Rossettis) as an illustration or enactment of Keats's metaphor of
life as a "Mansion of Many Apartments" and of the imagination as
"Adam's dream." The poem thus becomes a metaphysical progression
culminating, with the lovers' union, in the demonstration of "the truth
of Imagination—What the imagination seizes as Beauty must be
truth" (1, 184). Stillinger's essay skillfully analyzes the shortcomings
of Wasserman's method. Yet he makes his case only to move to the
opposite extreme by reading the poem as antiromance, an instance of
Keats's later skepticism and disillusionment with the imagination. Thus
with a little shift of emphasis Romeo becomes Lothario, romance
becomes seduction, and the lovers' passion little more than the culmination of a rake's sordid stratagem. The interpretation seems hardly
less one-sided than the one it would correct. Both discussions tend to
reduce the poem to the value of a simple thesis, a representation of the
imagination as either good or evil, truth or deception.

Agnes is above all dramatic (Keats himself saw it as a step toward a chief ambition, "the writing of a few fine Plays" [II, 234]); and while it tends to sacrifice depth of character to richness and suggestiveness of background, it skillfully achieves a rich interplay of dramatic emotions, a complex texture not lacking its own kind of playfulness, irony, and even humor. Of course we are seduced, along with Madeline, each time we return to the work, as we submit to its suggestions of mystery, the rapture of young love, and its high, romantic spell; that is all part of its deeper playfulness, and part, too, of its deeper point. Yet at the same time we are hardly unmindful that the machinery by which we are taken in is conventional, not to say thin. The castle, for all its monumentality, is shadowy, insubstantial. The dwarfish Hildebrand and old Lord Maurice (some of the "fine mother Radcliff" types Keats was himself particularly amused by [II, 62]) and their kinsmen, whose very dogs howl execrations, rage savagely, only to subside in the end into a harmless, drunken stupor, "be-nightmar'd" as if by fairies. There is the lovers' usual go-between, a tottering, cackling crone, and a solemn Beadsman, both of whom seem to dissolve simultaneously into ashes, along with the rest of the castle, when the lovers depart. There are dusky galleries, arched ways, silken chambers, and, near the end, a drunken porter and a bloodhound.

It is no wonder Keats found the poem "smokeable" (II, 174).[3] Yet it is not, at the same time, merely ingenious to suggest that our consciousness of artificiality, at times of deliberate contrivance, makes up a necessary part of our enjoyment of the work and constitutes a vital element in its effect. For if at first glance Keats's romance strikes us as thoroughly conventional in its melodrama, we are soon aware that the conventions it employs are hardly of a piece, indeed that they are used at times with beguiling inconsistency.

---

[3] Keats actually applied the adjective to *Isabella*, but the context of his letter makes it clear he thought the objection true also of *St. Agnes*, "only not so glaring."

Madeline is sober and demure, "St. Agnes' charmed maid" (192), rising, beneath her solitary candle's gleam, to pious observances. Yet the rites she must observe ("supperless to bed . . . Nor look behind, nor sideways" [51, 53]), while rooted in folk superstition, suggest a little child put to bed early with visions of sugar plums. Porphyro is soft-voiced and trembling, yearning for his lady in the darkness while loath to interrupt her slumbers. Yet he is brought on at the outset, crowding stage like a big Italian tenor, with unabashed hyperbole:

> He ventures in: let no buzz'd whisper tell:
> All eyes be muffled, or a hundred swords
> Will storm his heart, Love's fev'rous citadel.
>
> (82-84)

Even the element of mystery, or mystification, that pervades the poem is hardly of a piece. We begin with the somber, Christian devotions of the Beadsman, which lend at first a more serious color to the popular superstitions Madeline pursues. But it is not long before we are in a world of charms and dim enchantments, a world inhabited by elves and fairies. Religious ritual, the stately mysteries of high romance, the self-conscious theatricality of opera, and the improbabilities of folk legend and a child's fairy tale all proceed to merge impenetrably. However, if *St. Agnes* lacks the larger unity and cohesiveness that characterizes Spenser's world, if we are puzzled as to which species of "romance" it belongs, such doubts and questions make up an integral part of its effect and meaning.

All this is not to argue that in *St. Agnes* Keats was writing parody or burlesque. It is, however, to claim that in taking refuge from the contradictory pressures of the moment in the consolations of a new romance, he was doing so with heightened awareness of the tenuousness of the imaginative world into which he was withdrawing and with a view of the poet's role as conjurer that was at times ironic.[4] Like most of

---

[4] See Marian H. Cusac, "Keats as Enchanter: An Organizing Prin-

Keats's major efforts, *St. Agnes* is a poem about the etherealizing power of human desire and passion, a further attempt at the "material sublime." However the particular genius of the work lies in its comprehension of the kinds of evasiveness and disguise the imagination necessarily employs in accomplishing its transformation, an awareness of the poetic process as an act of sublimation now in some ways closer to its modern psychological sense than its older, chemical one. Although it is often taken as such, *St. Agnes* is not primarily a glorification of sexual experience or even, for all the condensed richness of its imagery, of the human senses.[5] It is, rather, an exceptionally subtle study of the psychology of the imagination and its processes, a further testing, pursued more seriously in some of the poet's later verse, of the quality and limits of poetic belief. More than anything else, perhaps, the element most central to the poem is its concern with wish-fulfillment, a fundamental aspect of romance that had fascinated Keats from the time of his earliest verse—often, as he himself was well aware (and as Byron, for one, pointed out with vulgar contempt) at the cost of particular embarrassments.[6] To describe *The Eve of St. Agnes* as a romance

---

ciple of *The Eve of St. Agnes*," *Keats-Shelley Journal*, xvii (1968), 113-19, a brief, suggestive study of the role of the narrator.

[5] For a different view, see Harold Bloom's discussion of the poem in *The Visionary Company* (New York, 1961), pp. 369-75. While essentially an independent one, my own reading of the poem is most indebted to the essays of R. H. Fogle and Arthur Carr cited below, as well as to C. F. Burgess's admirably rounded discussion of structure and technique in " 'The Eve of St. Agnes': One Way to the Poem," *English Journal*, liv (1965), 389-94. John Jones's argument, in his recent full discussion of the poetry, *John Keats's Dream of Truth* (London, 1969), that the "dream come true" / "just a dream" ambivalence is the major "axis" of Keats's verse (p. 170) is especially appropriate to the study of *St. Agnes*. Jones's later discussion of the poem as a more intense redoing of *Isabella* (pp. 232-42), however, curiously ignores virtually all the elements of technique, convention, and narrative focus that separate the two works in skill and maturity of control and consequently in their fundamental meaning.

[6] Byron wrote Murray on November 9, 1820: "Mr. Keats, whose

of wish-fulfillment is, of course, to expose oneself immediately to misunderstanding, for we are apt, even today, to
regard that activity as artless, not to say simple-minded,
whereas in actuality it is close to the root of creativity of
human culture and the arts and never more compelling or
intense than when acting through a consciousness of the
kinds of reality it would alter or circumvent. A wish is
double-natured: it lies somewhere between a desire and an
act of will, an impulse and its realization, the unconscious
and the conscious. It is, in fact, the imagination (in its
broader romantic sense) that serves to mediate between the
self-centered gratifications of phantasy and the awareness of
human limitation, between the pleasure and reality principles, and which, by creating the grounds for an accommodation, defines the kinds of beauty or truth we find at any
given moment acceptable or satisfying. What distinguishes
St. Agnes at the point at which it occurs in Keats's career is
the subtlety of its control over the psychological mechanisms
of repression and release, the fact that the perspective it
provides upon the reality it constructs is not simple but
complex and continually shifting.

In visualizing *St. Agnes* as a poem of wish-fulfillment, one
can hardly overlook either the defensive nature of its battle-
mented setting or the poem's whole nocturnal character. The
major action itself suggests by analogy the way in which the
defenses of consciousness are circumvented, the way in
which, as in dreams, awareness begins to take its shape from
the promptings of latent desire. Consider merely the plot.
An ardent young lover abducts a lovely maiden from a closely

poetry you enquire after, appears to me what I have already said: such
writing is a sort of mental ****—******** his *Imagination*. I don't
mean he is *indecent*, but viciously soliciting his own ideas into a state,
which is neither poetry or any thing else but a Bedlam vision produced
by raw pork and opium" (*The Works of Lord Byron, Letters and Journals*, ed. Rowland E. Prothero [London, 1901], v, 117 [Byron's
italics]; see also 109). In all probability, Byron had not seen *St. Agnes*
or the 1820 volume at this time but was basing his comments on
Keats's earlier verse.

guarded castle filled with rivals and violent enemies; and when at the end the two escape across the moors to some legendary home in the south, they make their way through chained and bolted gates, past watchmen overcome by drink and slumber. Porphyro enters furtively and by night and, with the help of a sole friend and intermediary, gains access to Madeline's chamber. Here he conceals himself. It is only when, after watching her enter, undress, fall into prayer and reverie, and prepare herself for bed, he hears the steady breathing of her slumber that he dares leave his hiding place. Despite the arguments of Stillinger,[7] the climax of the poem, the union of the two lovers, in no way resembles rape or even a seduction of any ordinary kind. For it is a part of Porphyro's task, as the overtones of stealth and anxiety make us feel, that he must not break the spell in which Madeline lies bound, that he cannot interrupt the current of her dreams, that merely to awaken her would be disastrous. He must rather, through the use of various suggestions—the feast of fruits and spices with its teeming odors, the music he plays on her lute, the sound of his voice, the touch, even, of his arm—*create himself* within her dream. The desire he represents and introduces must be partly disguised, partly transformed, in order to win admission to the dream where alone it can find fulfillment. How and where the two first met, how long they have known each other, the state of Madeline's affections, or even the degree of her awareness of Porphyro as a lover are all questions to which we are never given answers, although we are made to feel, somehow, that he has been implicitly in her thoughts almost from the start of the poem. But when she awakes, or half-awakes, from her dream (for the point is left deliberately ambiguous), she recognizes Porphyro, after a moment of painful confusion, not just as a mortal wooer in all his human limitations, but also as a part of her dream, a part of her vision and her desire, and she accepts him as her lover. There is an accommoda-

[7] See n.2, above.

tion, one that is neither easy nor untroubled, between imagination and reality.

There is no need for elaborate Freudian analysis to see that the major action of the poem is essentially a drama of wish-fulfillment, a testimony to the power of human desire to realize itself, to transform awareness, and to gain a measure of recognition and acceptance despite the thousand restraints—fear, disbelief, denial, propriety—excluding it. Only in the dream and its processes—by extension the domain of romance, poetry, art—and the shelter they afford from waking consciousness is there any hope for the recognition and appeasement that the most fundamental kind of human energy and instinct insistently demand; for the dream is conditioned and informed by the same human desire it transfigures and fulfills.

Such a formulation enables us to see the poem plainly for what it is, and yet paradoxically could cause us to miss its real artistry. For if within the literature of English Romanticism *The Eve of St. Agnes* is a supreme example of art as wish-fulfillment, it is, nevertheless, as we have party seen, a wish-fulfillment of an exceptionally practiced and self-conscious kind that gives the work its essential character. The poem, that is, achieves its magic, but only in such a way as to dramatize the particular tensions that oppose it and the kinds of device it must employ in overcoming them—repression, anxiety, disguise, censorship, sublimation. The very artistry that brings the dream swelling into reality draws our attention to itself in such a way as subtly to qualify, even to unsettle, its own effects. Once we go beneath the surface melodrama we discover a mixture of the naive and sophisticated, the sentimental and the disenchanted, fantasy and psychological realism.

II

"It shall be as thou *wishest*" (172) Angela tells Porphyro, and her words suggest the principle of causality within the lovers' universe the poem invites us to accept. Yet we are not introduced to Madeline or Porphyro directly; nor, as we discover at the beginning, are all forms of wishing equally efficacious. The inductions to the narrative poems and fragments of Keats's last great year are masterpieces of technique, and that of *St. Agnes* is no exception. The description of the Beadsman and the chapel's piercing cold prepares a series of contrasts the poem is steadily to develop and expand.

> St. Agnes' Eve—Ah, bitter chill it was!
> The owl, for all his feathers, was a-cold;
> The hare limp'd trembling through the frozen grass,
> And silent was the flock in woolly fold:
> Numb were the Beadsman's fingers, while he told
> His rosary, and while his frosted breath,
> Like pious incense from a censer old,
> Seem'd taking flight for heaven, without a death,
> Past the sweet Virgin's picture, while his prayer he saith.
>
> (1-9)

Keats ingeniously begins his drama of wish-fulfillment by presenting a familiar form of sublimation that is introduced only to be rejected as ineffectual. As worshiper and adorer, the Beadsman prepares the way for Porphyro by establishing a contrast that is ironical; for his primary role requires a form of wishing—that is, prayer. Indeed the images that first surround him suggest a certain ardor and devotion, just as his breath, rising like incense, and the lamp he carries convey a kind of perfume, light, and warmth. Long practiced, however, in the rites of penitence and self-discipline, he restrains his feeling while his passion, channeled into the forms of religious worship, seems powerless to animate a host of images that are lifeless and unyielding. The virgin to whom he prays, however sweet, remains a mere picture. The emprisoned knights and ladies praying in their frozen oratories, reflect, through Keats's brilliant use of sculptural imagery, the harsh repression of human warmth and feeling, the note from which the poem commences and ascends. One may compare them with the carved angels of the ballroom who, eager-eyed and expectant as if animated by the music and festivities around them, seem virtually bursting from the stonework of the cornice into human life. At the most critical moment of the poem, the moment of Madeline's apparent withdrawal from her dream and her awakening, Porphyro kneels as if frozen by her bedside, "pale as smooth-sculptured stone" (297), only to derive a new and almost preternatural vitality by his acceptance as the consummation of her vision, as he melts "Into her dream" (320). Throughout the poem we find Keats using the imagery of sculpture to express the way feeling is arrested or repressed, then liberated and fulfilled in a new onrush of emotion.

There is a similar logic at work in the poet's use of musical themes and images. The contrast between the constraint of the Beadsman's world and the glow and movement of the ballroom culminates in the single moment when he passes through the little door—the indication of another range of experience:

> Northward he turneth through a little door,
> And scarce three steps, ere Music's golden tongue
> Flatter'd to tears this aged man and poor.
>
> (19-21)

The image of tears, which drew Hunt's admiration and moved him to observe that "a true poet is by nature a metaphysician,"[8] defines a particular moment central to the poem's harmony. The image recurs twice at important turning-points in the poem—once when Porphyro first learns of Madeline's hopes for St. Agnes' night and again when Madeline weeps on awakening from her dream to observe her lover kneeling by her bedside—and thus perpetuates and extends, almost like a theme in music, the power of a single mood. In the Beadsman's sudden weeping we recognize an act of self-love, or, more exactly perhaps, self-pity, an instant in which the restraints upon feeling are momentarily dissolved and the

---

[8] Hunt, *Imagination and Fancy*, p. 332.

repressed desires and longings of the soul achieve an unexpected outlet to expression. The image thus defines, in a moment of sudden contrast, the gap that exists between desire and fulfillment, between potential and realization, a gap that, as the poem is to suggest, can be bridged only by a leap of the imagination. From the very beginning, then, Keats creates, almost as a kind of leitmotif, that specific quality of human yearning basic to the theme and structure of his poem. Nor should one overlook the fact that the Beadsman is moved to tears by music, for it serves to symbolize throughout the poem, as in the image of the "silver, snarling trumpets" (31) that summon and chide the guests, the power of aroused desire. Often, however, it is used, as in the great image of the ballroom, filled with "music, yearning like a God in pain" (56), to suggest emotion denied its full expression or unnaturally restrained. Whether it be the boisterous music from the revelers below that is silenced when the hall door closes, the hushed strains the trembling Porphyro plays so quietly on Madeline's lute, or the inner melody that Madeline, entering her chamber like "a tongueless nightingale," feels "paining" her side with longing for deliverance (205-206), music is throughout the poem a symbol of the tide of human feeling that seeks to overbear all efforts to contain it.

Despite the show of feeling that momentarily masters him and sets the keynote for the poem, the Beadsman turns his back upon the setting he has opened. He turns "Another way" (25), which is not the way the lovers take. As in the "Bright Star" sonnet, Keats moves toward the world of mortal rapture from an image of devout but cold and inhuman isolation. The Beadsman affords an effective transition to our first glimpse of Keats's heroine for further reasons. Both are bent on rites and meditation, for we find Madeline already engrossed by the ceremonies she intends to observe. Both shun the castle's glittering entertainment for prayer, fasting, seclusion, and the hope of their own

visionary fulfillment. The same questions of truth and sub-
stantiality, moreover, surround the world to which each is
drawn. Self-absorbed, Madeline does not seem to hear the
music, yearning in desire; nor does she heed the ardent
cavaliers, who approach her only to withdraw. She is oblivious to the looks of "love, defiance, hate, and scorn" (69)
around her. While she dances, her eyes are "vague, regardless" (64); she is already engrossed by her imagination—

> Hoodwink'd with faery fancy; all amort,
> Save to St. Agnes and her lambs unshorn,
> And all the bliss to be before to-morrow morn.
>
> (70-72)

Paradoxically, however, the courtly festivities Madeline turns
away from do not seem any more real than the world of her
fancies. The revelers burst in

> With plume, tiara, and all rich array,
> Numerous as shadows haunting fairily
> The brain, new stuff'd, in youth, with triumphs gay
> Of old romance.
>
> (38-41)

They seem ghostly, insubstantial, merely part of the trap-
pings of "old romance," an outworn spell. As R. H. Fogle
has justly observed, such effects are "complex and even self-
contradictory," certainly "not the poetry of a simple ro-
mancer."[9] If we are tempted to view Madeline as the prey
of her illusions, we are at the same time reminded that the
framework of the entire poem, the conventions of romance
themselves, are hardly above suspicion. From start to finish
we are in a world of make-believe where our habitual distinctions between reality and illusion no longer apply. Indeed the
reader is himself invited at Keats's own request not only to
accept but to take part in a world where wishing has the force
of willing:

[9] "A Reading of Keats's 'Eve of St. Agnes,'" *College English*, VI
(1945), 326.

These [the revelers] *let us wish away*,
And turn, *sole-thoughted*, to one Lady there.

(41-42)

Thus, as by the magic of a wish, the argent revelry is resolved back into shadows, and we give ourselves up to the charm of Madeline's endeavor, a bit of harmless conjuring that can take on a more sober cast simply through a willingness to take it seriously: "Full of this *whim* was *thoughtful* Madeline" (55). It is as if the poem were subtly arguing the power of the characters, the poet, and even the reader, to shape a kind of reality from the stuff of illusion by an act of will.

The same kind of sophistication underlies the histrionics of Porphyro's arrival on the scene. Filled with "barbarian hordes, / Hyena foemen" (85-86), the castle holds, beyond Madeline herself, no one from whom he can hope mercy, "Save one old beldame, weak in body and in soul" (90). And then immediately, as if in answer to his prayers—

Ah, happy chance! the aged creature came,
Shuffling along with ivory-headed wand.

(91-92)

Here again, Keats is both using and spoofing the conventions of romance—the suspension of all normal standards of probability—as the bumbling crone gropes for Porphyro's hand to greet him as well as to reassure herself of his identity. Indeed it is the variable identity of the characters that now proves so fascinating; for, beyond its obvious melodrama, the deeper interest of the narrative lies in the changing psychological relationships it develops—the way the characters react upon and modify each other. Badly frightened by Porphyro's impulsive threat to reveal himself to his enemies, Angela protests herself "A poor, weak, palsy-stricken, churchyard thing" (155), virtually a ghost already. Yet only a little while earlier, in her amazement at seeing him, she has bid him "flit! / Flit like a ghost away" (104-105) and gone on to liken his appearance to some supernatural visitation:

Thou must hold water in a witch's sieve,
And be liege-lord of all the Elves and Fays,
To venture so.

(120-22)

Though they are all creatures of the romance world of the poem, the characters nevertheless lay claim at various times to different levels of existence or reality that continually play off against, challenge, or modify each other.

There is, for example, the enchanting scene in which Porphyro is led through many a winding corridor into Angela's little chamber, "Pale, lattic'd, chill, and silent as a tomb" (113), where the garrulous dame, as if through a sudden start of recollection, first reveals her mistress's intention:

St. Agnes' Eve!
God's help! my lady fair the conjuror plays
This very night: good angels her deceive!

(123-25)

There follows one of the brilliant "camera stills" the poem makes such effective use of:

Feebly she laugheth in the languid moon,
While Porphyro upon her face doth look,
Like puzzled urchin on an aged crone
Who keepeth clos'd a wond'rous riddle-book,
As spectacled she sits in chimney nook.

(127-31)

Dominated by the pallor of the chamber and the old dame's mocking laughter, Porphyro is momentarily transformed, as if before our eyes, into a child held spellbound by the enigma of a nanny's bedtime riddle, the pastime of a winter evening, while Madeline's intention appears nothing more than an empty piece of childish self-deception. Yet it is at this moment that he is moved to tears by his recognition of her adventure's unfulfilled potential, the solution to the puzzle's

mystery which lies in his own power to supply. Immediately
the pallor of the scene is filled with imagery of color:

> Sudden a *thought* came like a full-blown rose,
> Flushing his brow, and in his pained heart
> Made purple riot.
>
> (136-38)

It is, of course, not the formulated "thought" but the wish
that underlies it, or rather the sudden flowering of the one
into the fullness of the other, that Keats conveys in the dynamic image of a rose's unfolding. Transformed, Porphyro
rises up brilliant-eyed to assume his proper role as lover with
his enterprise fully formed in the reality of his imagination.
It is at such moments of alternate contraction and expansion,
when Keats takes daring freedoms with the whole decorum
of romance, that we sense within the shifts of background
and convention the maturity of his control over the focus of
his narrative and the intimate connection it establishes between technique and meaning.

The impulse toward contraction immediately resumes with
Angela's expressions of pious horror on first construing his
intent. His enterprise is now a "stratagem" (139) and the
adoring lover "cruel" and "wicked" (140, 143)—"Thou
canst not surely be the same that thou didst seem" (144).
Her words, for all their commonplaceness, have a further
point; for through its sudden changes in background, mood,
convention, the poem continually creates new contexts for
visualizing the characters and their actions, among which we
find it difficult to decide which are the most probable, believable, "real." Angela's objections now have the effect of
forcing Porphyro partly to conceal, partly to disguise his full
intention. He must swear "by all saints" (145), disavow all
"ruffian passion" (149), and hope for grace "When my weak
voice shall whisper its last prayer" (147), even threatening
to reveal himself to his foes and so call down upon himself a
kind of martyrdom. He must, in short, attempt to sublimate
the more questionable aspects of his enterprise by proposing

it in terms acceptable to religious or moral orthodoxy. It is somewhat ironical to reflect that the hero's plight was in certain ways similar to Keats's own when he discovered that passages in the completed manuscript of the poem offended the scruples of his publishers and he was forced to revise them, partly unwillingly, to bring them into conformity with the demands of propriety.[10] We miss the point of how details in the history of the poem's publication serve to illuminate one of its major thematic preoccupations when we see the problem in terms of mere prurience, duplicity, hypocrisy, or cynical expedience. The devices of disguise and censorship perform an integral and even aesthetic function throughout the whole formation of the work—well before Woodhouse and Taylor required their particular changes—for they have to do with Keats's larger grasp of human psychology, his mastery of the interplay between the various levels of human intuition, both unconscious and conscious, and the means by which they achieve accommodation.

It is in the portrayal of Madeline and her dream that Keats's treatment of such deeper concerns becomes more difficult and subtle. His famous declaration to Bailey over a year earlier in November 1817 that "the Imagination may be compared to Adam's dream—he awoke and found it truth" (1, 185) has an undeniable yet inconclusive bearing on the meaning of *St. Agnes*. For the relationships within the poem are too complicated to be resolved into the simple terms of the earlier equation. For one thing Madeline never fully awakens from her dream; and if she partly wakes as her "blue affrayed eyes" (296) open, that awakening is not an altogether happy one.

> Her eyes were open, but she still beheld,
> Now wide awake, the vision of her sleep:

---

[10] See *The Letters of John Keats*, ed. Hyder Edward Rollins (Cambridge, Mass., 1958), II, 162-64, 182-83, for the reactions of Woodhouse and Taylor. The relation of Keats's revisions to earlier versions of the poem is discussed in Stillinger's "The Text of 'The Eve of St. Agnes,'" *Studies in Bibliography*, XVI (1963), 207-12.

> There was a painful change, that nigh expell'd
> The blisses of her dream so pure and deep,
> At which fair Madeline began to weep,
> And moan forth witless words with many a sigh;
> While still her gaze on Porphyro would keep;
> Who knelt, with joined hands and piteous eye,
> Fearing to move or speak, she look'd so dreamingly.
>
> (298-306)

Like the knight-at-arms of Keats's famous ballad written later in the spring, Porphyro is "pallid, chill, and drear" (311), momentarily isolated from the sustaining warmth and vitality of her dream, which, in the fullness of its imagined blisses, has outrun the vision of her human lover. Marked by her tears, there is the same recognition of a gap between desire and appearance, a moment of painful contraction followed immediately by a more intense reintegration of vision and reality in which the lovers are united.

> Into her dream he melted, as the rose
> Blendeth its odour with the violet,—
> Solution sweet.
>
> (320-22)

Porphyro's success comes not through any shattering of the dream or diminution of its spell, but through his power, sensed almost from the moment of his first appearance, to suggest and to inform its content, to bring it slowly to the point of consciousness and recognition where, while it still remains a dream, he can become a part of it and find acceptance. In his infinite persistence and resourcefulness, he expresses the power of human desire, of the wish, to create its own fulfillment, to achieve, relative to other things, its own kind of truth.

Yet the inherent relativity of the poem, the shifting use it makes of subtly different conventions and attitudes which continually puzzles us and makes the work impossible to summarize in terms of any single statement, is never clearer than when we look more closely at its treatment of Madeline's dream. Her soul "Flown, like a thought, until the morrow-day" (239), she fades into sleep, into that state of benign unconsciousness where the powers of intelligence recover a measure of their innocence and instinctual vitality —"As though a rose should shut, and be a bud again" (243). Porphyro is free to emerge from his concealment, to proceed to his "complainings dear" (313), the expressions of his desire muted by the tide of unconsciousness. Yet he emerges, in Keats's marvelously suggestive phrase, "Noiseless as fear in a wide wilderness" (250); and the note of anxiety relates not merely to his fear of interrupting her slumber but also to the awe we sense, on peering with him through the bed-curtains, at the profundity of her repose, "where, lo!—how *fast* she slept" (252). For her sleep, and the dream already begun to form within it, which before had seemed so warm and protective, now, by a slight variation in imagery, is made to appear aloof, cold, almost inhuman. There is indeed something frenetic in the way Porphyro, "half anguish'd" (255), proceeds to heap up in abandon the fruits and syrups, and something somber in the way they stand, forlorn and apart, "Filling the chilly room with perfume light" (275). For the charm that holds Madeline, for all Porphyro's attempts to soften it, is now "Impossible to melt as iced stream" (283), seemingly impervious even to the touch of his "warm, unnerved arm" (280) as it sinks into her pillow. She lies "entoil'd in woofed phantasies" (288). Confronted by a situation calling for Prince Charming to awake his sleeping princess with a kiss, we have instead a heroine who appears to have gone over the line where sleep turns into coma and dreaming into endless fantasy.

The continual modulation between such different sets of contexts and conventions keeps us perpetually off balance and prevents our settling into any simple attitude in reading *St. Agnes*. True it is that the brief terror of Madeline's awakening and its moment of schizophrenic anguish is rapidly dissolved within the lovers' rapturous union and flight. Yet in another way the sense of Madeline's dilemma, the momen-

tary rift the poem opens between the Porphyro of her dream
and the mortal lover isolated by her human vision, retains
its haunting power, so that the sexual culmination the poem
proposes, however "sweet," remains a "Solution" (322), a
resolving of difficulties that does not so much command as
entreat our willing suspension of disbelief. We accept the
romance of the poem—in a sense we *will* it—in its triumph
over the oppositions that confront it, even while we recognize the way in which the adequacy of such means are called
in question. Nor is it possible to ignore the way the poem
lets us down from its heights of magic quite deliberately and
in a fashion that to some degree anticipates Keats's other
great poem of sleep and awakening, the "Ode to a Nightingale." The beating of the sleet upon the panes rouses the
lovers:

> 'Tis dark: quick pattereth the flaw-blown sleet:
> "This is no dream, my bride, my Madeline!"
> 'Tis dark: the iced gusts still rave and beat:
> "No dream, alas! alas! and woe is mine!
> Porphyro will leave me here to fade and pine.—
> Cruel! what traitor could thee hither bring?"
>
> (325-30)

Porphyro's words have a triumphant ring, as though they
heralded an emergence from dream into reality. Their immediate effect, however, is an unhappy one, for they momentarily place Madeline in another role familiar to us,
although now from popular romance—that of the damsel
robbed of her maidenhead by a faithless lover who departs at
dawn, the type of the forsaken Gretchen. Porphyro, nevertheless, is "no rude *infidel*" (342). He has already twice
called Madeline his "bride" (326, 334) and has a home
awaiting her across the southern moors. The poem, in fact,
seems virtually on the point of ending on a note of domesticity, with the storm, for all its icy gusts, marking a return to
the world of the natural elements and breathing humanity.
Such homely expectations, however, are quickly lost amid

the onset of some final magic. "Hark! 'tis an elfin-storm from faery land" (343), Porphyro exclaims. The lovers are not destined for a return into the mortal world but for some nebulous transcendence of their own. And while they steal away through the familiar stage-props of the castle, they flee as "phantoms" (361, 362), unfelt, unheard, unseen by all but the wakeful bloodhound, a descendant of Sir Leoline's supernaturally sensitive old mastiff.

> And they are gone away: ay, ages long ago
> These lovers fled away into the storm.
>
> (370-71)

While Angela, the Beadsman, the Baron and his guests are carried off by death or nightmare, the lovers may, as Arthur Carr has argued, take flight into "a happier and warmer reality." Nevertheless there is something sad about the way they flee away, almost like ghosts, into the storm, just as the immemorial realm they gain is strangely vague, remote, and insubstantial. Nor, as Carr himself has pointed out, are they permitted to escape without the poet's reminder "that we have been listening to a fairy-tale, with its formula of happiness after danger."[11] Thus we remain charmed but also perplexed by the poem and its blend of domesticity, elvishness, gothicism, realism, courtly romance, riddle, fairy tale, and legend, a combination that remains to the last deliberately anachronistic and refuses to relate itself to what we commonly mean by "reality" in any way that can be readily defined. If the poem continually suggests the transforming power of the aroused imagination, the logic of "Adam's dream," it simultaneously exposes, through the heterogeneous devices and conventions it employs, the kinds of stratagem to which poetic magic must resort.

[11] Arthur Carr, "John Keats' Other 'Urn,'" *The University of Kansas City Review*, xx (1954), 241. A directly opposite view is expressed by Herbert G. Wright in "Has Keats's 'Eve of St. Agnes' a Tragic Ending?" *Modern Language Review*, xl (1945), 90-94.

III

Largely in reaction to the apparent sentimentalism of earlier readings, modern criticism of *The Eve of St. Agnes* has been sharply pointed, topical, and dogmatic. It has felt compelled to elaborate, even at the expense of some confessed distortion, a tightly thematic framework for the poem rather than to conclude with what must at all costs be avoided—a view of the work as "a mere fairy-tale romance, unhappily short on meaning."[12] Yet if *St. Agnes* has any "meaning" at all, it lies precisely in its quality as romance. As in the case of the later odes, it is the way we are taken into the world of the poem, what happens to us there, and the way we are let out again that matters most. As readers we cannot permit the statements in the letters, however useful, or our own preconceived notions of the poet's intellectual development to substitute for the experience of the work itself, the way it summons up and operates upon what Keats, near the end of his life, was to call "the knowledge of contrast, feeling for light and shade, all that information (primitive sense) necessary for a poem" (ii, 360).

St. Agnes is above all a poem of contrast, of light and shade, a poem informed from the opening of its initial stanza by "primitive sense." Moreover its real concern is equally primitive and fundamental to the nature of romance, as well as to "romanticism," in all its various forms: the power of wishing, willing, and the kind of fulfillment it can bring in fiction, love, and art. Yet while *St. Agnes* is remarkable for the power of the desires and expectations it arouses, the satisfactions it offers are consistently qualified or restrained. For Keats's narrative, even while enrapturing us, progressively reveals the kinds of dislocation toward which romance, by its very nature, tends. The real triumph of the poem lies in the self-conscious mastery and artifice of its technique, which grants both poet and reader a vital measure of detachment

[12] Stillinger, "The Hoodwinking of Madeline," pp. 533, 534.

from the very spell it casts, which tests the limits and the dangers of its own devices even while employing them, and which marks the beginning of that ironical perspective on imaginative experience Keats was steadily to develop in "La Belle Dame sans Merci," the great odes of the spring, and *Lamia*. True it is that the temporary dissonances that develop at each stage are resolved in larger harmonies within the rising movement of the poem, after the manner of romantic music later in the century. Keats's treatment of the Romeo and Juliet theme, however, utilizes something of the playfulness and arch-sophistication of the scores of Berlioz and Prokofiev, as well as the high dramatic climaxes of Tchaikovsky's. For the particular kind of "intensity" *St. Agnes* achieves is less the result of any pure or final commitment to imagination than a complex awareness of the strains and tensions that are bound to develop within any romantic attempt to satisfy the sum of human expectations once aroused. In this sense the poem lies somewhere between the self-indulgent pathos of *Isabella* and the cynicism and self-mockery of *Lamia*, a poem that begins, as we shall see, with a parody of a number of the imaginative processes of poetic creation the poet had earlier affirmed. Briefly, what *St. Agnes* requires us to consider is the narrow line that separates sublimity from sublimation.

In reconsidering his earlier poetry for inclusion in the 1820 volume, Keats wrote disparagingly of *Isabella* to Woodhouse: "If I may so say, in my dramatic capacity I enter fully into the feeling: but in Propria Persona I should be apt to quiz it myself—There is no objection of this kind," he went on, "to Lamia—A good deal to St. Agnes Eve—only not so glaring" (II, 174). The comment, one must remember, was written in September 1819; and, as Bate has observed, nothing better illustrates the bitter mood of disillusionment in which the poet later returned to *St. Agnes* than his revisions for its final stanza, changes that go far toward destroying the delicate balance between sentiment and detachment the work progressively maintains.[13] For the sense of ambivalence Keats noted in his comment to Woodhouse and took as an "objection" to the work is one the poem by its very technique largely anticipates and turns to positive account, one that explains in no small measure the immense advance it marks over *Isabella*. *St. Agnes* blends the spontaneous and timeless allure of traditional romance with a modern and sophisticated self-consciousness as regards convention and technique, one that enraptures us and at the same time exposes to examination and analysis the very devices it employs. If one can read the poem as a sublimation of the particular tensions under which Keats was suffering in the winter of 1818-1819, one must add that it achieves its end with an artfulness and self-awareness that reveal a new maturity of realization. That realization concerns, more than anything, the infiniteness of human desire, the wish-fulfilling power of the imagination, and the beauty as well as the tenuousness of the spell that power casts.

[13] See *John Keats* (Cambridge, Mass., 1963), p. 443n., and *Letters*, II, 162-63. Keats revised the ending of the poem to read:

> Angela went off
> Twitch'd with the Palsy; and with face deform
> The beadsman stiffen'd, 'twixt a sigh and laugh
> Ta'en sudden from his beads by one weak little cough,

a change to which Woodhouse objected as an affectation of "the 'Don Juan' style." The revision was not adopted in the 1820 volume.

CHAPTER NINE

FROM *THE EVE OF SAINT MARK*
TO "LA BELLE
DAME SANS MERCI"

THE impetus developed in the *Eve of St. Agnes* was sufficient to carry Keats into *The Eve of Saint Mark,* an apparent companion piece he wrote in February 1819, the same month the longer poem was completed. However the fragment of *Saint Mark* is only the backdrop for a narrative that never materializes, and Keats's plans for continuing the poem, if, indeed, he had definite ones, are impossible to guess. The work has always taken on a special significance from Dante Gabriel Rossetti's conviction that Keats would have gone on to treat the popular belief that an individual stationed in the porch of a church on St. Mark's Eve would see the apparitions of those fated to severe illness or death in the coming year.[1] Rossetti's intuition was suddenly, if not conclusively, corroborated by the discovery, only in this century, of sixteen additional lines of pseudo-Middle-English verse that recount the superstition preserved in Keats's own hand and again in a transcript of the poem made by Woodhouse:

> Gif ye wol standen hardie wight—
> Amiddes of the blacke night—
> Righte in the churchè porch, pardie
> Ye wol behold a companie
> Approchen thee full dolourouse
> For sooth to sain from everich house
> Be it in City or village
> Wol come the Phantom and image

[1] See Ernest de Selincourt, *The Poems of John Keats,* 5th ed. (London, 1926), p. 525.

Of ilka gent and ilka carle
Whom coldè Deathè hath in parle
And wol some day that very year
Touchen with foulè venime spear
And sadly do them all to die—
Hem all shalt thou see verilie—
And everichon shall by thee pass
All who must die that year Alas.

The lines in Keats's holograph appear, however, only on a
random scrapbook leaf, on the verso of which, written in a
similar style, appear the sixteen lines that have always been
taken as an integral part of the poem.[2] In the transcript
Woodhouse carefully isolates the passage relating the particular superstition by a wide gap at the very end without
explaining its relation to the work as a whole. Nor does the
questionable passage appear in either of Keats's surviving
manuscript versions. Up to the present day, we find editors
who print the lines—sometimes without any explanation—
as a part of the poem and those who relegate them to the
footnotes. Similarly we find critics who argue they are vital
to interpretation of the work and those who consider them
totally irrelevant.[3] What we have in *Saint Mark* is a work

[2] The Sabin scrapbook leaf is described in *The Poetical Works of
John Keats*, ed. H. B. Forman (Oxford, 1906), p. 1. For a description
of Woodhouse's transcript of the poem, see Mabel A. E. Steele, "The
Woodhouse Transcripts of the Poems of Keats," *Harvard Library Bulletin*, III (1949), 250-51.

[3] Gittings, for example, includes the lines without any comment in
his text of the poem in *Selected Poems and Letters of John Keats*
(London, 1966). Bush, who considers the superstition an "afterthought," places them in a footnote and observes that Rossetti's "conjecture has no legitimate bearing on our reading of the unfinished poem
we have" (p. 342). More recently David Luke has argued that the
passage and the legend are of formative and interpretive importance in
"*The Eve of Saint Mark*: Keats's 'ghostly Queen of Spades' and the
Textual Superstition," *Studies in Romanticism*, IX (1970), 161-75,
which reopens the issue.

wherein, somewhat like the later *Fall of Hyperion*, all the inherent difficulties of dealing with a fragment are complicated by a passage of disputed verse.

Saint Mark raises anew the same questions of design and intention that haunt so much of Keats's narrative verse. If many of them appear finally insoluble, they nevertheless illuminate, through the context in which they arise, the poet's mood and temper as he approached the early spring. It is difficult to imagine, to begin with, that, having just finished *St. Agnes*, a poem based (whether or not at the suggestion of Isabella Jones)[4] on a superstition he could find in any number of sources, he could the same month begin a poem entitled *The Eve of Saint Mark* in ignorance of the second legend. The superstition must have been in his mind from the outset as a possibility for developing a narrative involvement, and not, as critics continue to argue, a kind of afterthought. To be sure there is no trace, other than the title, of the superstition in the poem as Keats transcribed it on September 20 to send to George and Georgiana, where "the legend of St. Mark" (52) that Bertha reads is the history of the saint's life, travels, and death. However the lines relating to the superstition appear at the end of Woodhouse's transcript, above the notation "Written 13/17 Feby 1819 R.W." While it is still conceivable they were written later, in September, as some scholars argue,[5] quite the opposite seems most likely. The fact that Woodhouse's carefully dated transcript includes the lines of imitative verse that have an accepted place in the work while relegating the disputed lines to the end suggests the latter were ones the poet had decided to exclude. It is possible to read the two sets of sixteen lines on recto and verso of the scrapbook leaf con-

---

[4] In *John Keats: The Living Year* (Cambridge, Mass., 1954), pp. 60-62, Robert Gittings reveals that she was responsible for suggesting to Keats the legend of St. Agnes. He later argues (pp. 85-86) on less conclusive evidence that she also suggested the legend of St. Mark. See also Gittings, *John Keats* (London, 1968), p. 287.

[5] See n. 8, below.

secutively.[6] But it is also possible to regard them, as Wood-house's transcript suggests, as alternative possibilities, and to conclude that Keats deliberately decided to withhold the lines dealing with the specific legend of Saint Mark's Eve ("Gif ye wol standen hardie wight— / Amiddes of the blacke night—") or to replace them with an equal number of a more broadly superstitious character ("Als writith he of swevenis, / Men han beforne they wake in bliss") as a way of opening up the poem to other possibilities for development.[7] Virtually all the evidence indicates that Keats began *The Eve of Saint Mark* with the idea of treating a popular legend similar to the one he had just dealt with in *St. Agnes* but that the project changed in character as he proceeded. The poem represents not so much the failure of a narrative intention as its gradual withering away.

In late September, in the few days following the composition of "To Autumn," Keats found his thoughts returning to the fragment he had left uncompleted. The two Sundays, the two seasons of the year, and the two cathedral cities, Chichester and Winchester, together with the differences in mood and harmony between them, inevitably suggested to him something of the distance he had come in the intervening months. "How beautiful the season is now," he wrote Reynolds on the twenty-first.

> How fine the air. A temperate sharpness about it. Really, without joking, chaste weather—Dian skies—I never lik'd stubble fields so much as now—Aye better than the chilly green of the spring.
>
> (II, 167)

[6] Luke argues that their "arrangement . . . urges sequence and continuity" (p. 163).

[7] The oft-noted fact that the opening line of the latter set, "Als writith *he* of swevenis" (my italics), becomes meaningless without some antecedent can be explained simply by the way Keats introduced the passage in his September letter to George and Georgiana: "What follows is an imitation of the Authors in Chaucer's time" (II, 204). He was not, at least at this point, concerned to make a more integral connection between the passage and the body of the poem.

He was taken back in imagination to the beginning of *Saint Mark* and its description of a cathedral town and the surrounding countryside on an early spring evening:

> Upon a Sabbath-day it fell;
> Twice holy was the Sabbath-bell,
> That call'd the folk to evening prayer;
> The city streets were clean and fair
> From wholesome drench of April rains;
> And, on the western window-panes,
> The chilly sunset faintly told
> Of unmatur'd green vallies cold,
> Of the green thorny bloomless hedge,
> Of rivers new with spring-tide sedge,
> Of primroses by shelter'd rills,
> And daisies on the aguish hills.
>
> (1-12)

A day earlier he had written his brother and sister-in-law:

> The great beauty of Poetry is, that it makes every thing every place interesting—The palatine venice and the abbotine Winchester are equally interesting—Some time since I began a Poem call'd "the Eve of St Mark quite in the spirit of Town quietude. I th[i]nk it will give you the sensation of walking about an old county Town in a coolish evening. I know not yet whether I shall ever finish it—I will give it far as I have gone. *Ut tibi placent!*"
>
> (II, 201; Keats's italics)

Here he copied the poem in what is, for all intents and purposes, its final form, lacking the disputed passage and the last four and one-half lines which he thought perhaps too tangential or transitional to include.[8]

---

[8] Aileen Ward argues (*John Keats: The Making of a Poet* [New York, 1963], pp. 320, 435n.) that Keats wrote both Chaucerian passages in September together with the fragmentary final paragraph (115-19), which represents, she believes, his attempt to resume the poem at this time. For reasons I have cited, it seems to me more

Despite its incompleteness, the poem, as he transcribed it, has a certain unity, but it is a harmony of mood and tone, or, to use his own word, of "sensation," rather than of narrative event. As critics like Bush and Walter Houghton have commented, the poem builds upon a series of deliberate contrasts: the cold of the early spring landscape and the warmth of the hearth, the bustle of the crowded streets and the silence of Bertha's lonely chamber, the sobriety of communal worship and the transports of her solitary reverie.[9] As in *St. Agnes*, one finds Keats using a flow of subtly different contexts and perspectives to effect what amounts to a dislocation in our sense of everyday reality. However his means for doing so are entirely different; for the medieval coloring of the poem is only the background for the creation of a sense of consciousness that strikes us today as essentially modern, a medievalism that is, as Rossetti and the Pre-Raphaelites observed, of a chaste and more subtle kind than anything in the earlier work. Indeed, by comparison with the gothic props and mystification of *St. Agnes*, *Saint Mark*

---

probable that, in transcribing the poem for George and Georgiana, Keats slightly abridged an earlier draft or drafts in the version he sent them. Luke gives Miss Ward partial support by arguing that the holograph in George Keats's notebook (British Museum MS Egerton 2780), which contains 115-19, was actually a *later* draft of the poem. He disregards the testimony of both M. R. Ridley (*Keats' Craftsmanship* [Oxford, 1933], p. 276) and Gittings (*John Keats*, p. 287 and n.) that the changes and revisions in the notebook version bear every indication of an early draft in favor of a single fact. "It would seem physically impossible," he writes, "for Keats to have copied out E [the notebook version] for George prior to the September version (and indeed for some time after), for George was and had been in America since June, 1818, long before Keats had even begun to consider the poem" (pp. 164-65n.). As Joseph L. Mills has pointed out to me, however, there is no indication that the notebook was in George's possession or, for that matter, even belonged to him at this time. It bears George's name but followed by the date, 1820.

[9] See the headnote in Bush's edition, p. 341; and Walter E. Houghton, "The Meaning of Keats's 'Eve of St. Mark,'" *English Literary History*, XIII (1946), 64-78.

seems antisuperstitious and even antimedieval in its effect.
As she reads, Bertha is surrounded by fantastic, mocking
forms that play about her and that seem on the point of
luring her, like the dreaming Madeline, into some realm of
mysterious enchantment; but the effect is clearly only that
of her shadow cast by the glare of the fire. While she dreams
over the curious volume and the accounts of martyrdom and
sainthood that engross her, the dazzling play of sacred imagery is set off by the staid propriety of the cathedral streets
and at the same time by the opulent and bizarre details of an
eclectically modern interior:

> Her shadow, in uneasy guise,
> Hover'd about, a giant size,
> On ceiling-beam and old oak chair,
> The parrot's cage, and panel square;
> And the warm angled winter screen,
> On which were many monsters seen,
> Call'd doves of Siam, Lima mice,
> And legless birds of Paradise,
> Macaw, and tender Av'davat,
> And silken-furr'd Angora cat.
>
> (73-82)

It is the juxtaposition of these different contexts, the complex patterns they assume in the fading Sabbath light, that
more than anything suggests the grounds for her perplexity.
She is a "poor cheated soul" (69); and if we are never told
exactly why, there is a sense in which there is no need for
explanation. For the poem, without asking them, implicitly
raises questions we can best understand in terms of the
poetry of our own day that virtually picks up from where
Keats's poem leaves off:

> Why should she give her bounty to the dead?
> What is divinity if it can come
> Only in silent shadows and in dreams?
> Shall she not find in comforts of the sun,

In pungent fruit and bright, green wings, or else
In any balm or beauty of the earth,
Things to be cherished like the thought of heaven?

In its use of sensuous tones and contrasts to create a deepen-ing sense of subjectivity and inwardness that speaks virtually for itself, *Saint Mark* is the most characteristically modern poem Keats had yet written. In an important sense, Bertha's Sunday afternoon is the prologue to Wallace Stevens's "Sun-day Morning."[10] Keats may have begun with the idea of writing a companion piece similar in kind to *St. Agnes.* However it is clear that as he worked on it, *Saint Mark* took on a very different style and character. The thrust of narrative or the framework of popular superstition was no longer necessary to the kinds of poetic effect now of most interest to him and finally irrelevant to the little atmospheric idyll he was content to abandon.

II

The next several months of relative poetic inactivity were ones during which Keats's creative energies accumulated before their remarkable efflorescence later in the spring. Among the shorter pieces, two sonnets written in April reveal both his steady dependence on and his increasing ambiva-lence toward the unconscious mind's creative processes. "To Sleep" and more especially the sonnet "On a Dream" reveal a deepening psychological complexity. The former sonnet celebrates the luxury of mere obliviousness, the relief of escaping from the multiplying sorrows of the daytime world and the probings of a conscience "that still lords / Its strength for darkness, burrowing like a mole." "On a Dream" dramatizes the actual mechanism of escape and the rapture of the dream-experience. Yet the sonnet is pervaded by a haunting sense of sorrow in its way more profound than anything in Keats's earlier verse.

[10] *The Collected Poems of Wallace Stevens* (New York, 1955), p. 66ff.

The sonnet was inspired by a re-reading of the story of Paolo and Francesca in the fifth canto of Dante's *Inferno* and by a vivid dream Keats described in some detail to George and Georgiana. "I had passed many days in rather a low state of mind and in the midst of them I dreamt of being in that region of Hell," he wrote them.

> The dream was one of the most delightful enjoyments I ever had in my life—I floated about the whirling atmosphere as it is described with a beautiful figure to whose lips mine were joined at [*for* as] it seem'd for an age—and in the midst of all this cold and darkness I was warm— even flowery tree tops sprung up and we rested on them sometimes with the lightness of a cloud till the wind blew us away again—I tried a Sonnet upon it—there are fourteen lines but nothing of what I felt in it—o that I could dream it every night—.

Here he wrote out the sonnet in what is virtually its final form:

> As Hermes once took to his feathers light
> When lulled Argus, baffled, swoon'd and slept
> So on a delphic reed my idle spright
> So play'd, so charm'd so conquer'd, so bereft
> The dragon world of all its hundred eyes
> And seeing it asleep so fled away:—
> Not to pure Ida with its snowcold skies,
> Nor unto Tempe where Jove grieved that day,
> But to that second circle of sad hell,
> Where in the gust, the whirlwind and the flaw
> Of Rain and hailstones lovers need not tell
> Their sorrows—Pale were the sweet lips I saw
> Pale were the lips I kiss'd and fair the fo[r]m
> I floated with about that melancholy storm—.
>
> (II, 91)

The sonnet must be taken up in the light of Keats's commentary on it, for one is immediately aware of striking and significant differences between them. In a way similar to sections of *Endymion*, both the prose account and the sonnet use the sexual embrace as a metaphor for the creative process—the fertilization of the poetic intelligence by the unknown female figure to whose lips the dreamer's own are joined within a buoyant, floating realm below the level of the conscious mind. However Keats's account of the experience in his letter, for all its clarity and suggestiveness of detail, is one-dimensional, a simple dream of wish-fulfillment. The sense of warmth and efflorescence is only intensified by the surrounding cold and darkness; for the lovers are protected, endlessly it seems, from any deeper consciousness, nor is the landscape recognizable as hell.

Keats's outcry, "o that I could dream it every night," is hardly appropriate to the experience as represented in the sonnet. The poem, in emerging from its origin in the dream, engages a far more complex range of awareness as its more elaborate symbolism testifies. The introductory episode, in which Hermes charms Argus and his hundred eyes to sleep, dramatizes the victory of the imagination over the tyranny of the mind and its conscious powers. Yet the larger effect of the poem lies in the contrast between the ease and facility of the god's escape and the somber pallor and disquiet of the sestet and the underworld where the dreamer finds himself, a description that combines the lightness and voluptuousness of the prose account with an ominous turbulence and instability. The spirit takes its flight not to "pure Ida," the realm of cold, inhuman sublimation, or to Tempe, where "Jove grieved that day" in resignation to the loss of his beloved Io whom Juno set Argus to guard from further violation. It finds alleviation in the warmth and rapture of a love that is human but seems both prohibited and desolating. The lovers float in an embrace, but they hover above a region infiltrated by a consciousness of guilt and hidden sorrows only the more poignant because they cannot or need not be told. The lips the dreamer kisses are sweet, but their pallor suggests that, for all its gratifications, the love they offer is seductive, enervating, perhaps even killing.

The sonnet "On a Dream" is really a miniature allegory of creative experience, a work all the more fascinating because we can, to an extent that is unusual with Keats, trace its roots to a striking event in the poet's psychological life. Yet, as we have seen, the differences between the dream and the sonnet and the stages of creativity they represent are more compelling than their similarities. The sonnet expresses, to be sure, the extraordinary fecundity of Keats's unconscious at this point in his career and the extent of his reliance on it. Yet the poem also reveals the ability, at some secondary level of creativity, to elaborate his original experience, to develop its possibilities and hidden implications without destroying its essential vitality, and to reinvest the whole with a significance that is both profoundly ambivalent and ironic.

III

The far greater work Keats composed a few days later, the first of his undoubted masterpieces of the spring, "La Belle Dame sans Merci," distills within its brief dramatic form a more moving and pervasive sense of irony. The poem is the most condensed and suggestive he ever wrote, a narrative in which we sense, in ways about which it is hard to be explicit, a large degree of personal identification. Over the years it has been read (with an eye to the poet's growing involvement with Fanny Brawne) as a study in the wasting power of sexual attraction and love, as an intimation of the toils of disease and early death, and as an expression of the poet's infatuation with and enslavement by his own muse. To these one would want to add another kind of fatality—Keats's ever-present concern with the nature of poetic fame (underlined by the composition this same month of two sonnets on the subject), a theme now assuming its own ironic significance from its inseparability from love and death. Certainly the poem derives its power from a wealth of hidden feelings and forebodings. At the same time, in the brevity and sparseness of its narration it is the most impersonal and detached of all the greater lyrics. It is the most purely "archetypal" poem he ever wrote, the most resistant to "reductive" readings. More than anything, it is the perfection of its style and form that is intriguing, an assimilation that refines a whole new apprehension of the medieval spirit.

One way of crystallizing what is most characteristic or essential in "La Belle Dame" and the side of Keats's genius it represents is by returning to the judgment of the greatest of his earlier critics, Matthew Arnold. It was Arnold who more than anyone established Keats's reputation for all time by ranking him alongside Shakespeare "in one of the two great modes by which poetry interprets." Arnold's term for this power of interpretation was "natural magic," the ability, as he elsewhere put it, of "catching and rendering the charm of nature in a wonderfully near and vivid way," and which, he stated, Keats particularly possessed "by virtue of his feeling for beauty and of his perception of the vital connection of beauty with truth."[11] Arnold's criterion of "natural magic" as a way of defining Keats's primary power, his "indescribable *gusto*," is bound to remind us of the poet's own ideal of "intensity." It is a major strength of Arnold's criticism that the premises and concepts by which he judges Keats are in many respects remarkably congenial to the poet's own. Yet Arnold's apprehension of the particular quality of Keats's genius is of further value in that it enables us to see the poet and portions of his work in relation to the persistent themes and values of a major current of Western literature. For within the broader context of Arnold's criticism "natural magic" is something more than mere intensity of imaginative perception, more than the ability to distill an aspect of na-

[11] "John Keats," *Essays in Criticism*, 2nd series (London, 1921), p. 119; "On the Study of Celtic Literature," *On the Study of Celtic Literature and on Translating Homer* (New York, 1883), p. 102.

tural beauty through the power of sympathetic response. As his other criticism makes clear, especially his long essay "On the Study of Celtic Literature," Arnold had in view traits of temperament, of culture, even of race, and a beauty of a more specific kind, a beauty strongly tinged with melancholy, nervousness, excitement, and a certain wild grace. "Magic is just the word for it," Arnold wrote, "the magic of nature; not merely the beauty of nature,—that the Greeks and Latins had; not merely an honest smack of the soil, a faithful realism,—that the Germans had; but the intimate life of Nature, her weird power and her fairy charm."[12] Throughout the whole of nineteenth-century literature there is no work that better exemplifies what Arnold meant by the "Celtic Strain" and its centrality to English verse than "La Belle Dame." Arnold's phrase illuminates the heart of Keats's poem and its preoccupations, for "natural magic" is more than anything else what "La Belle Dame" is about.

Following the completion of *The Eve of St. Agnes* and his work on the fragmentary *Eve of Saint Mark*, Keats made one more attempt at a poem of a medieval character. However, "La Belle Dame" represents an infinitely more profound assimilation of the medieval spirit, or, more accurately perhaps, the transformation of that spirit within the terms of an essentially modern style and sensibility, than anything in the pseudogothicism of *St. Agnes* or the architectural background of *Saint Mark*. In many respects the poem represents the culmination of his absorption over a number of months with a variety of medieval styles and attitudes, a complex of possibilities that suddenly, perhaps in the course of a single evening, achieved a formal and thematic definition through a pressure of deeply felt and personal concerns.

Just as it remains impossible to limit those concerns to any single issue of his private life, so it is equally impossible to describe the medieval quality of his ballad of fairy enchantment and loss in terms of any single analogue, such as the ballad of "Thomas Rymer" or the story of *Sir Launfal*, how-

[12] "On the Study of Celtic Literature," pp. 120-21.

ever suggestive anyone of these may prove. Those critics who
have repeatedly tried to explain the poem by means of any
single source have generally concluded, despite occasional
insights, with results as barren as the landscape that en-
velops Keats's knight. Undoubtedly Douglas Bush is right
that as regards imagery, phrasing, and general suggestiveness,
The Faerie Queene presents the closest parallels: not merely
the episodes involving Cymochles and Phaedria and the
False Florimel, but Duessa's seduction of the Red Cross
Knight and, by significant contrast, "Arthur's wholly inspiring vision of the Faerie Queene."[13] Yet to compare any
one or all these episodes with "La Belle Dame" is to sense
immediately how much Keats has made contact with an
ethos that lies very much in the background of Spenser's
romance and on which the older poet drew throughout—the
world of Arthurian legend and more particularly its source in
Celtic lore. To feel, as every reader has, the elfin grace and
cunning of Keats's fairy enchantress, the wild and touching
beauty of her secret ways, is to feel how much the mystery
and desolation of the poem transcend the patent villainy of a
Duessa or a Phaedria, how much closer we are to the ambivalence of such divinities as Rhiannon and Morrigan and
the heroes they alternately adopted and beguiled, a race of
whom Arnold wrote, "the moment one goes below the surface,—almost before one goes below the surface,—all is
illusion and phantasy, double-meaning, and far-reaching
mythological import. . . . These are no mediaeval personages;
they belong to an older, pagan, mythological world."[14] There
is no reason to imagine Keats was ever deeply versed in the
whole of Arthurian legend or the folklore that informs so
much of it, although the standard sources, such as Malory,
were available to him, and there is evidence that he became
increasingly interested in the ballad and its lore during his
walking tour into the north country, Scotland, and Ireland.

[13] See the headnote in Bush's edition, p. 344; and Bate, *John Keats*,
p. 478n.
[14] "On the Study of Celtic Literature," p. 46.

It is simply characteristic of his genius that he was able, by a process of unconscious assimilation and in the brief space of forty-eight lines, to distill the essence of the magic that, as Arnold saw, pervades from its origins a whole current of English literature. It is in this larger sense that the poem is truly archetypal.

With all the swiftness of its narrative, its ballad-like compression, "La Belle Dame" owes much of its power both to an extraordinary clarity and to a suggestiveness of detail. The autumnal lake, the silent birds, the knight's pacing steed, the meal of strange forest fruits, and the sudden vision of the company of death-pale warriors and the dread name they utter: these and other details have the sharp distinctness and contraction of images remaining from a dream, as though they held the clue to a larger drama of partly hidden significance. The major subject of the narrative, the story of the fairy enchantress who comes from the other world to grant her love to a mortal, to destroy or to save him, is a stock feature of a multitude of Celtic lays and Arthurian romances. "La Belle Dame" is remarkable for the way it achieves its peculiar effectiveness, the power actually of a kind of resonance, by analogy not with any single tale or romance but with the whole tradition of the fairy mistress as it has come down to us from any number of sources, a tradition whose details and implications Keats has developed in his own individual way. We find, for example, that the fairy enchantress is commonly represented throughout Celtic lore as an inhabitant of lakes and other bodies of water,[15] a hyperborean, perhaps, but fundamentally related to the race of naiads who had fascinated him from the time of

---

[15] The close association between such supernatural creatures and lakes and fountains has often been commented on by medievalists. See, e.g., T. P. Cross, "The Celtic Elements in the Lays of *Lanval* and *Graelent*," *Modern Philology*, XII (1915), 599ff.; and Roger S. Loomis, "Morgain La Fee and the Celtic Goddesses," *Speculum*, XX (1945), 198ff. See also Bernice Slote's "La Belle Dame as Naiad," *Journal of English and Germanic Philology*, LX (1961), 22-30, which develops the connection.

"Sleep and Poetry" and whom he had connected from the first with the mythological beginnings of poetry. Instead of "many a Nymph who wreaths her Brows with Sedge,"[16] however, we now see only withered reeds around a desolate lake. We find also that one of the manifestations of the fairy enchantress's power is the singing of the magic birds that often accompany her—the song, for example, of the enchanted birds that cast Cuchulinn into sleep, or the music, as Arnold himself recalled, of "the birds of Rhiannon, whose song was so sweet that warriors remained spell-bound for eighty years together listening to them."[17] Such melody is like the music of the Val des Faux Soulas in the romances, "a valley of surpassing loveliness, the home of singing birds, green and fresh even in mid-winter."[18] This otherworldly paradise to which knights are lured by their fairy lovers, however, is closely akin, perhaps inseparable from, the Val sanz Retor, where the knight may be given the task of un-spelling other, earlier captives but frequently is himself imprisoned forever in a curtain of druidic mist suggestive of the grave. It is the whole complex texture of these relation-ships, together with the note of ambivalence and foreboding of departed magic that surrounds them, that Keats's poem conveys and that we sense behind the simplicity of the re-frain, "And no birds sing."

One should note, moreover, that the fairy goddess of Celtic lore, especially the divinity of lakes and streams, is not simply a baneful enchantress, luring knights to their doom. She is also, by a curious paradox, the nurturer and foster parent of heroes, the donor of precious gifts who instructs them in magic and the arts of prophecy. Among the most common of her gifts are a horse and a coat of arms. Thus La Dame du

[16] William Collins, "Ode to Evening," l.25.

[17] "On the Study of Celtic Literature," p. 46. Lucy A. Paton has shown a number of instances in which singing birds are associated with sleep, enchantment, and the hero's vision of a fairy mistress in *Studies in the Fairy Mythology of Arthurian Romance*, 2nd ed. (New York, 1960), pp. 29, 31, 96, 211n., and passim.

[18] Paton, *Fairy Mythology*, p. 96.

Lac gives a spirited white horse and a coat of arms to her hero, Lancelot.[19] In a number of romances the fay appears to her lover riding a mysterious horse and takes him up with her, a relationship Keats appears to have reversed in his ballad. As scholars such as Roger Loomis have pointed out, however, La Dame du Lac, the benevolent fay, is in reality Morgan la Fée, the malevolent enchantress, in another guise; the two are parts of a larger duality and trace their ancestry to a common source.[20] There is an obvious fatality in all this: the divinity who protects and instructs the hero fulfills her love by seducing and destroying him. In a similar way Keats's "elfin grot" corresponds to the cave where, time and again in Celtic story, the hero is lured by his enchantress and their relationship is, in one way or another, consummated. As Lucy Paton has shown, there is an evident connection between such Celtic material and the classical story of Endymion, the shepherd cast into dreaming slumber on the hillside by Diana.[21] The hillside of classical legend becomes the cave of Celtic fable, closely associated with the funeral barrows of the dead (Keats actually has both cave and hillside in his ballad). Rather than a dream of heavenly love, however, the vision now becomes a journey to the underworld and a visit to the souls of the departed, a perilous adventure since it can result in perpetual imprisonment, as indeed Merlin is eternally bound by Niniane, the Celtic fay and dweller by the Lac du Dyane.[22]

Without a need for further particulars, one can see from a number of details that "La Belle Dame" is an original assimilation of a closely knit body of early northern legend, a network of stories connected more or less subterraneously

[19] See Loomis, "Morgain La Fee," pp. 188-89; Cross, "Celtic Elements," p. 631ff.; Paton, *Fairy Mythology*, p. 161.

[20] This is the major theme of Loomis's discussion and recurs, also, throughout Paton's.

[21] Paton, *Fairy Mythology*, pp. 216-18, 238-39, 275ff., 298.

[22] We know the Merlin legend was in Keats's mind from *The Eve of St. Agnes*, 170-71: "Never on such a night have lovers met, / Since Merlin paid his Demon all the monstrous debt."

with classical mythology and many of the themes that had been at the center of Keats's visionary preoccupations in *Endymion*. It is possible to account for his shift of interest from southern to northern mythology through the extraordinary complexity and ambivalence of so much Celtic legend, its darker coloring and Christian overtones, particularly its suggestions of the story of the Fall, an event that, in its various implications, had begun to haunt his imagination. Primarily, no doubt, it was the supremely enigmatic quality of the Celtic fay, together with her relevance to a complex of personal concerns, poetic and otherwise, that was most compelling. Summing up the nature of the Celtic goddess under the type of Morgan la Fée—"a female pantheon in miniature"—Loomis has described her in words that are worth quoting:

> She was a sort of naiad or nereid, haunting springs, rivers, fords, lakes, and seas, or dwelling beneath their surfaces; she was a foster-mother of heroes, who took them in their infancy, trained them for high adventure, and watched over them in peril; she showered wealth on her favorites; . . . she foretold the future; she was both a beneficent and a sinister power; she lay in wait for mortals, offering them her love; she possessed a very swift and powerful horse.[23]

Some understanding of the Celtic fay and the extraordinary richness and ambivalence of her character provides important clues for the interpretation of "La Belle Dame." Thus it is clear that Keats's ballad is nothing so simple as a tale of guileful seduction and betrayal. Nor can it be taken purely in the opposite sense, as Wasserman would have it—as the knight's initiation into the mysteries that lie beyond "heaven's bourne," a state of spiritual elevation that, through the fallibility of his mortal powers, he is unable to sustain.[24]

[23] Loomis, "Morgain La Fee," pp. 200-201.
[24] See Wasserman's discussion of the poem in *The Finer Tone: Keats' Major Poems* (Baltimore, 1953), esp. pp. 76-77.

To some degree both sets of implication are present. Indeed it is the larger irony of the poem that it joins them inseparably.

Such relationships can be seen most directly in the feast of strange fruits the maiden provides her lover prior to his sleep within her cave. Beginning with the realm of "Flora, and old Pan," with its "apples red, and strawberries" on which the youthful poet feeds, to the angelic meal of "summer fruits" in the *Fall of Hyperion*, a banquet Keats endows with sacramental overtones, the feast of fruits, like the suggestion of love-making that follows it in Keats's ballad, is the usual prelude to visionary experience. Like the apple, so common in Celtic story, by which the fay entices the lover to her domain,[25] the strange roots and honey, the "manna dew" she offers him, are clearly symbolic of what anthropologists have for some time described as "mana," the magical power of transmuting or transcending external nature, Arnold's "natural magic," the transforming power of the poetic imagination.

Yet we know that "mana" is also "taboo": the two are one and the same, positive and negative aspects of a single power. Mana, that is to say, is magic taken as a sacred and creative energy; taboo is the same force considered in its terrifying and minatory, if not necessarily prohibitive, implications.[26] It is notable that Celtic tales and later romances dealing with the fairy mistress make frequent use of the theme of the *ges* or taboo she places on her lover, suggestions of which cling to Keats's ballad. Thus, she sometimes forbids him to eat food on first entering her kingdom or after his return to the mortal world; more frequently she commands him, on leaving her, never to reveal her name.[27] Within the con-

[25] See Paton, *Fairy Mythology*, p. 39, n.3.

[26] The point is made by R. R. Marett in *The Threshold of Religion*, 2nd ed. (London, 1914), pp. 98-99.

[27] The *ges*, or taboo, in Celtic romance is described by Cross, "Celtic Elements," pp. 622ff. Paul Haeffner has revealingly discussed the theme of taboo in *Endymion* in connection with Keats's dependence on phantasy and the deeper levels of consciousness in "Keats and the

densed structure of Keats's ballad, the fruits she offers him clearly serve as mana and taboo in one, as an experience that is both initiatory and fateful, while the knight learns the name of his enchantress, the clue to her deeper identity, only in the dream of the starved warriors who have preceded him, only, that is, at the price of his own enslavement. One cannot dismiss the rites La Belle Dame lightly practices as mere deception; nor is the knight's dream the mere figment of a disordered imagination, a purely subjective response. Neither part of his narration, the "before" or the "after," is more believable or real than the other, for neither part has meaning without the other. The real significance of the events he relates lies in the irony of their juxtaposition, in the terrifying incongruity between the endless staring faces of his vision and the casual charm and rapture of the brief encounter that occasioned it.

Like so much of Keats's other verse, "La Belle Dame" is most of all about the essence of poetry itself, the gift of that "natural magic" that transforms common experience into enchantment and later vision. It is a miniature allegory of the growth and development of the poetic consciousness dramatized through the details of the knight's relation and the great central themes of love, death, and immortality. What is remarkable about the poem within the larger canon of Keats's work is the perfect blend of pathos and irony it achieves by its compression and simplicity together with the range of its suggestiveness. It is almost a reworking in miniature of the romance between Endymion and Cynthia in darker, northern colors. It broaches the theme of fairy captivation to which Keats was to return in a more cynical and bitter way in *Lamia*. Nevertheless, we miss a further, major

---

Faery Myth of Seduction," *Review of English Literature*, III (1962), 20-31. Charles Patterson has briefly alluded to the element of taboo in "La Belle Dame" and the poem's Celtic origins (p. 138), while stressing *Palmerin of England* as a possible source, in *The Daemonic in the Poetry of John Keats* (Urbana, Ill., 1970), p. 138, a discussion notable for its analysis of the ballad's narrative form.

range of implication unless we see the ballad's relationship to a later work to which it is rarely, if ever, compared: *The Fall of Hyperion.* For both poems deal with the growth of tragic knowledge and awareness from their first roots in mere sensuous enchantment, the fall from innocence into experience the muse of poetry inflicts, in her designingly capricious way, on those she favors most. Keats's fairy enchantress is also, in her darker guise, Fata Morgana, a role he was to seek to make endurable through the intervention and instruction of Moneta and by recasting the pagan fable into the form of a Christian allegory of divine redemption. However, the realization "La Belle Dame" leaves with us is of a simpler but ultimately perhaps more truthful kind: the transience of bliss, the community of individual desires and dreams, the finality of death, and the eternal hunger for renewed experience even in the face of tragic awareness. If at the end Keats's knight seems blind to such conclusions, if he can only turn back to the fading landscape with words that are an inconsequence, that is only the culminating irony of the poem.

CHAPTER TEN

ROMANTIC IRONY: THE
GREAT ODES
OF THE SPRING

THE great odes have for long been placed at the center of
Keats's achievement and, for that matter, at the center of
the English Romantic achievement as a whole. They are by
nature ideally suited to the kind of close analysis that was
the radical innovation of the New Criticism in England and
America and has become the prevailing mode of critical
exegesis today. In recent years they have been steadily en-
riched by a series of sensitive and revealing explications, and
it can be fairly said they have benefited more from modern
elucidation than the poet's other verse. At the same time,
and perhaps inevitably, there are aspects of the odes that
have been unduly neglected. By its very method, the New
Criticism was dedicated to the reading of each poem individually, within the context it alone created. Despite some
notable exceptions (in particular the distinguished discussions of Bate and Perkins), recent attempts to establish a
basis for reading the odes as a group, for understanding the
ways in which they interrelate with and qualify each other,
have never been as successful as individual readings.[1] Equally

[1] See Bate, *John Keats* (Cambridge, Mass., 1963), pp. 486-524; and
David Perkins, *The Quest for Permanence: The Symbolism of Wordsworth, Shelley, and Keats* (Cambridge, Mass., 1959), pp. 217-57, 282-
94. I agree with John Holloway, another exception to the common
trend, that "if the Odes really are a unified sequence" (and he thinks
they are), "the best way to understand them fully is to treat them as
such, and make them interpret each other. So far, this has hardly been
done—in part because critics have been too ready to think (as Garrod
did) that *To Autumn* stands quite by itself, and in part because they

important has been the tendency (again with significant exceptions) to consider the odes in relative isolation from the poet's other work and the course of his career. The methods and techniques of the New Criticism have never been as successful with the long poem as with the lyric, and interpretation of Keats's narrative poetry has notably lagged behind the modern reappraisal of the odes. The fact is evidenced merely by the number of recent studies that neglect much of the later narrative verse altogether or pass over it with cursory attention. The result has been that the odes have come to seem to us today the center of Keats's achievement—indeed, for many, the essential Keats—but a center curiously isolated from the larger development of his career, as though the sudden and seemingly effortless outburst of high lyricism in the spring (together with its brief autumnal coda) represented a happy and inexplicable deliverance from the longer, tortured, and at times embarrassingly incoherent labors that surround it.

Ultimately the odes have most to tell us when they are taken not only together as a group but as an integral part of Keats's total achievement, as a mature reflection of the particular concerns with which he wrestled throughout his career. Very broadly, they are best considered as a series of closely related and progressive meditations on the nature of the creative process, the logical outgrowth of his involvement with Negative Capability. Needless to say, the latter phrase must now be taken to encompass something more than the capability "of being in uncertainties, Mysteries, doubts, without any irritable reaching after fact & reason" (I, 193); it now

---

have thought *On Indolence* too bad to deserve much attention" ("The Odes of Keats," *The Charted Mirror* [London, 1960], ch. 3, p. 40). Even Holloway, however, is more concerned with the odes as a *unity* rather than a *progression*. The common view is that expressed by Gittings: "The order does not matter greatly; there is no progress of thought from one ode to the other" (*John Keats*, p. 311). Holloway's brief, suggestive discussion takes "On Indolence" as its center as the expression of the mood of creativity from which the other odes spring and which they in various ways explore.

embraces a set of related premises and attitudes, including even certain questions deriving from them. The larger formulation involves his habitual distrust of "Dogmas" and "seeming sure points of Reasoning" (1, 282), his preference for "sensation" and "speculation" as opposed to thought, his ideal of the "camelion Poet" (1, 387), and his commitment, above all, to creativity as an expression of an evolving state of consciousness. By this time the principle involves, too, as we have seen, certain questions—the problem, for example, of whether the poet, in exerting his imaginative power, intensifies and distills the actual identity of his materials or whether he transforms them into abstractions from experience that are in certain ways unreal. All these conceptions and the questions surrounding them had for some time been a source of steadily deepening preoccupation. In the great odes one finds Keats taking up and rigorously exploring through verse itself the central assertions put forward so casually and sanguinely as far back as the winter of 1817-1818 in order to test further the capacity of the imagination's informing power and with it the adequacy of his earlier theoretical speculations.

One way of approaching such a complex of related issues is through a consideration of the odes as the culmination of that ironic sense that, in its development, has been a major theme throughout this study. The fact that the odes employ a strong measure of paradox and irony has hardly gone unobserved in modern criticism. The shift that takes place, for example, in the conception of death at the climax of the "Ode to a Nightingale," the more obvious turn upon the word "forlorn," or the revelation of a wealth of quietly mocking implications in such words as "shape," "attitude," "brede," "marble," and "overwrought" at the beginning of the final stanza of the "Ode on a Grecian Urn"—these and a number of other devices that we recognize as "ironic" have been examined by a host of critics to elucidate the parabola shape of these poems, the rising and falling movement of imaginative engagement and disengagement they embody.

Nevertheless it must be clear that the conception of irony we have been approaching as a background for the odes is something that ultimately transcends the use of any literary device. We might, for example, take Jonathan Swift as an undisputed master of the entire range of ironic technique but nevertheless find the notion of irony I am seeking to define altogether alien to that writer in his doctrinal allegiance and satiric intention. Irony, in this further sense, is not so much technique as a state of mind or disposition, a whole mode, in fact, of conceiving experience. Within the movement of nineteenth-century European literature we call "Romanticism" there develops a new conception of irony, one we are just beginning to explore today in relation to the younger generation of English Romantic writers, a conception that with them develops more individually and spontaneously than in the case of their more philosophically oriented German counterparts. Irony in its Romantic sense is related to Shelley's habitual inability to choose, his recognition, after a point, of the irrelevance of choosing, between skepticism and "mild faith."[2] It is akin to the state of sensibility Byron, who at least by the time of *Don Juan* had come to some of the same conclusions, described as "mobility."[3] In Keats's case we are apt to fall back on the poet's own phrase, Negative Capability, but if we had to use one of our own, we might describe it as a state of perpetual *indeterminacy*.

The spirit of irony I have been seeking to define, one that we sense as a characteristic part of the life and art of our own century, derives from the recognition that those concerns and questions that matter most to us, however pressing or however intently we pursue them, are ones that cannot be brought to any final determination. Although it has antecedents at least as far back as Socrates, it is a spirit that finds

[2] See Shelley's "Mont Blanc," ll. 76ff.

[3] Byron uses the word in *Don Juan*, xvi.97. See also his remarks on the term in his notes to the poem, and George M. Ridenour's discussion in *The Style of Don Juan* (New Haven, 1960), pp. 162-66.

its fullest expression in Romanticism. What makes its expression in the work of the younger English Romantic poets so fascinating is that it arises, not as in Germany, from prior philosophical conclusions, but from the actual experience of writers seeking to use their work as a serious means of discovering or evolving a faith sufficient to replace creeds that have become manifestly outworn—to use poetry in the way that Arnold was to urge later in the century. The ironic recognition to which such an undertaking leads—the sense of failure, irrelevance, or human and artistic limitation—can culminate in any number of effects. It can give rise to the comic exuberance and liberation we find in a work like *Don Juan,* or the sense of tragic fatality we feel in *The Triumph of Life.* In Keats's later writing we find an irony of an equally broad range but one that finds its purest expression in the great odes, for it arises through what is most central to the ironic sense—through the poet's involvement with process, and more specifically the creative process.

It is at this point useful to reconsider one particular aspect of Keats's reliance on the creative process, a difficulty that had troubled him in the past and was to continue to haunt him throughout the brief remainder of his career: the difficulty of bringing the most important of his longer poems to a satisfactory conclusion. The problem emerges merely when we measure his longer narrative work against the best of his lyrics or when we reflect upon the modern critical predilection for the odes. The reasons for the failure of *Endymion* have been analyzed at length in an earlier chapter. In *Hyperion* we have seen another work that altered in shape and direction as Keats worked on it, that outgrew the limits of its original conception. Much of the problem derived from one aspect of his characteristic honesty, his insistence on the integrity of the creative process and the life of the work, that the poem must to a large degree evolve its own values and implications as it proceeded, that it must discover its own significance and create its own conclusions. All too often he discovered, however, that the fullness and complexity of experience the work sought to encompass could outrun, in the kind of intricacy and contradiction they involved, its means for doing so. One could hardly argue with the premise that the work should determine its own shape, that it should evolve organically from a wealth of sensation to a distillation of thought—not the other way round. Even overlooking the problem of eliminating "disagreeables," however, how was one to deal with the fresh insights and complications that were continually arising, suggesting not ways of bringing matters to a satisfactory conclusion but rather the need for a new approach, a whole reformulation of experience?

The perception of this kind of irony, the sense of elusiveness and indeterminacy of so much of what intimately concerned him, was hardly new to Keats. Indeed it was a state of things, an aspect of the "Mystery" he had celebrated with gusto not only in the Negative Capability letter but as far back as his first real breakthrough with the ode, in the "Hymn to Pan" in the first book of *Endymion*. The irony, however, had its less appealing aspects, as he now realized when he could see with increasing clarity the real unsatisfactoriness of *Endymion* as he had completed it, or while, after so many months of thought and work, he was starting to persuade himself of the necessity of recasting the *Hyperion* into a totally new form. The failure of the latter project, or at least its temporary breakdown, was steadily depressing. Nevertheless his special sense of the dilemma, however distracting in the face of the urgent need he felt for returning to the major task, was proving fruitful in another direction. For the kind of irony of which he was now conscious, while unsettling to the long, didactic work, was beginning to provide a powerful source of inspiration for the series of shorter, meditative lyrics that attempted not any final escape from the problem but merely to crystallize the paradox as it existed. The great odes of the spring are the mature expression of that irony to which his adherence to Negative Capability as a principle had gradually led him.

Since, as already stated, one intention of this chapter is to

247

bring the odes into closer relationship to each other, a preliminary indication of the pattern they collectively assume may prove useful even at the risk of some anticipation. Briefly, the "Ode to Psyche" can best be taken as a general introduction to the problem examined more specifically in the odes that follow it, for it is here that Keats broadens out from a sense of his own dilemma to a consideration of the position of the modern poet generally in his relation to the conflicting forces of mythology and history and the relatively somber prospects for poetry that lie ahead. In the "Ode to a Nightingale" he tests the possibilities and limits of the creative imagination by confining his attention to a single image, one deliberately of the most conventional stamp, in the effort to endow it with a fullness of identity and the permanence of art. In the "Ode on a Grecian Urn" he shifts his attention to an artifact created in the past, one already endowed with an enduring form, in the attempt to determine the meaning or identity such a work can possess for a later age or state of human development. The process of inquiry is collateral to that of the former ode but moves in the opposite direction. However, in the concluding stanza of the "Ode on a Grecian Urn," the greatest of the lyrics written in the spring, the central paradox is crystallized with an energy and succinctness that carry the art of Romantic irony to its extreme. In the "Ode on Melancholy," the most tangential of the series, he takes up a subordinate aspect of the paradox by returning to his old fascination with "intensity" as the essence of poetical experience and its ability to dissolve the most basic oppositions in human feeling. The "Ode on Indolence" pictures him momentarily drawn to an even more ambitious task by the impulse to pursue the identities of three favorite and compelling abstractions, Love, Ambition, and Poetry, as they appear before him. After an instant's hesitation, however, he declines a further effort in order to resume enjoyment of a flow of free and unconstrained associations and with a sense that the task of imaginative inquiry has reached its limits. Given its different perspective and emphasis, each of the odes actively involves us in a process of imaginative intuition that leads to a cumulative recognition of what, within the terms of art and human experience, such a process can and cannot achieve.

II

The "Ode to Psyche," which there is good reason to take as the earliest of the odes of the spring,[4] is also the broadest in the variety of its implications. Its attempt is both to trace and to reinterpret, in some sense to recreate, the identity of the mythological goddess, taken as the patroness of creative inspiration throughout the course of time, by means of a dramatically shifting set of historical perspectives. The ode can readily be divided into three sections or movements between which there are tonal differences that are more pronounced than in any of the odes that follow. This customary division, however, must be qualified in one respect, for the poem is given a kind of circularity by its opening lines, which both prefigure and complete the irony of its conclusion. Thus the point at which the action of the ode might be thought to begin, "Surely I dreamt to-day, or did I see," is preceded by a brief apostrophe that raises a series of implicit questions that can be answered only through an understanding of the whole poem:

> O GODDESS! hear these tuneless numbers, wrung
> By sweet enforcement and remembrance dear,
> And pardon that thy secrets should be sung
> Even into thine own soft-conched ear.

(1-4)

4 From its place in Keats's long journal letter to George and Georgiana (II, 106-108), "To Psyche" can be dated in late April. Although the remaining odes of the spring cannot be precisely dated or ordered, the overwhelming evidence, internal and external, indicates they were composed later. Some of the hazards of interpreting the odes as a progression are usefully discussed in Robert F. Gleckner's "Keats's Odes: The Problems of the Limited Canon," *Studies in English Literature*, v (1965), 577-85.

Why, we must ask, does the poet sing in "tuneless" numbers secrets already known to the goddess he entreats? The note of mystery, together with an undertone of tender concern and reluctance, is deepened by the force of "wrung" and the oxymoron "sweet enforcement," as if to excuse a votary who knows he can address his deity only in ways that violate the very godhead he seeks to celebrate and commend.

Such questions, however, are dispelled amid the wonder and amazement of the vision suddenly granted the poet of the goddess and her lover, Cupid:

> Surely I dreamt to-day, or did I see
>   The winged Psyche with awaken'd eyes?
> I wander'd in a forest thoughtlessly,
>   And, on the sudden, fainting with surprise,
> Saw two fair creatures, couched side by side
>   In deepest grass, beneath the whisp'ring roof
>   Of leaves and trembled blossoms, where there ran
>   A brooklet, scarce espied:
> 'Mid hush'd, cool-rooted flowers, fragrant-eyed,
>   Blue, silver-white, and budded Tyrian,
> They lay calm-breathing on the bedded grass;
>   Their arms embraced, and their pinions too;
>   Their lips touch'd not, but had not bade adieu,
> As if disjoined by soft-handed slumber,
> And ready still past kisses to outnumber
>   At tender eye-dawn of aurorean love:
>   The winged boy I knew;
>   But who wast thou, O happy, happy dove?
>   His Psyche true!
>
>   (5-23)

It is impossible to grasp the full significance of the scene and its figures, which we take in gradually like a painting, without returning to Keats's first treatment of the story of Cupid and Psyche in "I Stood Tip-toe." In the earlier poem he had, to be sure, touched on the legend only briefly, but it is there closely bound up with his conception of the birth of mythology as the origin of verse. Indeed it is the same wonder of mythological discovery, the amazement of the poet who first "pull'd the boughs aside, / That we might look into a forest wide" ("I Stood Tip-toe," 151-52), that Keats recaptures in a far more intense way in the opening stanza of "To Psyche."

Briefly, what Keats renders in the scene is the wonder of discovery—in one of its many versions—of the primal story, the primal myth. It is as if the whole relationship between the two divinities, the mystery of their love, were in a moment revealed and rendered timeless, full of its infinite implications and possibilities for further discovery. The scene is among the most purely pictorial in the odes, for painting, unlike verse, music, dance, or even sculpture, which demand a temporal medium, conveys all it has to give the observer massively and at once, even if the eye requires time to elaborate a multitude of details and relationships that are at first "scarce espied." The question of whether the vision is dreamed or actually seen (significant only as an act of retrospection, the poet's looking backward on "to-day") never intrudes upon his present sense of awe. For in the mythopoeic mode of apprehension there is no division between past and present, sleep and waking, the image and its content or "conception," sensation and thought. The primitive form of understanding comprehends as a totality all that intellection and investigation may, in their innumerable ramifications, subsequently educe. What the scene distills is the wonder of that kind of apprehension that constitutes the essence of myth, in which everything is given implicitly and at once, even if the poet may not at first recognize the identity of the goddess herself. For the loss of such understanding and the prospects for a poetry that would advance without the hope of recovering it are the ode's major preoccupations.[5]

The picture of Cupid and Psyche has often been accused

[5] The contrast between the worlds of myth and history is a basic theme throughout the works of Mircea Eliade, such as *The Myth of the Eternal Return* (New York, 1954) and *The Sacred and the Profane: The Nature of Religion* (New York, 1957).

of a certain lushness or prettiness characteristic of an earlier stage of Keats's development,[6] and there is an undeniable truth to the charge but also a deeper justification. For the scene exists both as a cultural and a personal kind of reminiscence. Within the structure of the ode as a whole, it looks back not only to an earlier stage of culture when the kind of understanding and belief that characterizes myth were possible, but to an earlier Keats who actually experienced such moments of infinitely expanding awareness and hoped for a time to recapture and perpetuate them in his verse. Thus the ode's last stanza, which outlines the hopes for the future, the possibilities that now lie ahead, takes on its full significance and its darker features only in the light of the dawning radiancy of the opening vignette. There was for Keats a certain justness, perhaps even a necessity, in beginning the first of the odes of the spring by a return upon himself.

The shift in tone between the first and second stanzas, among the most remarkable in all the odes, comes as a modulation to rapt elegy for the past:

> O latest born and loveliest vision far
> Of all Olympus' faded hierarchy!
> Fairer than Phœbe's sapphire-region'd star,
> Or Vesper, amorous glow-worm of the sky.
>
> (24-27)

It marks the exchange of innocence for knowledge and experience, for, as Kenneth Allott has written, " 'To Psyche' is about a kind of Fall."[7] Fundamentally the change is from a mythopoeic conception of experience, that most genial to art, to an historical one. For if myth seeks to gather up and universalize human experience in terms of the images it creates, history continually intervenes to unravel them by

---

[6] See Douglas Bush, *John Keats: His Life and Writings* (New York, 1966), pp. 130-31.

[7] "The 'Ode to Psyche,' " *John Keats: A Reassessment*, ed. Kenneth Muir (Liverpool, 1958), p. 91. Allott's fine essay is one to which I am particularly indebted.

defining each act it scrutinizes as a particular and unique event, and the paradox of this antagonism is a major theme throughout the odes. Thus we proceed from the opening vision of the lovers, which seems, in its timelessness and openness to contemplation, almost unrelated to the Cupid-Psyche myth conceived as an account or story, to an awareness of the completed legend, the events that in "I Stood Tip-toe" Keats had compressed to a few couplets:

> The silver lamp,—the ravishment,—the wonder—
> The darkness,—loneliness,—the fearful thunder;
> Their woes gone by, and both to heaven upflown,
> To bow for gratitude before Jove's throne.
>
> (147-50)

Yet the process of temporal or cultural elaboration as we find it represented in the ode is even more far-reaching, for not only has Psyche been deified and canonized but she has outlived the cult of her worshipers:

> O brightest! though too late for antique vows,
>   Too, too late for the fond believing lyre,
> When holy were the haunted forest boughs,
>   Holy the air, the water, and the fire.
>
> (36-39)

Not only have her wonder and mystery been formalized as ritual but the secrets of her rites have been all but lost; and the fact that she was "not embodied as a goddess before the time of Apulieus the Platonist" and therefore too late to be "worshipped or sacrificed to with any of the ancient fervour," as Keats explained to George and Georgiana (II, 106), only makes the irony of her involvement in history more complete. From the timeless domain of the first stanza, the realm of "Flora, and old Pan" with its rapt discoveries and wide-eyed contemplations, we are transported to a world where mythology has been swallowed up by history. The delicately winged and breathing creature has withered to a mere historical abstraction.

Yet even in these days so far retir'd
  From happy pieties, thy lucent fans,
  Fluttering among the faint Olympians,
I see, and sing, by my own eyes inspired.
So let me be thy choir, and make a moan
    Upon the midnight hours;
Thy voice, thy lute, thy pipe, thy incense sweet
    From swinged censer teeming;
Thy shrine, thy grove, thy oracle, thy heat
    Of pale-mouth'd prophet dreaming.
                                            (40-49)

If she retains, here or there, a solitary votary, nevertheless
the pallor of her dreaming prophet suggests that the "heat"—
the kind of "fervour" or intensity necessary to renew her
presence within an age of disbelief—may prove exhausting
for even the most devoted of her followers.

Thus the simple, dove-like creature so instantaneously
revealed to the poet in the opening vision must now at a later
day be invoked as Psyche, the goddess of the poetic soul, the
Muse. The task is no easy one, for the progression from the
pure wonder of revelation through religious worship to disbelief suggests the distance that separates the poet, writing
in an age far gone from "happy pieties," from the object of
his inspiration and something, too, of the sacrifice and ardor
now necessary for one who would become her priest and
struggle to envision her anew. The change between the first
and second sections of the ode, between the playful, light-
some creature and the high, forlorn divinity, partly suggests
the change that, in the course of time, has overtaken poetry:
the change between the poetry of the mythical golden age, a
poetry of instant discovery and unquestioning belief, and a
poetry of established, even ritualized, order—the poetry of
high commemoration which, ever since the Renaissance, it
had become steadily more arduous for poets to intone.[8] Nev-

---

[8] Strong Miltonic echoes, especially of "On the Morning of Christ's
Nativity," have often been noted within the second and third stanzas.

ertheless the fires of poetic devotion must be kept burning even in an age of disbelief: Keats is fully committed to the task of serving Psyche even while he knows the burden her worship imposes. However he now intimates the necessity of a new kind of poetry, one, as Bate has done so much to suggest, of an increasing inwardness and subjectivity. One of the most remarkable aspects of "To Psyche" is the way the transition to the consideration of a poetry of growing modernity at the beginning of the closing stanza of the poem is prepared for by a recapitulation of a whole stage of poetic evolution including major aspects of Keats's own development.

The task, then, is the necessary one of cultivating the poetic garden, of re-exploring the Psyche story and the kinds of possibilities it offers from a new standpoint, that of the modern age.

> Yes, I will be thy priest, and build a fane
>   In some untrodden region of my mind,
> Where branched thoughts, new grown with pleasant pain,
>   Instead of pines shall murmur in the wind:
> Far, far around shall those dark-cluster'd trees
>   Fledge the wild-ridged mountains steep by steep;
> And there by zephyrs, streams, and birds, and bees,
>   The moss-lain Dryads shall be lull'd to sleep;
> And in the midst of this wide quietness
> A rosy sanctuary will I dress
> With the wreath'd trellis of a working brain,
>   With buds, and bells, and stars without a name,
> With all the gardener Fancy e'er could feign,
>   Who breeding flowers, will never breed the same:
> And there shall be for thee all soft delight
>   That shadowy thought can win,

However, as Allott has remarked, "nobody has stopped to explain why Keats thought of Milton at this point in his poem" (p. 87). As he points out, Keats was probably recalling Milton's jubilant, at moments tender, depiction of the downfall of the pagan deities in the "Hymn." One might add, in a more general way, that he was thinking of a whole tradition that culminates in Milton.

255

A bright torch, and a casement ope at night,
  To let the warm Love in!

(50-67)

Yet it is just at this point—in the interpretation of the significance and tone of the important closing stanza—that
responsible critics have been and remain most liable to diverge. It is possible, for example, to agree with Bloom that
there are aspects of the ode that epitomize the poet's myth-
making or myth-revitalizing faculty. Nevertheless it is hard
to accept either his view that the ode rises to the triumph
of a "rhapsodical climax" or that of Kenneth Allott that it
finishes "with exultation at its climax."[9] It is necessary, first
of all, to describe what exactly the last stanza depicts. What
one discovers is a process of interiorization by which the
poetic garden, the fane of Psyche, and the forms of primitive
mythology are incorporated and subsumed by the mind and
its processes. One might say that the Psyche myth, now
internalized, becomes the object of the poet's deliberate
contemplation, a matter to be digested and elaborated from
the viewpoint of the various implications it affords, until
what is implicit becomes explicit, until myth is extrapolated
into "thought." Within the logic of the ode and its development, such is virtually the only direction that remains for
the modern poet to take. One can add, too, that the process
is described in an involuted and metaphysical style that
sharply contrasts with that of the earlier sections and that
verges in some of its effects on the macabre.

For the prospect the last stanza unfolds is hardly one of
unqualified optimism. The wild and steeply rising mountains,
reminiscent of some of the poet's descriptions of northern
scenery during his walking tour the preceding summer, form
an ominously brooding background for the idyllic region of
soft zephyrs and streams that enclose the "rosy sanctuary,"
a landscape where the creatures of classical mythology are

    [9] Allott, "The 'Ode to Psyche,'" p. 93; Harold Bloom, *The Vision-
ary Company* (New York, 1961), p. 395.

256

happily repopulated only to be *"lull'd* to sleep." Fancy, the gardener, cultivates a cerebral trellis where exotic buds in infinite profusion burst into thought "with pleasant pain." The description combines the quaint simplicity of a child's nursery rhyme,

> Mary, Mary, quite contrary
> How does your garden grow?
> With silver bells and cockle shells,
> And pretty maids all in a row,

with something of the lurid incongruity of surrealist art. If the natural landscape with which the poem opens appears at times too lushly sensuous, that at the conclusion seems consciously artful and anachronistic.

This is not to argue that the task as Keats presents it in the final stanza is not a serious one. It is just that the possibilities for a continuation of poetic development, as he is now impelled to envision them, are so darkly qualified. One can say that the poet is now no longer the same as the one who in the first stanza wandered "thoughtlessly." He has by definition left "the infant or *thoughtless* Chamber"; whether he likes it or not he has entered the darker "Chamber of Maiden *Thought*." There is no hope of recovering the state of poetic innocence, of rediscovering the great myths of the past in the fullness of their simplicity. The only possibility for further progress lies in the expectation of following out their various lines of implication in a more specialized way. Ultimately the poet must confront the ambiguous value of advanced knowledge, accept his place within the present state of cultural evolution, the "grand march of intellect" (1, 282), and resign himself to the task of extending the reaches of poetic consciousness into the wilderness surrounding it on all sides.

Hence the emphasis in the concluding stanza falls on the *"mind*," and, more narrowly, the "working *brain*." The major poetic effort is now the production of "branched thoughts," a kind of intellectual elaboration attended with as much difficulty as pleasure. For the organicism of the image is immediately qualified, not merely by the phrase that follows ("new grown with pleasant pain") but by the involution of the whole gardening metaphor, which as it develops gradually suggests more the kind of artifice that leads to forced growth ("wreath'd trellis," "gardener Fancy," "*feigns*") than cultivation. The work of rearing and training the productions of the poetic garden proceeds, but it is accompanied by the same hints of enforcement for which the poet apologized at the commencement of the ode.

Over and beyond the particular ironies of style and technique that complicate the texture of the ode's conclusion there emerges, however, the further kind of irony I have attempted to define at the outset of this chapter. That irony, it may be recalled, can be thought to reside in a sense of perpetual *indeterminacy*. Here it is useful to return once again to the "Mansion of Many Apartments" letter to Reynolds of the preceding spring, a letter whose tentative conclusions become the subject of vital reconsideration in Keats's ode. One major premise of the letter, it may be recalled, had been his conviction in an orderly assimilation of poetic knowledge, the belief in a steady growth in "intellect," if not in excellence, between, say, Milton and Wordsworth, so that the fresh insights for which the modern poet struggles, far from being merely idiosyncratic, can be seen to play a meaningful role in the history and advancement of human culture. "The truth is there is something real in the World," he had concluded his letter of May 3, 1818, to Reynolds. "Your third Chamber of Life shall be a lucky and a gentle one." "To Psyche" returns through a related set of metaphors to treat the burden of the modern consciousness and the "many doors" opening before the poet "on all sides." Yet the direction it suggests for further progress, for a continuation of the task of poetical investigation and discovery, is neither clear nor certain. Indeed the recognition the ode finally intimates is that for the poet of the present day there can be no escape from shadowiness and subjectivity, that the effort to push further into the region of the unknown leads only to the perception of further passages and implications, that it results in a sense of ultimate inconclusiveness that is ironic.

While the poetic garden exists for the cultivation of consciousness and the fruits of "a working brain," the kinds of "thoughts" we find elaborated there are forever in a process of becoming, forever changing, forever "new grown." If the poem's earliest flowers, "Blue, silver-white, and budded Tyrian," are richly, perhaps too richly, sensuous, these are disconcertingly ephemeral and tenuous—"buds, and bells, and stars without a name." The progression from "buds" to "bells, and stars," from nature to artifice, suggests comparison with those related kinds of development the logic or illogic of which was, as we have seen, at one time or another so preoccupying: the change from material substance to essence, from sensation to thought, from life to poetry. Such flowers may be of a superior breed, but at the same time they are too hybridized and delicate even to support the bare identity of a name.[10] They bear witness to the inexhaustible inventiveness of the gardener, Fancy, who, while forever "breeding flowers, will never breed the same." The garden affords the promise of infinite profusion and fertility but little suggestion of the order and coherence that "growth" usually implies, those indications, as Keats had briefly pondered them in an earlier letter to Bailey, of "a *complex Mind*—one that is imaginative and at the same time careful of its fruits" (I, 186). For any end to the process of continual proliferation is quite literally unthinkable. If the teeming garden of the ode's final stanza is Keats's metaphor for the modern poetic psyche, one can say the possibilities it

---

[10] A number of the particular ironies latent throughout the final stanza have been perceptively observed by David Perkins in *The Quest for Permanence*, pp. 226-28. For a different reading of the ode, see James H. Bunn, "Keats's *Ode to Psyche* and the Transformation of Mental Landscape," *English Literary History*, xxxvii (1970), 581-94, which largely disregards them.

offers for cultivation are either limitless or depressingly circumscribed, depending on the state of one's hopes and expectations as regards the function of verse. What we have is a Romantic Garden of Adonis with a vengeance.

In the end Psyche emerges as the patron spirit of "all soft delight / That shadowy thought can win." The emphasis on thought, which grows throughout the stanza, remains to the last; but the importance of the qualifying adjective is obvious. For what such kind of thinking can finally "win" remains, at best, problematical. The delights over which she presides are undeniable and unceasing, for she represents the spirit of perpetual creativity and unconscious generation. Yet the kind of awareness she fosters is closest to what Keats habitually means by "speculation"—the kind of "reasoning," as he had declared only a month earlier, that, while "erroneous" (in both the older and newer senses of the word), still "may be fine." "This is the very thing in which consists poetry" he went on, adding significantly, "and if so it is not so fine a thing as philosophy—For the same reason that an eagle is not so fine a thing as a truth" (II, 80-81). The "Ode to Psyche" represents, in ways the earlier letter helps suggest, a mature and qualified reappraisal both of the major premises of Negative Capability and of the role poetry can hope to play within the contemporary world. In structure it is closer than is usually recognized to the two greater odes that follow it, for like them it proceeds toward a series of expectations it cannot finally fulfill. It leaves us with a realization both of the amplitude and the limits of the poetic imagination as Keats had come to conceive of it.

At the last Keats returns briefly to the Cupid-Psyche legend, almost lost sight of in the evolution of the final stanza. As patroness of "shadowy thought," the goddess will at least be forever welcome to the poet, and there is even the hope that the early love of Cupid and Psyche can actually be reborn within the poet's consciousness. The casement of the mind stands fully open "To let the warm Love in," suggesting, as Bloom has noted, the continual accessibility of the

poetic imagination.[11] Yet we are given occasion to pause
when we remember that the love between Cupid and Psyche
originally took place in secrecy and darkness and that the
identity of the celestial visitant was forbidden to be known.
Now the anticipated guest, frankly welcomed as "the warm
Love," is guided back to the open window by a bright torch
where the lovers' rites are to be reenacted in the light or
half-light of the modern consciousness. Compared with the
mystery and excitement of the earlier romance, there is a
touch of the calculated or rehearsed about the scene. Such a
reading may be oversubtle, but there are aspects of the setting
that remain profoundly saddening. At least one should stop
to measure the distance between the "warm Love" as a symbol of returning rapture in "To Psyche" and the role the god
assumes in *Lamia*, where Keats uses him to introduce the
mixture of anxiety and boredom that creeps into the poem:

> Besides, there, nightly, with terrific glare,
> Love, jealous grown of so complete a pair,
> Hover'd and buzz'd his wings, with fearful roar,
> Above the lintel of their chamber door,
> And down the passage cast a glow upon the floor.
>
> (ii.11-15)

It is an aspect of "To Psyche," and not the least important,
that it takes us one step forward toward this kind of disillusionment.

III

Contrary to my general intention, I have dealt with the
"Ode to Psyche" in some detail. This is because it has been
among the most neglected of the great odes and because the
relationship between its major sections and consequently the
coherence of the work as a whole have often been misinterpreted. More important, it serves to introduce the central

[11] Bloom, *Visionary Company*, p. 397.

problem that all four of the later odes of the spring touch on in more particular ways.

In the "Ode to a Nightingale" and the "Ode on a Grecian Urn" Keats concentrates more narrowly on the poetic symbol. This is not to say that the concern with the conflict between myth and history disappears, for in the two great odes the symbol is explored as a possible means for bridging the division between the two realms, as a potential *tertium quid* combining the different values of both the worlds of timelessness and time. Each symbol provides the focus for a new and searching test of the nature of the creative process and now especially, to return to a central preoccupation, of the kind of identity it can and cannot impart. For the task in both odes is to create or preserve for the object each considers a higher or *essential* reality without destroying its quality and uniqueness as an existent being or thing. The problem for Keats, as we have seen, is that of the creative process itself. In the first case the task is to invest the nightingale with values that are permanent without losing the sense of its living reality for the present. In the second instance the poet begins not with a living object but with a work of art created at a distant time and by a different artist—one working, perhaps, with expectations similar to his own—in the attempt to define its identity for his own generation. The "Urn" moves from the world of mythic oneness in the effort to engage the concerns of the present. The "Nightingale" works from a point in history, the standpoint of the speaker in his heartache and loneliness, in the effort to regain the world of timelessness and myth. The myth in question is not, of course, any single legend like that of Endymion or Psyche, each with its different emphasis, but the archetypal myth of Plato's realm where antinomies are resolved and values are perceived as one. The thrust of the one ode is complementary and reciprocal to that of the other. As a record of intense imaginative experience, a "voyage of conception," each concludes in a form of recognition that is profoundly ironic.

Since its primary concern is for synthesis, that is, for the creation of the bird as an evolving symbol, "Nightingale" more directly confronts the problem of the creative process. As with so much of the earlier verse, the process begins gradually and through a sustained play of associations. The poem takes shape within that familiar, shadowy world of vague and confused sensation but in a mood troubled by discontent and longing. The bird, singing in its ease and immunity from pain, draws the poet into that act of imaginative identification that is the beginning of poetic activity. The mere voice in its simplicity becomes the focus about which a rich train of associations starts slowly to gather:

> O, for a draught of vintage! that hath been
> > Cool'd a long age in the deep-delved earth,
> Tasting of Flora and the country green,
> > Dance, and Provençal song, and sunburnt mirth!
> O for a beaker full of the warm South,
> > Full of the true, the blushful Hippocrene,
> > > With beaded bubbles winking at the brim,
> > > > And purple-stained mouth;
> > That I might drink, and leave the world unseen,
> > And with thee fade away into the forest dim.
> > > > > > (11-20)

"Throat" (from the end of the preceding stanza) suggests wine, and "vintage" leads on both to Flora, suggesting the primal world of "Flora, and old Pan," and "the country green," the homely, familiar world of commonplace actuality. The longing for the "warm South" leads backwards to the Provence of the medieval poets and then to classical antiquity and the fabulous Hippocrene that will permit the poet to "fade away" to join the bird within its forest haunts. Already the progression has begun to suggest a wealth of subtly different implications and at the same time that kind of attenuation that is to overtake the whole poetic effort.

"Ode to a Nightingale" is the supreme expression in all

Keats's poetry of the impulse to imaginative escape that flies in the face of the knowledge of human limitation, the impulse fully expressed in "Away! away! for I *will* fly to thee." However, the process is far from an unthinking one. The third stanza openly confronts those "disagreeables" the imagination must somehow deal with—sickness, sorrow, age, and finally death. For it is, of course, the recollection of Tom's last days that lends a special poignancy and also a kind of weakness to the stanza. The burden of such tragic knowledge seems deadening and inescapable. In the face of it the poet can only "dissolve." The verb may briefly recall the chemical analogy and the whole process by which discordant associations are "evaporated" in the distillation of a more intense conception of reality; but it is clear from the full context that the force of the word is now more vaguely psychological and escapist: "*Fade* far away, dissolve, and quite *forget*." The poet is transported "on the *viewless* wings of Poesy." The stanzas that immediately follow gain much of their extraordinary intensity from the conscious and willful exclusion of knowledge (but a knowledge that, as in *St. Agnes*, can be only temporarily suppressed).

Thus the illusion of recovering the primal garden of eternal spring is only the more compelling for the unobtrusive hints of change that underlie it, the fading violets and coming musk rose, just as the beauty of the region is the more seductive because it cannot be seen:

> I *cannot see* what flowers are at my feet,
>   Nor what soft incense hangs upon the boughs,
> But, in embalmed darkness, guess each sweet
>   Wherewith the seasonable month endows
> The grass, the thicket, and the fruit-tree wild.
>
> (41-45)

The elimination of the primary sense intensifies the others; in Keats's phrase, it leaves "so much room for Imagination" (II, 19). The loss only gratifies the imagination in its desire to enlarge the fullness of the season in a way that outruns the power of the senses, as the extraordinary effects of synesthesia partly suggest. In this region of half-lights and shadows the poet is for a time able to control the flow of associations that surround the bird so that the process of imaginative assimilation, whatever the hints of contradiction that subtly run counter to it, maintains unity and momentum. The process reaches its climax in the sixth stanza. For now the poet daringly returns to the idea of death, the chief among the besetting evils of the third stanza, to pursue its connotations further but in such a way as actually to reinforce the notion of the bird as an ideal of tranquillity and permanence ("embalmed darkness," "easeful Death," "rich to die," "high requiem"). For a moment death, conceived of as an eternal present, the prolongation of the ecstatic moment, is reconciled with the other values—love, beauty, enjoyment—that the bird expresses.

But for a moment only. The various different connotations of death cannot be long suppressed, nor is the bird, in its evolution as poetic image, able to assimilate them as they now gradually reemerge to consciousness. As David Perkins has shown, the bird, taken as a poetic image, collapses from the sheer weight of implication it must bear.[12] To put it another way, the poet is gradually forced to recognize the bird as something no longer natural but essential, as primarily a work of art, a symbol, a value that exists in separation from the world of man:

> Thou wast not born for *death, immortal* Bird!
> No hungry generations tread *thee* down.
>
> (61-62)

Rather than uniting the earthly and the eternal, the bird now serves to emphasize the gap between them. The point is, however, that the bird, first as suggestive image then as symbol, cannot be isolated from the whole poetic process

[12] *The Quest for Permanence*, pp. 244-57. Like most recent critics of the odes, I am indebted to Perkins's excellent study of Keats's use of symbol, especially in the case of "Nightingale" and "Urn."

that creates it and inevitably outruns it. For the process, taken as a kind of speculation, a form, even, of "thinking," is one that exceeds any means the poet can set up to contain it. The controlled interplay of associations that swells the bird into reality, that gives it value and identity, at the same time inexorably exposes it to an ever-widening circle of human experience, a kind of complexity the bird cannot subsume. The very process that creates the bird inevitably rejects it as inadequate, just as any image, poem, or thought is inadequate to express the complex sum of human realization. In the transformation it undergoes, the bird is thus the symbol of the poem's achievement but also of its limitation.

Of course the recognition is not instantaneous. To some degree it is, as we have seen, latent from the very start in the way the imagination of the poet proceeds to operate on its materials. Nothing, in fact, is more characteristic of the ode than the way in which the central realization is restrained almost voluptuously and only gradually permitted to infiltrate awareness:

> The voice I hear this passing night was heard
> In ancient days by emperor and clown:
> Perhaps the self-same song that found a path
> Through the sad heart of Ruth, when, sick for home,
> She stood in tears amid the alien corn;
> The same that oft-times hath
> Charm'd magic casements, opening on the foam
> Of perilous seas, in faery lands forlorn.
>
> (63-70)

The poet's conviction of identification with the bird, the illusion of his hold upon its values as poetic image, is slowly dissipated. The voice he hears "*was* heard" by an infinity of others, by "emperor and clown," and will be heard again by future generations he will never know. It has heralded the opening of endless vistas into "faery lands"; but it has also sung to the biblical Ruth at a specific moment in time. Such diversity of experience exceeds the imagination's capacity to

distill and unify. The illusion of mythic oneness is dissolved
in the awareness of change and human history as the voice
of the bird recedes.

The point of the whole experience is driven home by the
closing lines and the questions they pose:

> Was it a vision, or a waking dream?
> Fled is that music:—Do I wake or sleep?
>
> (79-80)

For the questions only arise when the poem itself, considered
as a vital process of unfolding, has ended. They issue from
a standpoint outside it. The poet awakes to reflect on his
experience, to contemplate it as vision or dream. But the
very form of his questions and the distinctions they demand
are ones to which poetry, as a primal state of consciousness,
has never needed to submit. The questions seek to reduce
the life and potentiality of the verse, its continuity and infinite suggestiveness, to the value of a logical abstraction by
forcing on it the alien methodology of "either/or." Their
very inappropriateness, or irrelevance, serves to emphasize
the change that gradually has taken place within the poet's
consciousness. They dramatize the replacement of one kind
of comprehension (or at least the possibility of recovering
it) by another that is more familiar, the kind of busy common sense.

IV

A major contrast between "Nightingale" and "Grecian
Urn" is indicated by the different nature of their central
images—the difference between living creature and artifact.
As I have argued, "Nightingale" moves from mortality toward essence, from image toward symbol, from time toward
eternity. In "Grecian Urn" Keats begins, rather, from the
world of myth, or as much of it as any work of art can
capture, and seeks to elucidate its mystery within the terms
of human life and history, to make it speak to the impatient

needs and questions of his human situation. The exercise of imagination necessary to give the bird an essential meaning is the same as that required to penetrate the surface of the urn, to bring its scenes into full reality, and to pursue the numerous implications they suggest. The task of composition is, ideally at least, no more demanding than the critical and interpretive; the two functions are equally creative and ultimately inseparable.

One is impelled, however, to agree with Bate's judgment that the "Urn" is "in every way a more considered poem than the 'Nightingale,'" a poem where we sense "the concentration of a second attempt and . . . a conscious effort to learn from the first." If not necessarily a greater work, it is a more successful one, yet not, I think, for the major reason he ascribes—"partly because it is more limited in what it tries to say."[13] It is just that it declares what it has to say with more conciseness, energy, and wit, and ultimately with fuller clarity. It pushes home a logic and conclusions the earlier work had left largely implicit. In this respect it is, as John Jones has asserted, the "most ambitious" but surely not, as he goes on to add, "the least successful of the five major odes."[14] Such claims and counterclaims are, perhaps, pointless, except insofar as they remind one of the decisiveness of a context for reading the odes as a group and, more, as a progression.

From the beginning of the ode Keats turns to contemplate the same paradox—a paradox now symbolized in the urn itself—that he had more gradually developed in "Nightingale." Compared with the slow, sensuous beginning of the earlier ode, the "Urn" opens with images of exceptional compression (the Keatsian version of the metaphysical sublime):

> Thou still unravish'd bride of quietness,
> Thou foster-child of silence and slow time.
>
> (1-2)

[13] John Keats, p. 510.
[14] John Keats's Dream of Truth (London, 1969), p. 221.

The urn is a "bride" yet still (and always) virginal, "un-ravish'd." Like any work of art, the urn is inexhaustible to meditation, forever full of the wonder of young love and the promise of new and intimate discovery. The sexual metaphor is central to the wit and logic of the poem, for it suggests that vital penetration of imagination necessary to bring any object of regard into the fullness of aesthetic apprehension. In this sense the ode is the expression of Keats's love for the urn; in the same way we are invited to enjoy the ode he composed upon it each time we take it up as readers. Yet the initial limitation is clear from the start: the urn, though bride, is and forever must remain "unravish'd." There is a sense in which its mystery remains finally inaccessible. For the very *openness* of the urn as a physical object suggests a correspond-ing limitation—the fact that it can and will be explored from different standpoints, at different times, and by different indi-viduals, the fact that its potential implications are legion. In a sense, then, the urn remains perpetually inviolable, with-holding the essence of its mystery even from the poet's "sweet enforcement." Although a "bride," it can never be entirely fulfilled; it can never be brought to final conception.

Similarly the urn participates both in the eternal world of myth and in the world of process and human history, in time and beyond it. It is the "foster-child of silence and slow time," the ward of an incongruous match. The urn exists in time because it is only through time and its events that we can even begin to interpret the scenes it presents in their relation to our own experience. A sentence on the subject of Wordsworth from the "Mansion of Many Apartments" letter to Reynolds of just a year ago can, with very little adjust-ment, be applied to the urn: "we find what [it] says true as far as we have experienced and we can judge no further but by larger experience" (1, 279). However the implications of such potentiality are developed more complexly in the ode. The urn is a "Sylvan historian": it is the chronicle of our brief lives and their mystery, yet the shapes and figures it records remain within the pastoral, mythic world of "Flora, and old Pan." It speaks home to our present condition, but it has spoken so to all men since its creation and will continue to speak when we are gone to all who come after us, to those who will exist "in midst of other woe / Than ours," to those whose state of mind or being we can only begin to imagine. It derives its identity from our knowledge of life, yet transcends the identity we bring to it. It is equally true to the history of our time and to that of all ages. While perpetually relevant to the course of human events, it is yet immune to the kind of limitation history (taken as a record of choices, of paths taken) normally implies. It exists in its own kind of quiet indeterminacy.

My purpose is not another reading of the ode, for its paradox is apparent from the very opening lines if we read them, as I have attempted, within the context of the whole poem. Nor do I intend to analyze, as has been done so often before, the fine curve of Keats's imagination as it enters the surface of the urn to bring its scenes to life only slowly to withdraw, leaving the urn again in its silence and marmo-reality—the pattern of imaginative engagement and disengagement that defines the circular shape both of the urn and the ode. One can pause to admire again the profound and touching fourth stanza, where the tide of obstinate questioning, momentarily suspended, breaks in again:

> Who are these coming to the sacrifice?
>   To what green altar, O mysterious priest,
> Lead'st thou that heifer lowing at the skies,
>   And all her silken flanks with garlands drest?
> What little town by river or sea shore,
>   Or mountain-built with peaceful citadel,
>   Is emptied of this folk, this pious morn?
> And, little town, thy streets for evermore
>   Will silent be; and not a soul to tell
>   Why thou art desolate, can e'er return.
>   (31-40)

"Who?" "What?" "Why?" The picture of the sacrifice and
the little town sketched in the background (by the artist or
the imagination of the poet?) conveys a mysterious significance that demands to be translated into the logic of events
as they occur in history, into terms by which the human
understanding can fully comprehend it. Yet it is, of course,
just the context necessary for such a conversion that the urn
eternally withholds.

It is only when we turn to the ode's famous concluding
apothegm,

> "Beauty is truth, truth beauty,—that is all
> Ye know on earth, and all ye need to know,"
>
> (49-50)

that we come to grips with the deeper problems of interpretation it still poses for us. In all the vast body of criticism on
the ode, it has always been the concluding lines that have
assumed crucial importance, and they remain a major challenge in any attempt to reinterpret the poem or the odes as a
group. That challenge has been best summed up in T. S.
Eliot's well-known judgment of the declaration as "a serious
blemish on a beautiful poem." "The statement of Keats," he
went on to write, "seems to me meaningless: or perhaps, the
fact that it is grammatically meaningless conceals another
meaning from me."[15] The judgment is succinctly given, and it
may be useful to rephrase it. Eliot's objection derives, I think,
from the feeling—one many readers are bound to share—that
the concluding lines break decorum by making an assertion
the context of the poem is inadequate to support. It was, of
course, just this assumption Cleanth Brooks undertook to
refute twenty-five years ago in his brilliant and influential
essay,[16] and his method for doing so has often been re-

[15] Note to section 2 of Eliot's essay on Dante, *Selected Essays* (New
York, 1950), p. 231.
[16] "Keats's Sylvan Historian," *The Well Wrought Urn* (New York,
1947), pp. 139-52; reprinted in M. H. Abrams, *English Romantic
Poets* (New York, 1960), pp. 354-64.

adopted. His argument develops from a skillful and highly sensitive reading of the poem, an imaginative experience we are thereafter invited to consider by the critic (and presumably by the poet) as "beautiful" and "true" in the most usual sense of the words. What for Brooks is the meaning of the poem's final statement? Although it is admittedly unfair to take his words (like the poem's statement itself) from the context of his essay, he must at last be required to speak to the point. "The urn is beautiful," he writes, "and yet its beauty is based—what else is the poem concerned with?—on an imaginative perception of essentials. Such a vision is beautiful but it is also true. The sylvan historian presents us with beautiful histories, but they are true histories, and it is a good historian."[17]

There may be those for whom such a summing up seems justifiable. Nevertheless one feels more than ever today, without questioning the general excellence and seminal force of Brooks's exegesis, that his conclusion is inadequate. Throughout the years too many intelligent readers have come back to Eliot's opinion, and the dissatisfaction it expresses has been confirmed too often to be ignored.[18] Briefly, I think Eliot's judgment is both right and wrong or, more exactly perhaps, incomplete. He has once and for all defined a major source of dissatisfaction in our reading of the work. Yet he has not gone on to consider that dissatisfaction as a legitimate part of the poem's larger aesthetic and metaphysical effect, as a part of the total realization the work affords. The possibility we must consider is that the ode as a whole fulfills a larger conception of decorum precisely because its closing lines appear to violate the decorum the work has thus far established but do so only to make an essential point.

[17] *English Romantic Poets*, p. 363.

[18] See, e.g., Barbara Herrnstein Smith's interesting remarks in *Poetic Closure: A Study of How Poems End* (Chicago, 1968), pp. 229-32, a work that takes up the problem within a different context but that comments on the epigraph's "tenuous and perhaps spurious relation to the ode's structure" (p. 232).

At first glance "Nightingale" and the "Urn" appear to differ in one fundamental respect. "Nightingale" ends with a set of questions; the "Urn" comes to its close with an assertion. Yet the more one ponders the two devices Socratically, with an eye to their effects, the more he wonders if their ends are not much the same. As I have argued, the questions at the end of "Nightingale" invite the reader to reflect upon the poem but in a way that forces him to step outside its processes to a recognition of the incompatibility between such analysis and the inner life of his experience. The reader is offered two possibilities. He may conclude, "yes, it was a vision, not a mere dream," or, conversely, "no it was only a dream, not a real vision." As we have seen, the distinction is alien to the unity of consciousness the bird, as an evolving symbol, struggles to achieve, nor does it occur until the poem, properly speaking, is at an end. Either tack will take us back into the poem, but to push either set of possibilities is to destroy the vital rhythm on which the whole depends. What needs to be seen is that the assertion at the end of the "Urn" functions in a way that is closely similar.

While it stands as an assertion, the concluding statement actually serves to raise a number of crucial questions, the most fundamental of which develop out of the problem of how we are to take it. Are we to accept it as part of the urn's total expressiveness, to be pondered in the same way we contemplate the scenes depicted on the urn's surface, almost as if the saying were literally inscribed, a part of the "leaffring'd legend"? Or, alternatively, are we to accept it as the essence of the poem, a summation that, if we interpret wisely from the experience of our reading, contains its final meaning? To put the question a different way, are we to take the statement as one term or *proposition* that the "Urn" advances, a statement that, like "Heard melodies are sweet, but those unheard / Are sweeter," has meaning only in the context of the poem? Or are we to take it as a *conclusion*, in the sense not merely of a termination but as a distillation of the whole poem, a judgment that invites extension within a broader context? (Characteristically, Keats's favorite word in the letters is "axiom," one of those half-way terms, suggesting as it does qualities that place it potentially somewhere between the other two.) Or can we take it in both ways simultaneously? Far from being merely academic, the distinction I am attempting to draw takes us to the heart of the meaning of the "Urn" in order to indicate how it goes a step beyond "Nightingale" in crystallizing the problem both engage.

The questions I have asked are, of course, inseparable from some more familiar ones. There is the problem of how the final lines are to be punctuated; and, even presuming we can agree on this, who is speaking them? Is it the poet or the urn? Or the poet interpreting the urn?[19] Yet I do not think, however much they may distract us, these are the vital issues, for they all point forward to a larger one: what is the relationship between the formulated statement and the process of meditation that has preceded it? And here, regardless of whether we favor poet or urn as spokesman, or some combination of them both, I think we can be more definite. The fact is that the final statement of the "Urn" exists potentially both as a proposition and a conclusion in the sense I have attempted to define. It invites us to take it either way; it constitutes a paradox. It stands on the periphery of the poem, partly inside and partly outside the poetic process, just at the point where sensation, speculation, the language of poetry begins to give way to the processes of logical analysis, the language of thought. The concluding lines actually invite us to do two different things and to do them simultaneously. They ask us, first of all, to consider them as a proposition, the terms of which can be understood, and beyond that, have meaning only within the poem itself. If, however, we contemplate the

[19] The problems and possible solutions have been summarized in the appendix, "Who Says What to Whom at the End of *Ode on a Grecian Urn?*" in Jack Stillinger's useful compendium of modern criticism of the odes, *Twentieth Century Interpretations of Keats's Odes* (Englewood Cliffs, N.J., 1968).

statement within the full life of the poem, what we discover is a context for construing it but one that is by no means conclusive. For virtually every genial reading of the "Urn" has presented the ode (up to the final lines) not as an argument but a debate, a meditation on the power and limits of imagination. Considered purely within the context of the poem, as a proposition, the statement provides no final answer to the mystery of the urn or the scenes it depicts but rather complicates our response to them by inviting us to approach them in a different way.

For the temptation to take the statement as a conclusion is well-nigh irresistible. If the "Urn" is an abstraction of the sum of human experience, its ending seems an abstraction of an abstraction, the kernel of its tantalizing mystery, and the last line and a half, " 'that is all / Ye know on earth, and all ye need to know,' " especially invite us to consider it as such. Yet in order to do so we are obliged to abstract it from the poem, to take it up in the light of our own knowledge, to extend it within a broader, even universal, context, to turn it over in the mind. The poem itself takes us only so far, to that point where, as Keats writes, "we can judge no further but by larger experience." If the scenes depicted on the urn require an act of imaginative response to bring them to life, such is no less the case with the final dictum. Throughout, the ode demands that we meet it half way. Yet just like the picture of the empty town and the sacrificial procession proceeding from it, the apothegm resists our attempts to fathom it. The more we bring to it from the complexity of our own experience, the more elusive it appears, the more possibilities and implications it seems to possess. Contemplated long enough, the utterance assumes the shape of an absolute identity: two terms that circle endlessly back on each other. We have a statement that is, in Eliot's words, "grammatically meaningless." The contradiction of Brooks's interpretation, it seems to me, is that he wants to take it both as proposition and conclusion. While he maintains from the start of his essay that it can only be understood within the context the ode creates, he cannot in the end resist the impulse to elucidate it within a broader context as a statement of conviction. How else can one interpret his words about the truth and beauty of "an imaginative perception of essentials"? Perhaps the best comment on his method is the curious epigraph Keats penned to the first of his two sonnets "On Fame," which he copied for George and Georgiana just before writing out his transcript of the "Ode to Psyche":

> *You cannot eat your cake and have it too.*
> Proverb. (II, 104)

Of course it is just our human impulse, indeed our irrepressible desire to have it both ways, that the strategy of the "Urn" so effectively brings to realization in its closing lines. For the culminating recognition is one that, after all, has been building steadily throughout the poem. That recognition is simply that sensation, speculation, and the kinds of propositions poetry makes to us can never assume, force them how we will, the finality of reasoned thought. For the jump from proposition to conclusion that the "Urn" invites, almost demands, is thoroughly natural and human, indeed instinctive. It is the expression of our desire to invest the intimations art affords with the permanence of certainty. It is as if the poet, frustrated by the silence of the urn in the face of his human questioning, had forced it to speak beyond the power of its means. To extend the sexual metaphor, it is almost as if he had attempted a kind of rape. What he wrests from the urn is a conclusion in the older sense of the word—not a falsehood but a riddle or enigma. For the urn remains inscrutable to such interrogation: it literally "tease[s] us out of thought." It endures, "a friend to man," a source of endless and profoundly meaningful speculation on our own condition. However the terms in which it speaks to us, pursued beyond a certain point, give up their life and, like the figures on the marble surface, appear as mere abstractions.

Admittedly there is an easier way of reading the ode and its closing statement than that for which I have argued. It

276

depends on the conviction, expressed by readers and critics over many years, that in the "Urn" Keats was only re-expressing his declaration to Bailey of November 1817 in the "Adam's dream" letter that "I am certain of nothing but of the holiness of the Heart's affections and the truth of Imagination—What the imagination seizes as Beauty must be truth" (1, 184). As a means of concluding the ode, Keats fell back, it is often said, on that kind of ringing declaration one finds throughout the early poetry, for example in *Endymion*. Yet I do not think such explanations do justice either to the maturity of the ode or, more important, to its greatness as verse. What the "Urn" discloses is not a poet repeating earlier assertions, but rather discovering in them difficulties he had formerly ignored. If we require a gloss from the letters, it is best to return to the poet who, as we have seen, wrote of Wordsworth, "We find what he says true as far as we have experienced and we can judge no further but by larger experience," adding immediately, *"for axioms in philosophy are not axioms until they are proved upon our pulses"* (1, 279). I have already commented on the ambivalence of Keats's use of the word "axiom." However this is only to begin to grapple with the difficulties that the syntax of the statement presents ("axioms . . . are *not* axioms *until*"). Presumably Keats's meaning is that propositions do not become conclusions until they are fully experienced. Yet at what point and by what process, one may ask, is a proposition finally "proved"? Is it verified by an act of conscious recognition, or does Keats use the verb "to prove" primarily as a synonym for "to feel"? Perhaps both values are implied. But how can the process of feeling admit of any termination or how can it result in any conceivable conclusion without producing what it started from—an "axiom in philosophy," a mere abstraction? What Keats's "Urn" articulates is the larger paradox that has its origin in his whole conception of the creative process. More than anything, that paradox concerns a poetry of sensation that would become a poetry of thought.

The better our readings of the "Urn" become, the more

alert we grow to the particular ambivalence of its debate, the less apt I think we shall be to assign conclusive value to its final statement. What the ode expresses is the difficulty and yet the necessity of remaining content with the way art speaks to us, with the kind of "half knowledge" it offers. Once we demand the "Urn" to speak to us definitively, in a way commensurable with "fact & reason," we find we have destroyed its life. The very kind of imaginative response required to fulfill the urn, to give it depth and meaning, limits its value and separates it from us. What follows, however, is not that the final statement of the "Urn" is valueless or that it constitutes, in Eliot's words, "a serious blemish on a beautiful poem." Its very unsatisfactoriness is a vital part of a larger dialectic. For like all good poetry the ode makes a final point, if only indirectly and in a way that transcends the limits of any simple statement. Its realization has to do with what happens within the process of imaginative creation when we seek to refine our perceptions to the point where they approach the clarity of reasoned thought. At the last the "Urn" does speak to us directly and in words that seem, tantalizingly, the essence of its mystery. What it offers us is a sublime commonplace.

V

If beauty is truth and truth beauty, then joy is sorrow and sorrow joy. Such is the progression, to state it baldly, that leads from the "Ode on a Grecian Urn" to the "Ode on Melancholy." The latter presses and extends, in a more radical way, the logic of the earlier paradox. Of course we know that in real life it is impossible to equate joy and sorrow any more than we can equate beauty and truth. Certainly the fact was obvious to Keats. "It is impossible to prove that black is white," he wrote Mrs. Wylie in August 1818. "It is impossible to make out, that sorrow is joy or joy is sorrow" (1, 358). However it was clear that poetry could use axioms, like metaphors, in ways that appeared meaningless or illogical once one stepped back, as he was continually tempted to do, to examine them within a general context. One could agree with Byron that "Knowledge is Sorrow" and then "go on to say that 'Sorrow is Wisdom'—and further for aught we can know for certainty! 'Wisdom is folly'" (1, 279). Conceived within the terms of the poetic process, they were attitudes that were all equally "provable." Nevertheless, one longed after a time for some escape from such circularity and indetermination. One looked for the kind of "truth" one could define in a more permanent way. In an important sense "Melancholy" picks up at the point where "Grecian Urn" leaves off, for it seeks to push beyond the awareness of such paradox in order to isolate a more enduring element in our experience of life and poetry. The element it illuminates is the nature of intensity itself.

No less than the odes that precede it, "Melancholy" is the outgrowth of a deepening meditation, one that attains its fullness of realization only in the closing lines. However, one senses now the force of an acquired momentum, as well as a degree of deliberate foreshortening. It is the briefest of all the great odes. Keats wisely excised the original first stanza, and that which actually opens the poem serves only to anticipate, in a negative way, what the latter two declare, for it is these, as Bate has observed,[20] and more especially the last, that convey the sum of the ode's meaning. There is now no need for a controlling symbol and the gradual elaboration it might provide, for the paradox on which the poem builds appears all but crystallized in consciousness from the abrupt beginning and its exhortation:

> No, no, go not to Lethe, neither twist
> Wolf's-bane, tight-rooted, for its poisonous wine;
>
> .   .   .   .
>
> For shade to shade will come too drowsily,
> And drown the wakeful anguish of the soul.
>
> (1-2, 9-10)

[20] *John Keats*, p. 521.

Partly because it has been so often touched on by past criticism (as well as prefigured throughout the poet's earlier verse), the paradox that affords the focus of the ode's perception can be briefly summarized. It lies in the realization that our moments of most intense joy are inseparable, if only through our awareness of their impermanence, from sorrow, that joy and sorrow partake of and intensify each other, that after a certain point they become, indeed, indistinguishable. Of course to say this much is hardly to define the poem's "meaning," for such a statement reveals nothing about the way in which the paradox is employed—its whole dramatic and emotional effect.

Very broadly, "Melancholy" returns to the assertion at the end of the Negative Capability letter that "with a great poet the sense of Beauty overcomes every other consideration, or rather obliterates all consideration" (1, 194). It seeks to define the essential nature of the beauty and the joy distilled through that "obliteration" or "evaporation" that characterizes human apprehension at its most intense. For its technique the ode looks back to a key word at the beginning of the "Urn's" final stanza, the word "attitude," and with it our tendency to see the urn, finally, as a collection of images and gestures that are radically incomplete. For if "Melancholy" dispenses with the use of a dominant symbol, it achieves its end by presenting before us a steady progression of *attitudes* —if we grant the word a certain range—of an increasing complexity. Something of the suggestiveness the word had come to assume for Keats is indicated by an important section of his long journal letter to George and Georgiana written on March 19, 1819:

I am however young writing at random—straining at particles of light in the midst of a great darkness—without knowing the bearing of any one assertion of any one opinion. Yet may I not in this be free from sin? May there not be superior beings amused with any graceful, though instinctive attitude my mind m[a]y fall into, as I am en-

THE GREAT ODES

tertained with the alertness of a Stoat or the anxiety of a
Deer? Though a quarrel in the streets is a thing to be
hated, the energies displayed in it are fine; the commonest
Man shows a grace in his quarrel—By a superior being our
reasoning[s] may take the same tone—though erroneous
they may be fine—This is the very thing in which consists
poetry.

(II, 80-81)

On the one hand he was most intensely aware of the life and
animation around him, the "ellectric fire in human nature"
and existence, at those moments when the "instinctiveness"
and "animal eagerness" (II, 79-80) of living things were suddenly revealed through the characteristic pose or movement,
when arrested in "the alertness of a Stoat or the anxiety of a
Deer." However, he had now come to see that it was possible,
and even necessary, to regard axioms and opinions, the kinds
of assertion that were so frequent a preoccupation, as well as
abstractions like "joy" or "melancholy," as only a set of
further attitudes that needed to be realized and acted out in
order to achieve significance. For, as he went on to add in a
few sentences, "Nothing ever becomes real till it is experienced—Even a Proverb is no proverb to you till your Life has
illustrated it." What mattered finally to poetry was not the
abstraction but the gesture that embodied it and the particular grace or beauty of its realization—the way in which
the vital energies of life, whether of intellect or body (or, as
in a quarrel in the streets, the two taken together as inseparable) were given momentary identity. The essence of poetry
was something close to intensity itself.

In theme and imagery, "Melancholy" has sometimes been
criticized as the reflection of a weaker, overly sensuous side
of the poet's nature,[21] reminiscent of the Keats who gorged
down nectarines in all their "soft pulpy, slushy, oozy" rich-

[21] See, e.g., Bush's judgment that the ode expresses "a purely and
thinly sensuous aestheticism," one that "would support the old notion
of Keats as an epicure of voluptuous sensation" (*John Keats: His Life
and Writings*, p. 147).

ness (II, 179), the Keats who covered tongue and throat with Cayenne pepper in order to savor "the delicious coolness of claret in all its glory"—the bit of apocrypha recorded by Haydon[22] which, like one or two questionable emendations in Shakespeare, is too beautiful not to be true. However the deeper aestheticism of the ode lies not so much in the overt voluptuousness of certain of its images as in the implications of its argument and its deliberate and self-conscious attitudinizing, the method it employs to dramatize those implications, to examine them and put them to the test. As the ode proceeds, the flow of logic that connects its major figures becomes increasingly extreme and makes steadily greater demands on the reader to keep pace. Thus the second stanza works up through various images of natural transience to one of a more complex kind:

> But when the melancholy fit shall fall
>> Sudden from heaven like a weeping cloud,
> That fosters the droop-headed flowers all,
>> And hides the green hill in an April shroud;
> Then glut thy sorrow on a morning rose,
>> Or on the rainbow of the salt sand-wave,
>> Or on the wealth of globed peonies;
> Or if thy mistress some rich anger shows,
>> Emprison her soft hand, and let her rave,
>> And feed deep, deep upon her peerless eyes.
>>> (11-20)

The poet's fascinated stare upon his mistress's anger elucidates, in a new and suggestive way, that kind of "evaporation" that had long been for Keats a characteristic aspect of intensity. The poet's stare transcends the bitterness and pain of her resentment to find its center in a deeper play of forces. In one sense the source of her vexation, a sympathy with its causes, the awareness, even, of her as a suffering individual cease to matter. (Viewed in purely human terms, the situa-

---

[22] *The Diary of Benjamin Robert Haydon*, ed. Willard B. Pope (Cambridge, Mass., 1960), II, 317.

tion is the perfect one for a poet having his face slapped.)
For what absorbs him, what in a sense he lives in, is the
surging turbulence of her feeling, the flux and reflux of its
passionate working, the vitality that her anger in its various
expressions serves to reveal.[23] At such a time we recognize
Keats's ability to crystallize in a dramatic attitude, one that
can be entered into and explored, the characteristic views of
Hazlitt. "I affi[r]m, Sir," Hazlitt had written, as Keats transcribed his words for George and Georgiana on March 13,
"that Poetry, that the imagination, generally speaking, delights in power, in strong excitement, as well as in truth, in
good, in right, whereas pure reason and the moral sense
approve only of the true and good" (II, 74-75). Or as the
critic elsewhere put it in language the poet seems actually
to have echoed in the final stanza, the essence of poetry lies
in "the flowing, not the fixed," in "that uneasy, exquisite
sense of beauty or power that cannot be contained within
itself; that is impatient of all limit; that . . . strives . . . to
enshrine itself, as it were, in the highest forms of fancy, and
to relieve the aching sense of pleasure by expressing it in the
boldest manner, and by the most striking examples of the
same quality in other instances."[24]

This is not to deny the theme of human transience, which
deepens at the opening of the final stanza into the awareness
of death, but to argue that it is actually subordinate to a
further kind of annihilation. Within the intensity of the
poet's gaze the anger of his mistress is transformed into
beauty. Now the last stanza makes us apprehend the process
of gradual intensification in a different way by shifting our
perspective:

[23] Cf. Keats's remarks on "Charmian" (Jane Cox): "The picture
before me always gives me a life and animation which I cannot possibly
feel with any thing inferiour—I am at such times too much occupied
in admiring to be awkward or on a tremble. I forget myself entirely
because I live in her" (*Letters*, I, 395).

[24] "On Poetry in General," *Lectures on the English Poets, The Complete Works of William Hazlitt*, ed. P. P. Howe (London, 1930), V, 3.

She dwells with Beauty—Beauty that must die;
   And Joy, whose hand is ever at his lips
Bidding adieu; and aching Pleasure nigh,
   Turning to poison while the bee-mouth sips:
Ay, in the very temple of Delight
   Veil'd Melancholy has her sovran shrine,
     Though seen of none save him whose strenuous tongue
Can burst Joy's grape against his palate fine;
   His soul shall taste the sadness of her might,
     And be among her cloudy trophies hung.

(21-30)

We no longer find ourselves in contact with the natural images of the spring season, the April hillside and its budding flowers, or with the poet who still clasps his mistress in his living hand. Instead we find ourselves confronted with a succession of personified abstractions—Beauty, Joy, Pleasure, Delight, and finally Melancholy herself—who appear before us almost like actors in a pageant or figures on a sculptured frieze. Ever more closely interrelated through the poem's logic, they raise the question of the kind of meaning or identity they can possess for us once we attempt to apprehend them in themselves. For we discover we can grasp them only in terms of various attitudes and gestures we must interpret and fulfill. Consider for example, the figure of "Joy, whose hand is ever at his lips / Bidding adieu." One begins with "Joy," the abstract concept, and works toward the informing gesture, the "adieu" (the theatrical, slightly affected word that occurs in each of the odes of the spring, but not, where one might in some ways expect to find it, in "To Autumn"). Yet one realizes that the gesture is forever suspended, forever withheld, forever in the process of being made. Indeed its very suggestiveness almost compels us to imagine some fulfillment. One longs to see it performed or acted out. Perhaps we are tempted to imagine it rendered by the poet himself ("I can scarcely bid you good bye even in a letter. I always made an awkward bow" [II, 360]). In

284

any case we remember the fascination the manner of such parting tributes always held for him. One recalls Brown bidding goodbye to some old ladies at a party with Dilke throwing up windows to call after him, "Brown! Brown! They say you look younger than ever you did! . . . Brown! Brown! By God, they say you're handsome!" and Keats's wry comment: "You see what a many words it requires to give any identity to a thing" (II, 190-91). Or Reynolds in a doorway, embarrassed at some awkwardness in making his farewell, when "he put the tails of his coat between his legs, and sneak'd off as nigh like a spanial as could be" (II, 208). Gesture here becomes the pure expressiveness of poetry. Yet the figure "Joy" both acknowledges and resists our human desire for definition and completion. The curved arm, the fingers extended to the lips, convey a sense of power forever coming into being, potentially assuming an infinity of vital shapes and forms.

Similarly the real effectiveness of the image of "Joy's grape" lies not in its appeal to taste or savor, its quality as pain or pleasure; for joy and sorrow are transformed into each other while the bee-mouth sips. The essence of the image lies in the relationship it suggests between the unburst grape and the strenuous tongue compressing it, a joy of muscularity and expectation that transcends the boundaries of emotion and dwells in pure intensity, in the tension the image itself creates.

If the message of the "Urn" is that the propositions poetry addresses to us are generically different from the certainties of reasoned thought, the logic of "Melancholy" takes us one step further. The true "aestheticism" of the ode lies in its demonstration that the emotions themselves, taken in the way we generally consider them, as joy, sorrow, anger, or melancholy, are themselves abstractions that have no real identity, being only general contexts for apprehending something that is more fundamental. The essence of poetical experience lies in intensity itself, the force of pure poetical expressiveness, a power that, like electricity, exists between polarities and oppositions, that reveals itself in movement and in gesture, but that resists any human effort to define or limit it. As Keats had long before declared,

> 'tis the supreme of power;
> 'Tis might half slumb'ring on its own right arm.
> ("Sleep and Poetry," 236-37)

There are some critics who claim for the ending of the ode a depth of tragic realization,[25] as though it were necessary to rescue the work from the exaggerations of its partly playful, partly serious posturing into the aura of high seriousness. Yet we do not approach the shrine of Melancholy in the same spirit as we ascend toward Moneta's; nor do I think the tone of the conclusion, despite its elevated rhythm, is so much tragic as in the purest sense ironical.

> Ay, in the very temple of Delight
> Veil'd Melancholy has her sovran shrine.
> (25-26)

But the whole progression of the ode has brought us to the understanding that the inmost recess of that shrine is kept by Pleasure. What we are left with is one more version of the paradox all the odes collectively pursue. What we are made aware of is the endlessness of process and a power that exceeds the ability of any of the images the poem sets up to arrest it, a power that, in its essence, remains inexhaustible and undetermined.

VI

The disappointing "Ode on Indolence," which Keats did not think well enough of to include in the 1820 volume, appears to have been completed last, although in many ways it looks back to the beginning of the progression.[26] It finds

[25] See, e.g., the end of Bloom's discussion of the ode in *The Visionary Company*, p. 406.

[26] The place of "Indolence" within the sequence of the odes has been that most open to conjecture. Bate in his biography (p. 527) and

its seed in the section of March 17-19 in the journal letter to the George Keatses in which the poet distinguishes between "an easy and an uneasy indolence" (II, 77) and goes on to write of a mood in which

> pleasure has no show of enticement and pain no unbearable frown. Neither Poetry, nor Ambition, nor Love have any alertness of countenance as they pass by me: they seem rather like three figures on a greek vase—a Man and two women—whom no one but myself could distinguish in their disguisement. This is the only happiness; and is a rare instance of advantage in the body overpowering the Mind.
>
> (II, 78-79)

Keats alludes to the ode itself on June 9: "You will judge of my 1819 temper when I tell you that the thing I have most enjoyed this year has been writing an ode to Indolence" (II, 116). In view of the achievements of the preceding months, the latter comment appears willfully eccentric.

Bush in his life (p. 148) and edition (p. 351) place it last. In their biographies both Gittings and Ward put it second and date it in the first week in May. Gittings's explanation, "There can be little doubt that *Indolence* was written on Tuesday 4 May, since it describes a May morning between showers. This was the only day of such weather in a three weeks' fine spell" (p. 313), is open to obvious objections. Ward (pp. 280, 432 n. 15) dates it at about the same time through a complex of echoes but ignores the way the ode echoes or is echoed by Keats's letter of June 9 to Sarah Jeffrey. All in all, as Bush infers, the detailed arguments of the earlier biographers, Colvin and Lowell, seem more compelling. Thus Miss Lowell dates it last (II, 257-60), following up the ode's allusion to the mood of "summer-indolence" (16) and Colvin's contention that the "letter of early June shows that phrases of ['Indolence'] were still hanging freshly in his memory and seems to imply that it was a thing then lately written." She also agrees with Colvin's theory that either "Keats let the March vision . . . ripen in his mind until he was ready to compose upon it . . . or else that, having fallen some time in May into a second mood of drowsiness and relaxation nearly repeating that of March, the same imagery for its expression arose naturally again in his mind" (p. 353).

Nevertheless, after the fierce polarities and tensions of the earlier odes, "Indolence" comes not so much as anticlimax as relief.

The relationship of the ode to the broader sweep of the progression is clarified when we see it as a reaffirmation of the primacy of the state of mind from which the odes as a group emerge and to which the last stanza of "Indolence" is contented to return us: not apathy but a rich and nourishing immersion in the rush of pure sensation and its flow of stirring shadows and "dim dreams."[27] In many ways the ode marks both a beginning and an end. It is both the feeblest and potentially the most ambitious of the sequence. Yet its failure, if we choose to consider it that, is more the result of deliberate disinclination than any inability of means. The situation the poem rehearses is by now familiar, discernible, even, as a "mask," a "plot":

> How is it, Shadows! that I knew ye not?
>   How came ye muffled in so hush a mask?
> Was it a silent deep-disguised plot
>   To steal away, and leave without a task
> My idle days?
>
>   (11-15)

As Bate has pointed out,[28] one gets the feeling, partly from the way the poem echoes images and phrases from the other odes, of having been over the same ground before. The three shadows emerge out of the inchoate background to parade three times before the poet, pausing the last time to bend on him their averted glances. Then, tantalizingly, they disappear just at the instant he recognizes them. In their flight they briefly recreate the impulse central to all the odes:

> [They] faded, and to follow them I burn'd
>   And ached for wings because I knew the three;
> The first was a fair Maid, and Love her name;

[27] Cf. Holloway's contention (p. 43) that the ode "is really a poem about the mood from which Keats's poetry of that time sprang."
[28] *John Keats*, p. 528 and n.

The second was Ambition, pale of cheek,
    And ever watchful with fatigued eye;
The last, whom I love more, the more of blame
    Is heap'd upon her, maiden most unmeek,—
        I knew to be my demon Poesy.

                                        (33-40)

The temptation is, of course, to pursue the three shapes, to give them identity, to bridge the gap between their abstractness and the world of human concern, to rediscover the old polarities for one more journey of imagination. The temptation now is in some ways even greater than before, for the figures personify the three commanding passions of the poet's life.

The motive for fresh poetical adventure, however, is no sooner rediscovered than rejected. There is the sense of a gambit declined, a game no longer worth playing. The poet refuses to be lured again from the world of his shadowy visions. Beneath the mood of langor lies a sense of repetitiousness and predictability. The relaxation and detachment of the ode, its deliberate withdrawal from the kind of situation that, over the past few weeks, had proved so compelling, may represent merely a natural reaction to the strain of intense imaginative involvement. Nevertheless one suspects Keats had come to see the limits of a kind of experience whose possibilities he had, in fact, virtually exhausted. The final stanza seems more than a rejection of the opportunities of the passing moment; it contains overtones of a farewell, if only a temporary one, to a mode of poetical composition:

So, ye three Ghosts, adieu! Ye cannot raise
    My head cool-bedded in the flowery grass;
For I would not be dieted with praise,
    A pet-lamb in a sentimental farce!
Fade softly from my eyes, and be once more
    In masque-like figures on the dreamy urn;
        Farewell! I yet have visions for the night,
And for the day faint visions there is store;

> Vanish, ye Phantoms! from my idle spright,
> Into the clouds, and never more return!
>
> (51-60)

One senses an end to a whole process of intense inquiry that had absorbed Keats over a space of weeks, an investigation of the kind of definition the imagination can achieve in its endeavor to engage the central mystery of life and art.

Both in mood and expression "Indolence" is closely related, as we have seen, to passages in the letters of mid-March and early June, dates that lie on either side of the period of his composition of the great odes of the spring. It celebrates that mood of brooding inwardness and receptivity so necessary to Keats for sustained poetical creation. However the larger context of the poem recalls, if only by implication, another Keats that the odes as a group imperfectly represent. It brings to mind the poet who, in March, wrote of having

> come to the resolution never to write for the sake of writing, or making a poem, but from running over with any little knowledge and experience which many years of reflection may perhaps give me—otherwise I will be dumb. . . . I will not spoil my love of gloom by writing an ode to darkness.
>
> (II, 43)

It recalls the poet who on June 9, in the same letter in which he mentions "Indolence," wrote of a need for fresh "discipline" and went on to add:

> I have been very idle lately, very averse to writing; both from the overpowering idea of our dead poets and from abatement of my love of fame. I hope I am a little more of a Philosopher than I was, consequently a little less of a versifying Pet-lamb.
>
> (II, 116)

One is brought back to the poet who habitually shrunk from any hint of poetry as emotional exhibitionism or self-dramatization, who dreaded above most things "a Mawkish Popularity" (I, 267). We remember the poet who, when George was making copies of his verses during some very cold weather the following winter, could refer to the "Ode to a Nightingale" as "like reading an account of the b[l]ack hole at Calcutta on an ice bergh" (II, 243).

This is not to imply that the odes are other than what they clearly are, a magnificent achievement, judged by any standard. Still one can strongly doubt that Keats would ever willingly have accorded them the absolute and self-sufficient place among his verse that is often given them today. If there are those who argue in reply, as is still fashionable, that he either misjudged or permitted himself to be misled as to the true nature of his poetic talent, they do so at their own risk. Taken together, the great odes of the spring reveal an extraordinary development in self-awareness; yet the intellectual realization they afford is less valuable in itself than for what it anticipates: the need for some closer accommodation between conscious intention and unconscious creativity, thought and sensation, the kind of assimilation he would surely have attempted had he lived and gone on writing. Viewed from one perspective, their very triumph, the triumph of their organicism, becomes the limitation in the meaning they possess for us, their quality of inconclusiveness. They represent the purest expression of Negative Capability in Keats's verse. Yet they also demonstrate the way in which that negative precept, when adopted as a cardinal tenet of poetic composition, culminates in a pervasive irony.

CHAPTER ELEVEN

COMIC IRONY: *LAMIA*

THE personal uneasiness and discontents of the summer of 1819—the pain of the self-imposed isolation from Fanny Brawne, the pressure of financial worries, the compelling need to make headway with some work of major consequence—are not of themselves sufficient to explain the particular acerbity and divisiveness of *Lamia*. The apparent playfulness of the poem's opening only lends greater edge to a bitterness verging at times on sarcasm, a disconcerting quality of self-mockery. We have the sense of a poet pondering a major dilemma not with the end of resolving it but rather delighting perversely in its difficulties and embarrassments. Virtually from its beginning the poem is permeated by a sense of comic fatality—the sharp, unpleasant ring of old Apollonius's undeluded laughter: " 'twas just as he foresaw" (ii.162). In a number of respects *Lamia* is a work written by a poet against his better self.

An unusual quality of prescience is, in fact, the most striking aspect of the poem. Like all of Keats's major efforts, it must be taken primarily as an experiment or exploration, but one, now, of as controlled and predictable a kind as possible. The poem further engages the whole deeper problem of ironic awareness but more openly (and less profoundly) by adopting a manifest irony of surface and style as its technique. Time and reflection had shown Keats the need, above all, for greater detachment and control—the virtues of a new and necessary defensiveness. In the past he had approached the end of major poems overly involved in the process of composition only to find himself unsure of his final objectives, conscious of new possibilities and complications. Now, however, it was possible to anticipate such a state of affairs. Even better, one could convert the familiar predicament to positive advantage by accepting it frankly from the outset, by adopting the dilemma as the nucleus for a drama of divided impulses and sympathies whose very point would lie in its insolubility. Through a sharpening of aim and focus, through a superior degree of self-consciousness, it was possible to turn irony back upon itself. In fact the possibilities for self-parody were darkly exhilarating, especially when, back in the Isle of Wight, he recalled the quite different hopes and assumptions with which he had begun *Endymion* amid the same surroundings two years earlier.

Toward this end, as well as to avoid past confusions, the subject matter and its range of implication were kept tightly in hand from the outset. The story of Lycius and Lamia in Burton's *Anatomy of Melancholy*, a work he had read with an unhealthy fascination, as he himself realized, was from the first strikingly relevant to his own predicament, and its ending—its mixture of destruction and inconclusiveness— was ideally suited to the kind of satirical effect he could foresee. The very vulnerability and lack of depth of Burton's characters constituted a positive asset. His own talent had never been for strong characterization, and for what he wanted to achieve it was sufficient to play the weakness of one figure off against another. The way to succeed with the poem was by remaining deliberately ambivalent and detached, refusing to take sides while encouraging others (critics for example) to do so at their own cost. What was important, as he thought about it later, was not whether the poem gave the reader "either pleasant or unpleasant sensation" but that it give him one or the other, that it "take hold of people in some way" (ii, 189). It would be, as he hoped, purely in dramatic terms the most successful of the works he had composed.

Other advantages of such a plan were apparent. There was

no need, as there had been in the past, to struggle for an original assimilation of a given legend, to force the work toward the realization of some difficult and partly hidden significance. It was possible to conceive of the project, even, like one of Dryden's fables, as primarily a work of adaptation, and to encourage this impression the appropriate passage from Burton was printed directly after the poem in the 1820 volume. In line with his broader aim, he was beginning more and more to relish the control and detachment of Dryden's style and sensibility, a poet whose wit and urbanity, inseparable from a subtlety of versification within the tight limits demanded by the closed couplet, he had been intensively studying as a model. Rather than plunging impulsively into a subject or a theme, letting it shape itself, as it were, from the inside out, there were real advantages in beginning with a deliberate irony of stance and manner, in keeping on top of one's material simply by staying outside it. If the *Hyperion*, which preyed steadily upon his mind, was incomplete, perhaps incompletable, because it attempted too ambitious an assimilation of conflicting viewpoints and ideas, there was still the possibility of dealing with the concerns that mattered most by means of comic satire and analysis. For the moment, at least, there were better ways of writing a successful narrative than resigning oneself to the necessity of "strain[ing] my ne[r]ves at some grand Poem" (II, 113).

It is important to see *Lamia* from the outset as a work evolving in reaction to the recurring problems of the poet's art, a poem of greater self-consciousness and better considered limits than virtually any he had yet composed. Such a judgment need hardly blind one to the genuine brilliance of the work or to the high degree of originality it displays. Nowhere are these qualities more evident than in the fine induction Keats composed by way of prelude to the major action. The opening lines provide a framework for what follows by alluding briefly to what we quickly recognize as a compelling preoccupation: the loss of unified awareness, ultimately the breakdown of consciousness into disparate areas like "illusion" and "reality," that has taken place through time and the usurpation of mythology by history.

> Upon a time, before the faery broods
> Drove Nymph and Satyr from the prosperous woods,
> Before King Oberon's bright diadem,
> Sceptre, and mantle, clasp'd with dewy gem,
> Frighted away the Dryads and the Fauns
> From rushes green, and brakes, and cowslip'd lawns.
>
> (i.1-6)

In fairy tale fashion the poem commences, like Shelley's *Witch of Atlas,*

> Before those cruel Twins, whom at one birth
>> Incestuous Change bore to her father Time,
> Error and Truth, had hunted from the Earth
>> All those bright natures which adorned its prime,
>
> (49-52)

in a world pre-existent to historical consciousness and its various categories and divisions. Yet at the same time it recognizes the laws of temporal and historical progression, just as it moves toward a sense of time and place that is steadily more definite.

The poem does not begin with the events described by Burton but with the so-called Hermes episode, a piece of narrative chiefly of Keats's own invention which, while it has alternately perplexed critics and been dismissed by them as a mere curtain raiser, is vital to our understanding of the whole drama.[1] The episode has many puzzling aspects, but

[1] Earl Wasserman has presented the most coherent argument to date for relating the Hermes episode to the action that follows by noting the part it plays in establishing that "contrast between union with essence under the conditions of the ideal world and union with essence in the world of mutability" that he sees at the heart of the drama (*The Finer Tone* [Baltimore, 1953], p. 158). See also Edward T. Norris, "Hermes and the Nymph in *Lamia*," *English Literary History*, II

from the first our main questions have to do with Lamia and the nature of her mysterious power—the power concentrated in her serpent folds so astonishingly released during her metamorphosis, her power to dream and send herself abroad, the power by which she controls the invisibility of the Nymph whom Hermes seeks. The very emblems that characterize her are bewilderingly varied and contradictory, from the coolness of her silver moons and stars to the heat of her more passionate and dazzling colors, from the gentleness and pathos of her complaint to the incongruous mixture of feminine seductiveness and serpent guile with which she utters it. The range of implication that surrounds her extends from the earthly to the visionary, from the sensual to the spiritual, from the deceptive to the revelatory. It is not until she breathes upon Hermes' eyes that the god, whatever his own powers, can see his Nymph; yet she requires the touch of his serpent rod in order to escape from the labyrinth of her prison. Whereas she opens Hermes' eyes to a new range of experience, she later casts her beguiling spell over Lycius.

The chief effect of the episode is to establish at the outset a distinct perspective for viewing Lamia's ambivalence. For one must not overlook the fact that, unlike Lycius, we see her first before her metamorphosis, in her serpent form, and in part, at least, through Hermes' eyes. Indeed the particular cynicism of the episode, within the larger fatality of the poem, lies in the fact that the god's success in using Lamia's power to fulfill his own desire directly sets the stage through her release and transformation for Lycius's subsequent disaster. For it is difficult to explain why Hermes succeeds while Lycius fails except through the kind of priority he enjoys within the poem. Often in the past critics have distinguished between the two purely on the basis of the god's divinity, as if it were some isolated phenomenon, as if

---

(1935), 322-26. De Selincourt and Bush have shown that Keats drew a number of hints for the episode from Sandys's Ovid. See de Selincourt, pp. 454-55, and the notes to Bush's edition, pp. 352-53.

Hermes' immortality were not, as the introduction to the poem testifies, only the most obvious manifestation of a more significant advantage.[2] True the god is more purposeful and aggressive than the relatively passive Lycius, though Keats pokes gentle fun at the signs of his amatory distress.[3] Yet his chief advantage lies not only in the fact that he sees Lamia first but that he sees her when the diverse values she suggests are in a special sense undifferentiated. Her serpent condition, that is to say, comprehends a potential power for sensuous or spiritual enjoyment, for revelation or deception, for truth or falsehood. Yet these qualities, as she embodies them, are, whatever subtle overtones of antithesis may play about her, not clearly separated or distinguishable. They subsist together, however uneasily, as aspects of a larger potentiality; they account for the striking mobility and fluctuation of her serpent appearance. Hermes is never confused or deceived by her, for he understands and accepts, if only instinctively, the instability of her nature, the range of possibility that surrounds her. He is not, moreover, attracted to her for her own sake but only insofar as she can provide the means for fulfilling his own passionate aspirations; and the fact that the perfection and virginity of his Nymph are in some way dependent on her baser serpent nature in no way distracts him, though it may appear disconcerting to us. The bargain the two strike is artfully conducted on both sides, a meeting of minds, or rather the uninhibited cooperation and cross-fertilization of what have become for us quite different levels of perception and resourcefulness. Hermes is con-

[2] Such is a limitation of Wasserman's reading. See *The Finer Tone*, pp. 161-62.

[3] The poem's comic elements, especially in the first part, which older critics have often ignored, have been usefully illuminated by Georgia S. Dunbar in "The Significance of the Humor in 'Lamia,'" *Keats-Shelley Journal*, VIII (1959), 17-26. Her essay is a valuable corrective to overserious readings. She also discusses the way in which "the gentle, good-natured, happy teasing of Part I . . . becomes the angry, bitter sarcasm of Part II" (p. 24), although she is inclined to see too set a division between them.

cerned simply to attain the Nymph, and if he wins her only in dreams, the point, for him at least, has no significance:

> It was no dream; or say a dream it was,
> Real are the dreams of Gods, and smoothly pass
> Their pleasures in a long immortal dream.
>
> (i.126-28)

Clearly we are dealing in the case of Hermes with a realm of awareness where our habitual distinctions between reality and dream, consciousness and unconsciousness, truth and error, are simply irrelevant, while the narrator's tone of affected nonchalance contains more than a trace of bitterness. Hermes draws on Lamia's power to substantiate his vision of sufficient joy and truth while permitting her, by way of compensation, the freedom to assert herself more ambitiously, to exercise her power independently and, later, more dubiously on Lycius.

One cannot study the relationships between the actors in the Hermes episode without becoming aware both of their psychological complexity and of their close connection with Keats's larger concern with the nature of the poetic process—more specially, with the changes that have come about in its effect through time and the evolving character of human awareness. Virtually every critic has agreed that later in the poem Lycius comes to represent the poet as well as the lover. Moreover the famous passage in which Keats juxtaposes the symbol of imaginative transformation, the "awful rainbow" of the past, against its present dissolution at the killing touch of "cold philosophy" (ii.221-38) provides certain authority for interpreting the anguish of his situation —his divided allegiance to both Lamia and his harsh old tutor, Apollonius—as a comment on the predicament of the contemporary poet that Hazlitt, among others, had analyzed historically.[4] Indeed from the outset of the poem it seems

---

[4] As has often been pointed out, in declaring that "Philosophy will clip an Angel's wings" (ii.234) Keats was probably echoing Hazlitt that "the progress of knowledge and refinement has a tendency to circum-

clear that the "rainbow-sided" Lamia, in all her shifting lights and colors, her capacity for transformation, her ability first to conceal and then reveal, represents a power closely akin to the imagination. The drift of one set of implications of the episode seems unmistakable. As we have seen, Hermes derives his primary advantage from his mythological nature, from a state of awareness in which the divisions that haunt the modern consciousness do not exist. Like the earliest poets, the prototype of Homer or Ovid, he ventures upon the imagination in its full range of potentiality, when the ambivalences that characterize it for a later time are submerged or, at most, present only latently. He may, to be sure, require its intensifying energies but only to realize his own dream of beauty and truth. In drawing on its power, however, he also gives it a kind of necessary activation and, in performing his own part of the bargain, grants Lamia an autonomous existence, deceptively purged of her uglier but more material elements. One might say the result of Hermes' conquest is to release into the world the disembodied essence of romance, a power of mere enchantment by which Lycius, the later, weaker, characteristically "Romantic" poet, is seduced and, partly through the indecisiveness of his own nature, destroyed. There seems to be a fatal principle of compensation at work. On one level the drama of the episode depicts the transformation and attenuation of imaginative power from its first discovery to its modern degeneration to mere charm or spell.

To concentrate narrowly on the theme of the poetic imagination in *Lamia* is, of course, to run the risk of disregarding other aspects of the drama. No one would deny, for example,

---

scribe the limits of the imagination, and to clip the wings of poetry" ("On Poetry in General," *Lectures on the English Poets*, ed. Howe, v, 9). The theme is a common one in Hazlitt's writing (see, e.g., "Why the Arts Are Not Progressive?—A Fragment," in *The Round Table*, ed. Howe, iv, 160-64) and in the thought of the time. The following year (1820) Thomas Love Peacock published "The Four Ages of Poetry."

that the poem strongly reflects Keats's love for Fanny Brawne[5] or that the combination of apprehensiveness and fascination with which he found himself drawn to her is powerfully mirrored in his treatment of the central relationships. Yet here, as always in Keats, the various levels of thematic significance do not run counter to but illuminate and reinforce each other. In *Lamia*, as (in a more diffuse way) in *Endymion*, the poetic and sexual themes, both broadly imaginative in their concern, are inseparable. One can, for example, interpret Hermes' serpent rod, the means by which Lamia gains her release, as the poet-magician's control over the powers of the unconscious without gainsaying those who may want to read it, more obviously, as a phallic symbol. Throughout the poem such different kinds of interpretation are complementary rather than exclusive. Nothing better illustrates this fact than part of the comment Keats penned into the margin of his copy of Burton's *Anatomy* in disgust at the worldly mingling of "goatish winnyish lustful love with the abstract adoration of the deity." "Has Plato separated these loves?" he wrote. "Ha! I see how they endeavor to divide— but there appears to be a horrid relationship."[6] The comment undoubtedly sheds light on the divided nature of his attraction for Fanny Brawne. It indicates that the "two distinct tempers of mind" he had once sought clearly to distinguish—"the worldly, theatrical and pantomimical; and the unearthly, spiritual and etherial" (1, 395), the first ap-

---

[5] Bush has called Keats's letters to Fanny "the best commentary on the poem" (*Mythology and the Romantic Tradition in English Poetry* [Cambridge, Mass., 1937], p. 112). His discussion (see also his later *John Keats: His Life and Writings*, pp. 155-63) points out the poem's "central contradictions" and the limitations of any single approach. A similar warning echoes throughout Bernice Slote's long, suggestive discussion of *Lamia* in *Keats and the Dramatic Principle* (Lincoln, Nebr., 1958), pp. 138-92, which minimizes the poem's psychological complexities in order to deal with its affinities with Keats's dramatic interests.

[6] *The Poetical Works and Other Writings of John Keats*, ed. M. B. Forman (the Hampstead Edition), v, 309.

propriate to a Charmian or Cleopatra, the second to his sister-in-law, Georgiana—were in fact both perplexingly united in his love for Fanny. However the annotation in his copy of Burton takes us to the heart of the broader imaginative conflict of the poem and the root of Lamia's ambivalence, a quality that the self-confident Hermes is able to ignore or take for granted but that proves fatal to the poet-scholar Lycius, caught between "phantasy" and "reason" in a "twilight of Platonic shades" (i.235-36). Throughout the poem the glance of dazzled wonder and the voyeur's piercing stare are increasingly at odds. Nevertheless the dawning rapture of the lovers' union, the moment when the god first turns upon the "printless verdure" to discover the Nymph before him, perpetuates through its intermingling of chastity and voluptuousness what had for long been a major ideal of Keats's art and (witness "Bright Star") had taken on new personal significance through his relationship with Fanny Brawne. That he now chose to approach such ideals through the light intrigues of a mythological escapade, to subject them to a partly playful, partly caustic irony, is no evidence that he took them any less seriously than before. The new detachment bears witness, rather, to a recognition that former goals—"the yearning Passion I have for the beautiful, connected and made one with the ambition of my intellect" (1, 404)—were no longer achievable in the way he had once imagined them for reasons the poem goes on to demonstrate.

The pivotal importance within the poem of Keats's whole involvement with the creative process emerges if we pause to look more closely at what is in many ways the center of the Hermes episode—Lamia's metamorphosis. Her dazzling transformation from serpent to fairy has always fascinated but also puzzled critics. A bit of sensationalism, the description was one that struck Richard Woodhouse, when Keats read the work through for him, as "quite Ovidian, but better" (II, 164). Yet it has never been noted how the transformation Lamia undergoes when touched by Hermes' rod draws its significance, and much of its tone of subtle mockery, from its correspondence to some of Keats's favorite analogies for poetic creation. As she writhes, convulsed by heat and flame, emitting, rather ludicrously, sharp sparks of phosphorus, her brighter colors are quickly inundated:

> Her mouth foam'd, and the grass, therewith besprent,
> Wither'd at dew so sweet and virulent;
> Her eyes in torture fix'd, and anguish drear,
> Hot, glaz'd, and wide, with lid-lashes all sear,
> Flash'd phosphor and sharp sparks, without one cooling
> tear.
> The colours all inflam'd throughout her train,
> She writh'd about, convuls'd with scarlet pain:
> A deep volcanian yellow took the place
> Of all her milder-mooned body's grace.
>
> (i.148-56)

The description resembles nothing so much as the effects of a violent chemical reaction. Both in what it depicts and what it implies, the passage is marked by a brilliant, mocking irony. A sort of chemical analysis or separation of elements takes place. Lamia's bright emblems and colors are overrun and dwindle to a little pile of charred remains: "Nothing but pain and ugliness were left" (i.164). As we soon discover, however, she has only dissolved to ascend from the throes of her ordeal transformed. A moment later we hear her voice ringing softly through the trees as, "Borne aloft" like a vaporous distillation, she flies off, changed to a radiant but almost incorporeal lady, to lie in wait for Lycius:

> Still shone her crown; that vanish'd, also she
> Melted and disappear'd as suddenly;
> And in the air, her new voice luting soft,
> Cried, "Lycius! gentle Lycius!"
>
> (i.165-68)

Feigning aversion to his sudden love, she complains how "finer spirits cannot breathe below / In human climes, and live" and longs for "purer air" to soothe her "essence" (i.280-

83). While promising a secret power to "unperplex bliss from its neighbour pain," she nevertheless denies that the "subtle fluid" in her veins is different from the blood of human hearts (i.192, 307).

Viewed in one way, the episode is a brilliantly comic if somewhat bitter parody of Keats's whole early sense of the nature of poetic creation. It unmistakably suggests his discovery of the ironic possibilities latent in those "compositions and decompositions which take place" before "that trembling delicate and snail-horn perception of Beauty" (1, 265) and that intensity that makes "all disagreeables evaporate, from their being in close relationship with Beauty & Truth" (1, 192). To compare the fiery pangs of Lamia's etherealization with the "fierce convulse" and "wild commotions" of Apollo's dying into life at the end of *Hyperion* is to understand how a serious conception had become a subject for deliberate travesty. Indeed the Hermes episode and its aftermath can be taken in no small measure as a caricature of the "Pleasure Thermometer," of the whole notion of "intensity" that Keats had long pondered as an ideal leading to the achievement of happiness and truth. However fascinating, Lamia's beauty is too fragile and attenuated to survive for long in contact with the world—at least the world into which Lycius is bent on leading her, the world as Apollonius represents it.

II

Lamia's metamorphosis and the central logic of its governing metaphor are fundamental and determining factors in the larger rhythm of the poem. For if Lamia is transformed, however dubiously, at the outset, she is methodically and somewhat pathetically destroyed at the conclusion. By helping Hermes she gains the impetus necessary to free herself from the baser and anomalous elements that compose her nature. Her fiery distillation explains the fairy brilliance and intoxicating charm Lycius at first finds so irresistible. Yet it also leaves her weak and susceptible to the power of Apollonius's analytic gaze. When his withering glance looks through her and she vanishes with a scream, she does not seem to die so much as to evaporate. Both the mystery and potential tragedy of her sudden disintegration are comically subverted by the realization, if only implicit, of the virtually scientific logic that dominates the phases of her various transformations. Indeed Lycius's old tutor best fits the epithet most frequently applied to him if we take the word "philosopher" in its older sense of "natural philosopher" or man of science. He is, of course, the unlyric Apollo, the power of science and healing isolated from any saving touch of humor, compassion, or genuine benevolence, a cross between Apollo and Pollonius. As he makes his way toward Lamia's palace and the bridal chambers, chuckling to himself like someone who has just solved "some knotty problem" (ii.160), we are reminded of the self-satisfied researcher who has just discovered the solution to some puzzling phenomenon, ready now to elucidate the whole mystery before the common multitude with, like Linus Pauling, a flair for the dramatics of the occasion.

While the key to the significance of Lamia's transformation and rebirth is Keats's favorite image of the thermometer —the instrument essential to chemists for determining those intensities at which specific reactions occur—the image fundamental to her dissolution, as the major interpolation of the poem makes clear, is equally scientific—the prism. Indeed the imageries of optics and caloric are subtly interwoven throughout the whole of the poem. In his sensitive and acute discussion of *Lamia*, David Perkins has observed how much the work is dominated by the imagery of vision.[7] Lamia grants the Nymph invisibility and opens Hermes' eyes. From the moment when he first looks back, enraptured, when she calls him, Lycius is either "blinded" (i.347) or held captive by the eyes "Where he was mirror'd small in paradise" (ii.47). Apollonius's "quick eyes" (i.374) are repeatedly alluded to, and his glance, "Keen, cruel, perceant, stinging"

[7] *The Quest for Permanence* (Cambridge, Mass., 1959), pp. 263-76.

(ii.301), goes through Lamia utterly. Yet we partly miss the point of such consistency of metaphor unless we understand its intimate connection with a pattern of a different but complementary kind. Hermes burns with a "celestial heat" (i.22-23) and fosters the Nymph's "chilled hand," while she opens like a flower at the touch of his "warmth" (i.140-41). Lamia writhes in heat and flame; her transformation renders her ethereal but also critically weak, as Lycius intuitively senses when, at their first encounter, he complains that

> if thou shouldst *fade*
> Thy memory will waste me to a *shade*:—
> For pity do not *melt*!
>
> (i.269-71)

When the two lovers, hand in hand, hurriedly pass by old Apollonius on the street, Lamia's palm seems to "dissolve in dew" (i.370). Later the philosopher gloats when the problem of her identity begins "to thaw, / And solve and melt" beneath his scrutiny (ii.161-62). At no time do the two trains of images run more closely parallel than at the climax of the poem, the moment when Apollonius brings to light the serpent:

> The bald-head philosopher
> Had fix'd his eye, without a twinkle or stir
> Full on the alarmed beauty of the bride,
> Brow-beating her fair form, and troubling her sweet pride.
> Lycius then press'd her hand, with devout touch,
> As pale it lay upon the rosy couch:
> 'Twas icy, and the cold ran through his veins;
> Then sudden it grew hot, and all the pains
> Of an unnatural heat shot to his heart.
>
> (ii.245-53)

While "cold philosophy" unweaves the poetic rainbow, it also makes "The tender-person'd Lamia *melt* into a *shade*" (ii.238).

The thermometer and the prism, together with the imag-

eries of temperature and vision deriving from them, frame the
beginning and the end of *Lamia,* just as in many ways they
span the beginning and the end of the poet's career. At the
time of *Endymion* he could acclaim his discovery of the
"Pleasure Thermometer" as "of the greatest Service to me"
for "set[ting] before me at once the gradations of Happiness"
(1, 218)—an image that comprehended the creative possibilities latent in his whole commitment to the ideal of "intensity." In *Lamia,* however, the instruments of science play a
more analytic, eventually destructive, role, while Keats's insight into the nature of the poetic process is not only more
penetrating but, to say the least, ambivalent. Everyone knows
the story of Haydon's "immortal dinner" when Keats and
Lamb agreed that Newton "had destroyed all the poetry of
the rainbow by reducing it to its prismatic colours." There-
upon they drank "Newton's health, and confusion to mathe-
matics,"[8] and the equivocal nature of the toast is reflected
in the divided sympathies of Keats's poem. The account of
how Newton had demonstrated that when a single ray of
light passes through a triangular prism it divides into the
various constituent colors—red, orange, yellow, green, blue,
indigo, and violet—in accordance with a fixed mathematical
ratio was by Keats's day legendary. Doubtless it was just these
facts the poet had in mind when he wrote:

> There was an awful rainbow once in heaven:
> We know her woof, her texture; she is given
> In the dull catalogue of common things.
>
> (ii.231-33)

Yet Keats must also have known how one of his boyhood
heroes, Sir William Herschel, had carried Newton's discovery
one step further by showing that the various colored rays of
light differed in their power of rendering objects visible and
how, by placing thermometers in different parts of the spec-
trum, it could be proved that they differed in their caloric

[8] *The Autobiography and Memoirs of Benjamin Haydon,* ed. Aldous
Huxley (London, 1926), 1, 269.

intensities.[9] The story of Herschel's demonstration that the greatest heat was actually produced in an area beyond the red rays where there was no visible light was virtually as well known as Newton's discovery. Both the thermometer and the prism provided complementary means for measuring the intensity of those closely related concepts, heat and light. In *Lamia* the metaphor operates with a thoroughly ironic precision: what it creates it as readily destroys.

The consistency with which throughout his career Keats adopts analogies from contemporary science to express his own sense of the imagination and its creative processes is indeed striking. Yet the continuity of metaphor should not blind one to the radically shifting emphasis it comes in time to serve, especially in such a work as *Lamia*. In *Endymion* the scientific metaphor, so fundamental to the argument of the first book and, indeed, to the anticipated thrust of the poem as a whole, is largely affirmative and progressive in what it suggests. Even as late as May 1818, when Keats was looking forward to returning to his medical books, he could conceive of a useful and productive alliance between the arts and sciences. "Every department of knowledge we see excellent," he wrote, "and calculated towards a great whole" (I, 277). In *Lamia*, however, the fundamental scientific analogies serve the uses of the comic spirit, and, even more, of a pervasive skepticism and controlling irony. Lamia, taken as the essence of imaginative perception, is first distilled and then evaporated with all the brilliance of an experiment in chemistry but with little of the happy exuberance that characterizes Shelley's "The Cloud." Her appearance, indeed her value and significance, are relative to the changing circumstances of the poem, to the different viewpoints of the characters that surround her. For while the poem derives, from beginning to end, a balance and symmetry from the

---

[9] Sir Humphry Davy discusses Herschel's experiment immediately following his description of Newton's discovery in his *Elements of Chemical Philosophy*, *The Collected Works of Sir Humphry Davy*, ed. John Davy (London, 1839-1840), IV, 146.

logic of the thermometer-prism metaphor, it moves at the same time between the quite different historical poles represented by Hermes and Apollonius. Indeed the poem achieves its principal effect through the way in which it develops the poet's ambivalence toward science within a pessimistic view of history and the progress of human culture that is in sharp contrast to major aspects of *Hyperion*. Within Hermes' world, the lost domain of mythic unity and timelessness, Lamia's power of imaginative revelation possesses genuine effect. In Apollonius's world of science and analysis, she is no longer able to survive. The weak cunning of her "sciential brain," her power to "Intrigue with the specious chaos, and dispart / Its most ambiguous atoms with sure art" (i.191, 195-96), is child's play compared with the exact calculations of the molecular chemist or atomic physicist.

The pessimism of the poem's historical perspective, the steady polarization it establishes between science and the imagination, controls the movement of a drama where the play of character is quite secondary to a basic irony of situation. As all recent criticism genial to the poem has emphasized, there is little to choose between the three major characters: their weaknesses excel their strengths, and each emerges, in varying degrees, as misguided, ineffective, or disagreeable. Following the brief introduction, Lamia appears as the baneful serpent in disguise, Lycius's guileful seductress. In Part Two, however, Keats borrows a standard device of the Elizabethan history play, and tilts the balance of sympathy in her favor when she comes to appear persecuted and pathetic. One can readily blame Lycius for his unwillingness to remain content with a good thing; but his desire to marry Lamia publicly, to reconcile his love with broader and more active interests, is understandable, even if he has no conception of the anomalies the undertaking will involve. However perspicacious, Apollonius is repugnant and uncharitable, and the fact that he survives his pupil's death, presumably to moralize on the occasion, is only one more irony within the larger movement of the poem. The characters are throughout merely the creatures of the poem's framework and the changing stresses it brings to bear upon them, and they react predictably. The poet's invitation to the reader to join him in choosing and awarding wreaths to the three principals is partly tongue-in-cheek and partly a deliberate trap. For any reasoned balance of sympathies, not to mention taking sides, is out of the question. The characters and the attitudes they represent are all hopelessly inadequate. The dilemma they together represent is one which, within the terms the poem itself sets out, can have no conceivable resolution. The predicament, moreover, is clearly one of major relevance to Keats's whole approach to art and to experience. Of all his longer works, *Lamia* is the most patently and self-consciously—at times bitterly—ironic.

CHAPTER TWELVE

TRAGIC IRONY: *THE FALL OF HYPERION*

NEITHER the lyric questioning of the odes nor the dramatic fire of *Lamia* could long distract Keats from the task of returning to the uncompleted *Hyperion*. Indeed the kinds of success they represented only made a renewed attempt at the larger effort more imperative. Ever since the time of his schoolboy fascination with Virgil and Spenser, he had never ceased to look upon the long poem as the major criterion of poetic achievement—the mark of the great Elizabethans, those "Emperors of vast Provinces" (I, 224), and even, in his own time, of Wordsworth, who could look upon his shorter poems as "little cells, oratories, and sepulchral recesses"[1] embellishing the outlines of a grander structure. "Long," as he could now increasingly appreciate, meant something more than just "extended," nor was volume by itself the crucial factor. More important was the kind of resolution necessary to speak the way he knew the great poet always had—declaratively and affirmatively. It was this larger coherence—virtually a kind of world view—that he had sought to develop in his discrimination between the older Titans and the younger race of gods, in his treatment of the theme of progress and conception of a higher ideal of beauty, and most of all in his picture of the birth-throes of Apollo. Now in the late summer of 1819, and with a sense of time running out, he was deliberately steeling himself for a fresh assault, writing in his letters of a need for "Pride and egotism" (II, 144)—an odd phrase for the poet of Negative Capability and one misinterpreted by some of his friends who, unlike Wood-

---

[1] "Preface" to the 1814 edition of *The Excursion*.

house, failed to see its wealth of Miltonic significance (II, 150). His keen sense of his own particular shortcomings emerges again later in the special defensiveness of his some-what less than gracious reply to Shelley's generous invitation from Italy. "There is only one part of it," he wrote of *The Cenci*, which Shelley had had sent to him, "I am judge of; the Poetry, and dramatic effect,which by many spirits now a days is considered the mammon. A modern work it is said must have a purpose, which may be the God—*an artist* must serve Mammon." Behind the remark and its abrupt disclaimer lay a deeper awareness that the modern work must, ideally, serve both. Whatever his dislike for Shelley's more systematic and dogmatical approach to the task of composition, there could be no doubt that too often in the past his own mind had been "like a pack of scattered cards" (II, 322-23; Keats's italics).

In returning to the fragment of the poem, abandoned since early in the spring, and having to decide whether to make an entirely fresh start, to revise, or to attempt some compromise, the old, familiar problem emerged anew. It was not just that the role of Mnemosyne and Apollo's "dying into life" were, for reasons now more obvious than ever, dramatically inadequate to express the truth of his concep-tion. The deeper difficulty was that his conception itself had radically altered, in fact had been changing during the very time he had been at work on the poem. It was the dilemma he had faced at the end of *Endymion* all over again. Na-turally the problem involved a host of important subsidiary concerns—style, approach, structure. With respect to these, his dependence on Milton could not help but strike him now as more than ever forced and artificial. (How often in the past had he relied on the assimilation of another poetic sensibility—Milton's in *Hyperion*, Spenser's in *St. Agnes*, Dryden's in *Lamia*—as a means of dispatching formal prob-lems in order to make his own headway.) Merely in terms of structure, the parallel between the action of his first two books, the awakening of the overthrown Saturn and the council of the Titans, and the opening books of *Paradise Lost* was uncomfortably close. Even worse, however, was the way in which the expectations aroused by such similarities quickly collapsed. Whereas Milton, after the ascent to heaven in Book Three, was ready to prepare the background for his major action, the Creation and the Fall of man and its consequences, Keats could only lead his hero falteringly from the wings and propel him forward to his unaccountable, almost orgasmic, transfiguration. Such incongruities were manifest; nevertheless, the possibility of devising some alternative plan of development was at best uncertain. In recent months his trust in the reality of human progress had definitely wavered, while his conviction in the value of the poetic talent—the justification of which, through his treatment of Apollo, was a major premise of the whole undertaking—remained, but in a far more qualified and ambivalent way. If he were to succeed in achieving the kind of affirmative resolution to such questions that he wanted, he would have to deal with complexities in a way the earlier version did not permit. Several points in particular stood out. If he sought to retain the epic sections, he would have to get outside them in order to give them a perspective and significance they did not of themselves possess. At the same time he would have to involve himself more directly in the poem than he had, if only because the kind of resolution he was working towards was more subjective and personal than any he had heretofore anticipated. The truth was that for some time his conception of the work had been shading from epic into vision.

Hence the expedient, again a far from perfectly satisfactory one, of looking elsewhere for guidance—this time to Dante, whom he had been learning more from ever since the preceding summer and the walking tour with Brown when he had taken away with him all three volumes of the *Divine Comedy* in Cary's translation. Indeed the new induction Keats composed for *The Fall of Hyperion* reveals how useful Dante, and in particular the *Purgatorio*, was in helping Keats to break free from rote dependence on the action of *Paradise Lost* and at the same time to create a framework that gives genuine relevance to the old epic narrative. In the induction Apollo's (now the dreamer's) rebirth is expanded as a spiritual allegory, while his vision of Saturn and Thea comes as a logical fulfillment of the growth and new understanding he achieves through his travail. Mnemosyne (now Moneta) is no longer a lifeless abstraction but the dreamer's guide, admonisher, and judge, the supreme embodiment of the poetic conscience and humanitarian concern. The general shift from epic to allegory is marked by a variety of stylistic and structural changes that permitted Keats to eliminate or restrain a number of the more obvious Miltonic devices and mannerisms that fill the earlier version. Unlike *Hyperion*, *The Fall* is divided into cantos and narrated in the first person. Throughout the induction the dreamer, like Dante in the *Purgatorio*, is required to make repeated ascents by means of steps, while in her role Moneta resembles Virgil and later Beatrice. At the climax of the fragment Moneta parts her veils just as, in canto thirty-one of the *Purgatorio*, Beatrice reveals herself to Dante. These and other changes have been sufficient to persuade many critics that in *The Fall* Keats was rejecting Milton in order to embrace Dante as his new master.[2]

That supposition is, however, at best a half-truth. No one would want to disagree with Kenneth Muir that *The Fall of Hyperion* is "very much a purgatorial poem"[3] or that the new conception of its induction owes an important debt to Dante's quest for higher vision. Yet it is significant that Keats's letters during the very time when he was beginning to resume work on *The Fall* show that he was rereading

[2] John Livingston Lowes's announcement that "the structural background of the 'Vision,' to state it summarily, is the 'Purgatorio'" (*Times Literary Supplement*, January 11, 1936, p. 35) has remained largely unchallenged.

[3] "The Meaning of *Hyperion*," *John Keats: A Reassessment*, ed. Kenneth Muir (Liverpool, 1958), p. 111.

Milton intensively and, if possible, with greater admiration than ever. On August 14 he wrote: "I am convinced more and more every day that (excepting the human friend Philosopher) a fine writer is the most genuine Being in the World—Shakspeare and the paradise Lost every day become greater wonders to me" (II, 139). And ten days later: "I am convinced more and more day by day that fine writing is next to fine doing the top thing in the world; the Paradise Lost becomes a greater wonder" (II, 146). The importance of these remarks has generally been overlooked. Unquestionably Dante was vitally useful in the task of restructuring the poem within a new parabolic design. Nevertheless the fact remains that the key to the allegory of the revised fragment lies in a comprehensive and original assimilation of *Paradise Lost* that far transcends the manifest similarities of structure and style that dominate the earlier version. The chief evidence for this assertion lies within the poem itself. Nevertheless significant clues are not lacking in the letters.

In order to grasp the basis of Keats's fresh reformulation of Milton's theme and treatment in the light of his own concerns, it is necessary to return again to a familiar but important section, that of March 19, in the long journal letter to George and Georgiana of the late winter and early spring. "I am however young," he wrote,

> writing at random—straining at particles of light in the midst of a great darkness—without knowing the bearing of any one assertion of any one opinion. *Yet may I not in this be free from sin?* May there not be superior beings amused with any graceful, though instinctive attitude my mind m[a]y fall into, as I am entertained with the alertness of a Stoat or the anxiety of a Deer? Though a quarrel in the streets is a thing to be hated, the energies displayed in it are fine.
>
> (II, 80; my italics)

Brief and unobtrusive though it is, the italicized sentence raises a question that contains the seed of what was to de-

velop, some months later, into the sustained allegory of the
induction to *The Fall*. It reveals the poet already feeling his
way toward a whole new context for considering certain
aspects of imaginative experience that had come to seem
increasingly disconcerting. Only a few days earlier, on March
13, Keats had in the same letter copied out a long extract
from Hazlitt's brilliant and acid *Letter to Gifford*, a mixture
of personal vituperation and serious argument, that posed
some of those problems vigorously and in detail. "I affi[r]m,
Sir," Hazlitt declared, as Keats transcribed him,

> that Poetry, that the imagination, generally speaking,
> delights in power, in strong excitement, as well as in truth,
> in good, in right, whereas pure reason and the moral sense
> approve only of the true and good. I proceed to show
> that this general love or tendency to immediate excite-
> ment or theatrical effect, no matter how produced, gives
> a Bias to the imagination often [in]consistent with the
> greatest good, that in Poetry it triumphs over Principle,
> and bribes the passions to make a sacrifice of common
> humanity. You say that it does not, that there is no such
> *original Sin in Poetry*, that it makes no such sacrifice or
> unworthy compromise between poetical effect and the
> still small voice of reason—And how do you prove that
> there is no such principle giving a bias to the imagination,
> and a false colouring to poetry?
>
> (II, 74-75; my italics)

There is no need to continue further with the passage as
Keats proceeded to copy it. The point is that Hazlitt's argument, especially his idea of an "original Sin" peculiar to
poetry and the imagination, suddenly coalesced, in a highly
suggestive way, both with the major concerns of his poem
and with his whole approach to *Paradise Lost*. Time, of
course, was necessary for the insight to mature, just as certain
shifts of emphasis were inevitable. While Keats's question of
March 19, "Yet may I not in this be free from sin?" implies
the simple notion of immunity, what he was to develop in

The Fall was an allegory of poetic sin and expiation through
intensity of suffering. There were, after all, a variety of contexts in which Hazlitt's remarks might be taken up. What
was important, however, was that when, some months later,
Keats came back to *Hyperion* and his whole preoccupation
with Milton, the clue for continuing his poem was to come
through a new and deeply personal interpretation of *Paradise
Lost*. By this time Milton's grand conception of the Fall and
Redemption of man had come to assume a profound relevance to his own awareness of both the poet's plight and
dignity, the key for ordering his tragic sense of life and
human destiny into a meaningful allegory of the poetic soul.

II

   As prelude to the dreamer's coming vision, the brief paragraph of eighteen lines with which the induction to *The
Fall* begins clearly establishes Keats's major theme—the
dream itself, taken, as from the first he always had, as the
fundamental source of poetry:

> Fanatics have their dreams, wherewith they weave
> A paradise for a sect; the savage, too,
> From forth the loftiest fashion of his sleep
> Guesses at Heaven; pity these have not
> Trac'd upon vellum or wild Indian leaf
> The shadows of melodious utterance.
> But bare of laurel they live, dream, and die;
> For Poesy alone can tell her dreams,—
> With the fine spell of words alone can save
> Imagination from the sable chain
> And dumb enchantment. Who alive can say,
> "Thou art no Poet—may'st not tell thy dreams"?
> Since every man whose soul is not a clod
> Hath visions, and would speak, if he had lov'd
> And been well nurtured in his mother tongue.
> Whether the dream now purpos'd to rehearse

Be poet's or fanatic's will be known
When this warm scribe, my hand, is in the grave.

(i.1-18)

The passage advances two different and even partly contradictory ideas. The first, dwelt on by Wordsworth in *The
Excursion*,[4] concerns the *universality* of poetry. All men, from
the fanatic to the savage, are dreamers and hence potentially
poets. In one sense the poet is only he who can record his
dreams, who writes them down as verse; for "Who alive can
say, / 'Thou are no Poet—may'st not tell thy dreams'?" At
the same time, however, the passage strongly suggests a necessary criterion of value, a *qualitative* distinction between the
poet as mere dreamer and the dreamer as true poet. "In
dreams," Keats says with Yeats, "begins responsibility." The
fanatic, who speaks only to a sect, may discourse or write in
numbers but cannot claim the title of a poet, for poetry, in
this further sense, requires a meaning relevant to all mankind, a deeper universality. Nor can Keats himself be certain
whether the dream he is about to recite "Be poet's or fanatic's." The introductory paragraph thus sets forth a necessary but complex relationship between the dream and poetry.
Poetry commences with the dream, yet, in its further, ideal
sense, transcends it. Indeed it is just the mystery of this
relationship and the obvious questions that grow from it
that is the primary concern of Keats's allegory.

The description of the garden where the dreamer finds
himself is remarkable for its pastoral simplicity and quiet
beauty; but it possesses also a special range of significance.
Both in atmosphere and detail it recalls the Garden of Paradise and, more specifically, Milton's description of Eden in
Paradise Lost. The "trees of every clime," the "Palm, myrtle,
oak, and sycamore, and beech" (i.19-20), recall those cata-
logued in Milton's Garden; while the arbor, wreathed in
scents and flowers, brings to mind the bower of Adam and
Eve, with "flourets deck't and fragrant smells." The feast of

---

[4] See the notes to Bush's edition.

summer fruits, or what remains of it, suggests the meal Eve prepares to entertain the angel Raphael. Even should the reader miss these echoes, the references to Proserpine, recalling Milton's famous simile, and more obviously to the "angel" and "our Mother Eve" (i.31) cannot readily be overlooked.

The use of such allusions creates a special context for interpreting the events the dreamer proceeds to relate—his eating of the fruits, his thirst and drinking of the mysterious vessel of juice, his deathlike swoon and sudden starting up "As if with wings" (i.59). On one level the meal constitutes, as Brian Wicker has perceptively written, "a substantial and sacramental union" between the poet and his present condition of awareness and the lost state of human innocence.[5] For it is significant that the feast is only the remainder of a meal and that it contains, as the dreamer tells us, remnants of "pure kinds I could not know" (i.34). Through partaking of the fragments, he achieves communion with a former innocence and, specifically through Eve, with the universality of human experience that has descended from its loss.

The implications of the feast, however, are carried further in the effects it induces. The remnants the dreamer eats bring on a powerful yearning for the vessel and its juice:

> And appetite,
> More yearning than on earth I ever felt,
> Growing within, I ate deliciously;
> And, after not long, thirsted; for thereby
> Stood a cool vessel of transparent juice.
>
> (i.38-42)

---

[5] "The Disputed Lines in *The Fall of Hyperion*," *Essays in Criticism*, VII (1957), 40. I am indebted to Wicker's essay, which nevertheless presents a very different view from my own. For helpful clues as to Keats's reinterpretation of *Paradise Lost*, I am indebted to John D. Rosenberg's suggestive discussion of Keats's relationship to Milton in "Keats and Milton: The Paradox of Rejection," *Keats-Shelley Journal*, VI (1957), 87-95.

Like the glass of nepenthe in Shelley's *Triumph of Life*, a fragment that bears comparison in many ways with Keats's, the detail and its interpretation are of vital consequence. For the draught the dreamer drinks, pledging as he does so all the living and the dead, is the "parent" of his theme. Clearly Keats was partly returning to the ending of the old *Hyperion*, where Apollo longs for wings and gains divinity through the knowledge he reads in Mnemosyne's face—

> as if some blithe wine
> Or bright *elixir* peerless I had drunk,
> And so become immortal.
>
> (iii.118-20)

However the new setting of the garden in *The Fall*, with its reminiscences of Eden and its first inhabitants, provides a strikingly different context for interpreting the dreamer's desire and the events that follow. Thus the aroused "appetite" (i.38) that seizes him recalls both the "quick'nd appetite" of Eve in her prophetic dream of temptation (*Paradise Lost*, v.30-93) and the "eager appetite" that actually seizes her in the Garden (ix.740). The dreamer relates, immediately after drinking the potion, how "down I sunk" into his deathlike swoon, just as Eve relates to Adam how she *"sunk down, / And fell asleep"* (v.91-92) after tasting the fruit in her dream. Keats's dreamer starts up suddenly "As if with wings," as Eve herself is momentarily borne up into the clouds by her guide, and as the beguiled couple imagine "Divinitie within them breeding wings" (ix.1010) after they have both eaten of the tree.

In the induction to *The Fall* Keats was reworking his earlier conception of Apollo's longing for poethood and deification, but the allegoric framework he devised to dramatize that longing gives it a new and more profound significance. The remains of the feast of summer fruits the dreamer tastes provide substantial knowledge of lost innocence and man's subsequent decline throughout the course of history. But the draught he thirsts for and drinks and to which he owes the vision that immediately follows seems in its effects to represent his own re-enactment of the Fall itself—the poet's recourse to the transforming power of the imagination. Partly with the help of Hazlitt, Keats had come to see an important analogy between man's Original Sin and the primal act of poetical conception, between the fruit of the knowledge of good and evil and the power of the imagination. For it was possible to regard the latter faculty as something less than an unqualified blessing. Just here the subtlety and insight of Milton's larger treatment of the Fall was so suggestive. Satan had approached Eve first by night and in a dream tempted her with the promised power of the forbidden fruit:

> Taste this, and be henceforth among the Gods
> Thy self a Goddess, not to Earth confind,
> But sometimes in the Air, as wee, sometimes
> Ascend to Heav'n.   (v.77-80)

Later the erring pair had both been tempted to believe the fruit would prove

> of Divine effect
> To open Eyes, and make them Gods who taste.
>   (ix.865-66)

They had been cruelly misled. The fact remained, however, that the promise of new power had not been totally deceitful. The fruit of the tree had indeed proved a guide to higher knowledge but in a way that neither Adam nor Eve, in their innocence, could possibly foresee. Partly through Christ's merciful intervention and partly through Adam's acceptance of the hardship his progeny must endure, the apparent disaster of the Fall had been translated into a meaningful drama of spiritual progress and final Redemption. All of this, while hardly new to Keats, was more than ever germane to his preoccupation with the nature of imaginative experience. The *Fall of Hyperion* reveals the way in which the simple logic of his earlier metaphor of Adam's dream—"he awoke and found it truth"—could mature into a complex allegory of human suffering and tragic knowledge.

III

The change from the light and incense of the garden to the grim solemnity of the ancient sanctuary is vital to the sense of Keats's allegory. The change is that of moving from the realm of "Flora, and old Pan" to concern with "the agonies, the strife / Of human hearts," or from "the infant or thoughtless Chamber" to preoccupation with the "burden of the Mystery" (1, 280-81). It represents that growth from unthinking delight in pleasure to vision into the true nature and suffering of humanity that Keats, with "glorious fear,"[6] had eagerly anticipated from the outset of his career. Yet the development we sense in *The Fall* is not merely the change from immaturity to maturity, but from innocence to experience and responsibility, nor is it unmingled with misgiving and regret. The temple, with its store of treasures, houses the enduring remains of human art and culture, the artifice of eternity, but its interior is forbidding:

> The embossed roof, the silent massy range
> Of columns north and south, ending in mist
> Of nothing; then to eastward, where black gates
> Were shut against the sunrise evermore.
>
> (i.83-86)

The shut gates symbolize the impossibility of a return to innocence or to the garden; they bring to mind the great eastern gate of Paradise which closes behind the human pair following their loss of innocence and exclusion from bliss. Once inside there is no turning back. The only way lies forward toward the knowledge written in Moneta's face and to the struggle to achieve the understanding and transcend-

---

[6] "Sleep and Poetry," 128.

ence of her vision. The task is no longer glorious but stern and demanding.

The shift in tone and imagery between the first and second versions of *Hyperion* is a primary clue toward determining the bent of Keats's new allegory. In comparison with the earlier version, the induction to *The Fall* is more religious than classical in tone and detail, more Christian than pagan. The temple the dreamer must enter if he is to become the poet is the memorial of human achievement and therefore timeless and classic in feeling. Yet the "strange vessels," the "Robes," and "holy jewelries" it contains are all suggestive of religious ritual.[7] Nowhere can the change be seen more clearly than in the contrast between Mnemosyne and Moneta. In *Hyperion* Mnemosyne is a "Goddess benign" whose gift to Apollo is the poet's golden lyre. In *The Fall* Moneta is a "Holy Power," a "priestess" who is first seen ministering before an altar where the dreamer later fears his mere utterance to be "sacrilegious" (i.140). She is not only a guide but a stern admonisher and judge, while the emblems that surround her and the words she speaks are both austere and holy. The speech addressed to him before her altar,

> Thy flesh, near cousin to the common dust,
> Will parch for lack of nutriment,—thy bones
> Will wither in few years, and vanish. . . .
>
> (i.109-11)

recalls the sentence pronounced by Christ upon Adam—"know thy Birth, / For dust thou art, and shalt to dust returne" (*Paradise Lost*, x.207-208). Her altar, hidden at first from the dreamer by clouds of fragrant smoke, resembles Milton's description of the holy Throne, where "of incense Clouds / Fuming from Golden Censers hid the Mount"

[7] Lowes traced many details in this section of the poem to the description of the Covenantal Ark and Tabernacle of the Lord in the Book of Exodus, which Keats had probably been reading ("Moneta's Temple," *PMLA*, LI [1936], 1098-1113).

(vii.599-600). So also the golden censer she holds—except for her veils, perhaps her most important emblem—brings to mind the "Golden Censer" in which Christ, God's "Priest," mingles those "Fruits of more pleasing savour," the prayers of the repentant Adam and Eve, before his offended Father in *Paradise Lost* (xi.22-30).

Such parallels are important not because they suggest Keats had suddenly become a convert to Christian dogma but rather because they confirm that the framework central to the allegory of *The Fall* is the conception of sin and expiation. The dreamer's struggle, unlike that of Apollo, is now not merely for rebirth as poet but against an "unworthiness" (i.182) inherent in his very nature. As Moneta later makes plain, he is, like all visionaries, guilty of a culpability not fully realized until now, and his reprieve from death seems only partly the result of his own tremendous exertion and partly the intervention of something resembling divine grace. The life-and-death struggle with which the first *Hyperion* ends is carried over and expanded in the second, but its context is changed in such a way as to give it an entirely new significance.

Like Dante's *Purgatorio*, the structure and logic of *The Fall* is that of redemptive ascent. The altar toward which the dreamer advances represents the higher condition he must achieve in rising from mere visionary to poet. Just as the "floral censers" of the garden have given way to the golden one Moneta bears, so the "sweet food" she burns in sacrifice suggests a necessary transcendence of the sweet-smelling fruit the dreamer tasted earlier. It is precisely through the clouds of sweet but "sickening" incense, spreading abroad "Forgetfulness of everything but bliss," that he must ascend to clear perception of the pain written in her features. It is revealing to compare this progression to a passage from "Sleep and Poetry," the poem of purpose and self-dedication written three years before, at the outset of Keats's career, to which *The Fall* in so many ways looks back:

O Poesy! for thee I grasp my pen
That am not yet a glorious denizen
Of thy wide heaven; yet, to my ardent prayer,
Yield from thy sanctuary some clear air,
Smoothed for intoxication by the breath
Of flowering bays, that I may die a death
Of luxury, and my young spirit follow
The morning sun-beams to the great Apollo
Like a fresh sacrifice; or, if I can bear
The o'erwhelming sweets, 'twill bring to me the fair
Visions of all places.

(53-63)

Virtually all the major elements of the new induction are here—the notion of a poetic heaven or sanctuary, death and rebirth, sacrifice, the need to transcend the "o'erwhelming sweets" of verse, to achieve a point of vision—but jumbled incoherently together without the meaningful development and depth of Keats's allegory. For it is important to note that the draught the dreamer drinks—his rebirth in imagination—can lead as readily to a fool's paradise, the fate of those who rot upon Moneta's pavement, as to higher insight. His salvation is never possible until he has "mounted up" a *second* time: his swoon and starting up from the garden and his ascent of the stairs before Moneta's altar are central and contrasting movements.[8] Clearly Keats's meaning is that the luxury and ease of imaginative enjoyment can obscure the hardship of the struggle for vision into the tragic nature of human existence that is required of the poet who would live.

The redemptive aim of Keats's allegory as well as its assimilation of the old epic elements is further clarified if we pursue the suggested parallel with *Paradise Lost*, now in particular in terms of the drama of Milton's closing books. Thus the command to the dreamer to "ascend / These steps" (i.107-108) recalls the direction given by the angel

[8] David Perkins has commented on this relationship in *The Quest for Permanence* (Cambridge, Mass., 1959), p. 281.

Michael to Adam after the Fall, "Ascend / This Hill" (*Paradise Lost*, xi.366-67). And Michael and Adam "both ascend / In the Visions of God" (xi.376-77), just as Moneta, now the dreamer's guide, presents to him the vision of Saturn's desolation, a panorama of the past hardly less tremendous than the vision of the future Michael reveals to Adam. So also the plea the dreamer addresses to Moneta,

> "High Prophetess," said I, "purge off,
> Benign, if so it please thee, my mind's film,"
>
> (i.145-46)

brings to mind the relation, only a few lines later in *Paradise Lost*, that

> *Michael* from *Adams* eyes the *Filme* remov'd
> Which that false Fruit that promis'd clearer sight
> Had bred; then *purg'd* with Euphrasie and Rue
> The visual Nerve, for he had much to see.
>
> (xi.412-15)[9]

To some degree Eve's vain longing for divinity of knowledge is actually fulfilled through Adam's vision, but united now with full awareness of the tremendous agony and suffering he and his progeny must bear. In the same way the draught the dreamer consumes in the garden leads not to the experience of more intense enjoyment but to a deeper knowledge of human destiny and its pain.

IV

What Keats was attempting to accomplish in the latter part of *The Fall of Hyperion* is reasonably clear. He was

---

[9] My italics, except for proper names. Undoubtedly Keats also had in mind a part of the invocation to Book III:

> the *mind* through all her powers
> Irradiate, there plant eyes, all mist from thence
> *Purge* and disperse,
>
> (iii.52-54)

a passage of which he took special note in his copy of Milton.

seeking to interpolate important sections of the narrative of the earlier *Hyperion* into his text as a higher vision of human life and destiny. From the metaphor of the Fall and the account of the dreamer's struggle to ascend he fashioned an allegory of sin, expiation, and atonement that could give genuine relevance to the old epic action. Like Adam's vision from the mount, the knowledge the dreamer gains is not merely given but in great part earned, a vision dramatizing Keats's own peculiar sense of the hardships and compensations of imaginative experience. The dreamer may transgress by tasting the fruit of the imagination yet wins redemption, with Moneta's help and intervention, through dedication to the service of humanity. Like Dante's Beatrice or Milton's Christ, a major aspect of her role is that of a vicarious sufferer and redeemer. Although fated to survey "the giant agony of the world," he is to see it through her eyes and with her promise that what for her "is still a curse" shall be for him "a wonder," a vision "Free from all pain, if wonder pain thee not" (i.243-48).

As deeply relevant as it unquestionably is to Keats's new allegorical intention, the Christian story of the Fall and the various parallels it affords are insufficient fully to elucidate the fragment he again abandoned. For it is impossible to read *The Fall* through without realizing that the major issues it raises, and consequently its entire structure, are still in a process of evolution and that, as in so much of the earlier verse, its inner debate is never finally resolved. It is not just that the work is actively and progressively dialectical; the fact is that its dialectic is neither consistent nor conclusive. Much of the problem revolves around the conception of Moneta and the balance Keats had to strike between her role of interrogator and judge on the one hand and intercessor and redeemer on the other. The real difficulties become clear only when one examines in some detail the argument she addresses to her pupil.

Following his victorious struggle to ascend, Moneta makes the declaration that "None can usurp this height" but "those to whom the miseries of the world / Are misery" (i.147-49). However, when the dreamer looks about for others near him, those benefactors of humanity who, more like slaves than fellow men, "Labour for mortal good," he is disappointed in his search. Those whom he seeks are no visionaries, Moneta exclaims.

> They seek no wonder but the human face,
> No music but a happy-noted voice—
> They come not here, they have no thought to come—
> And thou art here, for thou art less than they.
>
> (i.163-66)

Thus far the meaning of her words is clear and inescapable. The "height" to which the dreamer's struggle has carried him is not as eminent as it might at first appear. For what Moneta is saying is that the state of innocence—the freedom from imaginative longing and the knowledge to which that longing leads—is after all the best. Never to have thirsted for the juice of the garden, never to have entered the temple and struggled up its steps, but to have remained content with humbly toiling for humanity would have been a greater virtue. The life of the selfless, unimaginative laborer for human welfare is best. The lesson Moneta reads is essentially the same as that with which Raphael admonishes the too curious Adam before the Fall:

> Heav'n is for thee too high
> To know what passes there; be lowlie wise:
> Think onely what concernes thee and thy being;
> Dream not of other Worlds, what Creatures there
> Live, in what state, condition or degree,
> Contented that thus farr hath been reveal'd
> Not of Earth onely but of highest Heav'n.
>
> (viii.172-78)

However, like Adam, the dreamer has fallen and cannot recapture innocence. As we have seen, the whole design of Keats's allegory is an effort to define the way of his atonement. Through his struggle he has been "saved from death" (i.138). Though still tainted, a mere "fever" of himself, he nevertheless looks to Moneta to be "medicin'd / In sickness not ignoble" (i.169, 183-84), and, when he finally glimpses her face, he finds it blanched by "an immortal sickness" progressing not to corruption but toward a terrible purity. The seed of redemption lies in the very root of his illness. The logic of this progression, however, is violated by the unexpected fury of Moneta's violent condemnation in a passage that reveals how much the main lines of Keats's allegory were still susceptible to the pressure of major doubts and questions. There is no point in reopening the textual problem of the disputed lines (i.187-210), so often wrangled over in the past, except to observe that Keats undoubtedly wrote them, that they throw a revealing light on the development of his argument, and that our chief clue to interpreting them remains the note the careful Woodhouse made in marking the passage in his transcript, that "Keats seems to have intended to erase" them. Woodhouse's supposition appears correct, for the distinction Moneta proceeds to draw is potentially disastrous to Keats's argument:

> Art thou not of the dreamer tribe?
> The poet and the dreamer are distinct,
> Diverse, sheer opposite, antipodes.
>
> (i.198-200)

Up to here the whole point of Keats's narrative has been that the poet *is* the dreamer but something more, that the essential distinction between them is qualitative, not generic.[10]

---

[10] The point has been convincingly argued by Murry in "The Poet and the Dreamer," *Keats* (London, 1955), pp. 242-43. In *Keats and Shakespeare* (London, 1925), Murry had earlier placed his finger on the major confusion the disputed lines introduced, "because the word 'dreamer' now bears an utterly different sense. The 'dreamer' here is the mere romanticist" (p. 179).

One may readily concede the probability that Keats recognized his error, that he clearly intended to omit the passage. Nevertheless there is little justification in therefore dismissing it as entirely irrelevant. The mere fact that he could compose the lines is of itself revealing. The passage suggests how much, despite the careful design apparent throughout the whole of the induction, the underlying question Keats had put so simply on March 19, "Yet may I not in this be free from sin," remained unsettled in his mind. It suggests how much, despite an undeniable consistency of metaphor, the deeper evolution of his poem was once again the product not of any fixed intention but of an active process of self-interrogation and discovery. What the passage prepares us for, if by this time we needed any special preparation, is another work whose argument is exploratory and probational and never fully secure from the ironies of genuine uncertainty and ambivalence.

Such irresolution, barely sensed in the dialectics of Moneta's debate with her disciple, emerges more clearly as the poem proceeds. *The Fall* is a visionary work, and its mystery is more than anywhere expressed within its single most important passage—the dreamer's vision of Moneta's face. At the end of the first *Hyperion* Keats had presented the deification of Apollo merely through the "Knowledge enormous" he reads in Mnemosyne's countenance. The rush of names, deeds, and legends suggests only an intellectual enlightenment. The description of Moneta's features in *The Fall*, however, evokes an emotion equivalent to the far greater vision of the fallen Titans the dreamer is about to behold through her eyes, and thus effectively conveys its pain and sadness:

> Then saw I a wan face,
> Not pined by human sorrows, but bright-blanch'd
> By an immortal sickness which kills not;
> It works a constant change, which happy death
> Can put no end to; deathwards progressing

To no death was that visage; it had pass'd
The lily and the snow; and beyond these
I must not think now, though I saw that face.
But for her eyes I should have fled away.
They held me back with a benignant light,
Soft mitigated by divinest lids
Half closed, and visionless entire they seem'd
Of all external things—they saw me not,
But, in blank splendour, beam'd like the mild moon,
Who comforts those she sees not, who knows not
What eyes are upward cast.

(i.256-71)

The passage is central to an understanding of the events that
follow, for the description of Moneta's features and the
scene upon which she stares are related to each other as
tragic perception and emotion are related to the essence of
human experience. It dramatizes the truth of Keats's earlier
conviction that "Knowledge is Sorrow" (I, 279) and that the
poet must be one "who has kept watch on Man's Mortality"
(I, 173). Only by sharing her vision of the downcast Titans
and comprehending its sorrow can Keats's dreamer gain
absolution from his curse and rise to the stature of a poet.

The description of Moneta's features seems calculated to
invite interpretation by analogy; and unquestionably the
most compelling has been that suggested by D. G. James,
who, like many critics after him, saw reflected in them the
agony of the suffering Christ.[11] The parallel is no less striking
than germane, for it supports the idea of her redemptive role
implied throughout the course of Keats's narrative. Nevertheless the more one studies the passage within the context of
what follows, the less such an interpretation seems, by itself,
sufficient. The conception of Moneta's suffering as an "im-

---

[11] See James's excellent study of the two *Hyperions* in *The Romantic
Comedy* (London, 1948), reprinted in Bate's *Keats: A Collection of
Critical Essays* (Englewood Cliffs, N.J., 1964), pp. 161-69.

mortal sickness" involves a paradox not ordinarily associated
with the finality of Christ's passion. Her suffering is a living
death, a misery that never ends but must endure through
countless ages. In the continuous wasting of her features, the
mutable and the immutable, the temporal and the eternal
are both contained and reconciled. Such agony is difficult
even to imagine; yet there have been other attempts to portray it. While suggesting the agony of the Crucifixion,
Moneta's suffering seems more nearly to recall the despairing
words Adam speaks near the end of Book Ten of *Paradise
Lost*, just as he begins to comprehend the destiny of his
offspring, which he is shortly to behold in vision from the
mount:

> But say
> That Death be not one stroak, as I suppos'd,
> Bereaving sense, but endless miserie
> From this day onward, which I feel begun
> Both in me, and without me, and so last
> To perpetuitie.
>
> (x.808-13)

Filled with new understanding and sympathy for his unfortunate progeny, while lacking any hope for their recovery,
Adam laments that he is doomed to "die a living Death"
(x.788), a fear justified by the epic spectacle of human
misery about to unfold before him. In a similar way, the
sorrow the dreamer finds in Moneta's face is the essential
knowledge of the plight of Saturn and Thea, understood as a
symbol of world fate, which he must perceive through her
eyes.[12]

What is most significant about the dreamer's rapt perception of Moneta and her contemplation is the way it
wavers between two orders of vision. The first is the type

---

[12] Cf. Murry: "The fate of Saturn is a symbol of the destiny of the
world, and Moneta is a symbol of the world made conscious of its own
vicissitude" (*Keats and Shakespeare*, p. 182).

of Adam's divinely mediated vision from the mount; the other is his unreconstructed view of the hopeless misery of his fallen offspring. As we have seen, the main development of *The Fall* unmistakably suggests the intention to represent the dreamer's sin as expiable, as, in fact, a kind of *felix culpa* bringing a knowledge of higher good as well as an inevitable pain and hardship. When, through parted veils, Moneta offers to reveal the scenes contained within her brain, the dreamer, like Apollo, seems on the point of ultimate comprehension. The vision she reflects, however, even while mitigated by the light of her benignant eyes, is singularly cheerless and somber, a realization that is closer to resignation—perhaps even despair—than to hope. In the earlier *Hyperion* the myth of the fallen Titans had served as the background for a view of universal hope and progress. Despite their cruel heartbreak, there is no doubt that a power prevails within their universe working through destruction and perpetual change toward ultimate perfection—the theme of Oceanus's great speech. Moneta's gaze, however, seems to comprehend only a consciousness of endless process, an eternal "deathwards progressing / To no death," an undetermined and interminable progression without apparent hope or purpose too terrifying to conceive ("I must not think now, though I saw that face"). It is the vision of the fallen Adam unrelieved by any promise of redemption, the vision of our modern age.

Keats's inability to dramatize any reconciling hope of comfort or assurance in Moneta's features is only too clearly reflected in what follows. The expected transcendence and breadth and grasp of vision are never realized. The power "of enormous ken," the ability to "see as a god sees" (i.303-304) which the dreamer feels growing within him as he stands upon the height he has won, is slowly lost within the shadows of the solitary vale. Instead there are the terrible lines, among the last Keats added to the older narrative, that describe the dreamer's prolonged agony as he beholds, hour after hour, the misery of Saturn and Thea:

> Oftentimes I pray'd
> Intense, that death would take me from the vale
> And all its burthens—Gasping with despair
> Of change, hour after hour I curs'd myself.
>
> (i.396-99)

The passage goes beyond the "vale of Soul-making," the speculation invented in the spring to justify and explain "a World of Pains and troubles" (ii, 102), to what Keats was to call his "posthumous existence" (ii, 359). Only in his final letters can one find the counterpart of such despair. "Is there another Life? Shall I awake and find all this a dream? There must be we cannot be created for this sort of suffering" (ii, 346). What had begun as the metaphor of Adam's dream was to end as the tragic and unfinished allegory of Keats's life, a drama mirrored in the inconclusive ending of *The Fall*. Throughout the agony of the dreamer's vigil one recollects the hardship of another spectacle and Adam's forlorn cry:

> O Visions ill foreseen! better had I
> Liv'd ignorant of future, so had borne
> My part of evil onely, each dayes lot
> Anough to bear.
>
> (xi.763-66)

V

There can be no disputing that, had he lived, Keats might have gone on to revise and to complete *Hyperion*. The possibilities it contains for further development are myriad. Nevertheless we are left with the fragment he abandoned and with the mystery of his inability to complete the project that so preoccupied him, on and off, during the whole of his great year of poetic achievement. Although still occasionally presented in such terms, the deeper problem was not one of technical considerations, any more than it was that of supplying a mere termination to the poem. It was the task of reconciling the need for a coherent framework of traditional allegory with an entire openness to the full complexity of man's experience and with an emerging sense of the desolating loneliness and isolation of the modern poet's view. The poem derives its primary impulse from a commitment to the value and discipline of a form of spiritual and allegorical progression that can be traced as far back as "Sleep and Poetry," a form characteristic of all the great narrative poetry Keats looked to as his models. At every stage, however, within the gradual evolution of *The Fall*, the challenges and hardships to which the dreamer must submit become more arduous, the promises of consolation more uncertain, and the ascent more terrifying and insecure. The visionary framework cannot sustain the weight of human need and questioning it must support.

The root of the problem really lies in the distinction posed at the very outset of the poem's induction: that between dream and vision. The poem turns upon Keats's desire, indeed his vital need, to discriminate between the two, while at the same time preserving the grounds of a common unity. Like so much of his earlier verse from *Endymion* onward, but in a way that is more urgent, moving, and humane, *The Fall* represents his last effort to *spiritualize* the dreamer into visionary. It embraces the attempt to achieve the clarity of vision—in the full sense Keats intended—through entire fidelity to the imagination and its processes, to the creative potential of the dream. Yet the prospect that rewards the dreamer at the end of his struggle, the vision of Moneta's eternally wasted features, seems to hold only a recognition of ceaseless change and process. There is no discernible end to his vigil and no resolution to the pain he beholds. While straining toward the redemptive promise of the second Adam, the vision expresses the tragic knowledge of the first. The image of Moneta that the dream distills transcends the visionary framework that would contain it. It is rather the expression of a deeper honesty—a recognition that the pain of human consciousness must be borne without the hope of any divine intercession. *The Fall of Hyperion* is the final triumph of the metaphor of Adam and his dream. It is the supreme expression of tragic irony in Keats's work.

EPILOGUE

"TO AUTUMN"

THE fallacy of using any single work, such as *The Fall of Hyperion*, either to predict or limit the shape of Keats's career or the direction of his evolution, had he lived, is nowhere better demonstrated than in the lyric he transcribed the same day he announced the final abandonment of *Hyperion*—the ode "To Autumn." As John Middleton Murry long ago observed, the two works are almost total contrasts in tone and spirit.[1] With its struggle for ascent through doubt and self-questioning to a point of visionary comprehensiveness above the human world, the longer work is fired with a Miltonic ardor and intensity. In its condensed but unhurried perfection, its contemplation of the actual, the ode is much closer to Shakespeare. The two works, to be certain, share one supreme concern: their common involvement with process. However as treatments of that theme they differ immeasurably. *Hyperion* fails through the inability to evolve a framework for transcending process, for reconciling man to the knowledge of sorrow and loss. "To Autumn" succeeds through its acceptance of an order innate in our experience— the natural rhythm of the seasons. It is a poem that, without ever stating it, inevitably suggests the truth of "ripeness is all" by developing, with a richness and profundity of implication, the simple perception that ripeness is fall.

The perfection of the ode lies chiefly in the care and subtlety of patterning within its three-part structure. The patterns are ones that partly connect "To Autumn" with the

[1] The contrast between the two works is the culmination of Murry's seminal study, *Keats and Shakespeare* (London, 1925). He juxtaposes the abandonment of *Hyperion* and the composition of the ode to assert his major thesis: "Shakespeare had triumphed in Keats' soul" (p. 168).

odes of the spring and partly mark a new development and vary in complexity. As critics have often pointed out, the three stanzas successively proceed from the last growth of late summer through the fullness of high autumn to the spareness of an early winter landscape, just as they suggest the progress of a single day through to its close in sunset. As Bush, among others, has noted, the imagery of the first stanza is mainly tactile, that of the second mainly visual, that of the last chiefly auditory.[2] In these and other respects the ode displays a deliberate symmetry and balance the earlier odes do not possess. At the same time it makes a more even and practiced use of devices developed in its predecessors. The personification of the season, introduced at the beginning of the first stanza in a way reminiscent of the opening of the "Urn," is developed in the second into a full series of tableaux, and then is briefly and elegiacally revived at the outset of the third before the ode returns us to the simple sounds and images of the natural landscape. There remains, too, but in a more subtle way, the pattern of lyric questioning, from the submerged "how" of the first stanza, to the rhetorical "who" at the outset of the second, to the more imperative "where" at the commencement of the third, that marks the gradual emergence into consciousness of the recognition the season both epitomizes and expresses. One must add, following Bate's observation that " 'To Autumn' is so uniquely a distillation,"[3] that the ode is Keats's last and most mature comment on the nature of the poetic process. For its whole development, from the imagery of ripening and storing in the first stanza, through that of winnowing and slow extraction in the second, to the subtle, thin, and tenuous music with which the poem rises to its close, represents his final adaptation of his favorite metaphor for poetic creation.

[2] *John Keats: His Life and Writings* (New York, 1966), p. 177.
[3] *John Keats* (Cambridge, Mass., 1963), p. 581. I am indebted to all the discussions cited in the footnotes to this chapter but particularly to Bate's, which is reprinted in his *Keats: A Collection of Critical Essays* (Englewood Cliffs, N.J., 1964), pp. 155-60.

The analogy Shelley makes explicit in his "Ode to the West Wind" is not less moving or real because it is left implicit in Keats's hymn. If the "wild West Wind" and its "mighty harmonies" express Shelley's sense of a universal force of spiritual creativity, the autumnal sounds that are borne away on "the light wind" that "lives or dies" at the end of Keats's ode converge to produce a music that is poignantly natural.

The ironies that pervade the odes of the spring are by no means missing in "To Autumn." However they are now resolved within an image that transcends them—the image of autumn itself. Virtually from its beginning the ode compels us to conceive of the season in two different ways: as a conventional setting or personified abstraction that has been depicted poetically and pictorially from time immemorial with a fixed nature and identity of its own;[4] and as a seasonal interval, a mere space between summer and winter that can never be abstracted from the larger cycle of birth and death.

> Season of mists and mellow fruitfulness,
>> Close bosom-friend of the maturing sun;
>> Conspiring with him how to load and bless
>> With fruit the vines that round the thatch-eves run.
>>
>> (1-4)

The homely, welcoming personifications seem to proclaim a role that is familiar and established. Nevertheless, as B. C. Southam has observed, the opening line, with its allusion both to "mists" and "mellow fruitfulness," already points to different and contrasting aspects of the year.[5]

While the first stanza concentrates upon the natural world through images of growth and process, the second

[4] In his chapter on "To Autumn" in *Keats and the Mirror of Art* (Oxford, 1967), pp. 232-43, Ian Jack has collected a sizable number of instances from both literature and painting.

[5] The line, Southam argues, looks forward to the "spectral, disembodied, chill feature of the season's end" even while it "glances at Autumn in her first capacity, fecund and beneficent" and thus anticipates a central progression in the ode ("The Ode 'To Autumn,'" *Keats-Shelley Journal*, IX [1960], 93).

stanza shifts to a more artful and stylized conception by presenting autumn as a figure captured and framed within a series of perspectives that are recognizably conventional. However the two conceptions of autumn, as process and abstraction, continually modify and interpenetrate each other. To take only one example, there is the depiction in the second stanza of autumn

> sitting careless on a granary floor,
> Thy hair soft-lifted by the winnowing wind;
> Or on a half-reap'd furrow sound asleep,
> Drows'd with the fume of poppies, while thy hook
> Spares the next swath and all its twined flowers.
> (14-18)

The picture is more than an intermingling of activity and stasis. For a moment the figure of the season is involved with and actually worked upon by the very processes she emblemizes, even while she remains careless and impervious to the changes they imply. Such juxtapositions convey a sense of irony of the most delicate and subtle kind.

Throughout the ode the play of irony is developed by the way in which the major patterns alternate and run counter to each other. In the first stanza the sense of process and maturing is carried forward by such active verbs as "load," "bend," "fill," "swell," "plump," "set budding." At the same time another pattern of words, concentrated near the end of the stanza, suggests the contradictory idea of a repletion that has already been attained: "fruit*ful*ness," "all," "more, / And still more," "later," "never," "e[v]er." In the second stanza, which, as Bate has written, is "something of a reverse or mirror image of the first,"[6] autumn is personified in a series of fixed poses—as thresher, reaper, gleaner, watcher—that, in their immobility, suggest an ideal of completion. Nevertheless the effect is in a measure counterbalanced by a sustained use of partitives—"oft[en]," "Sometimes," "care*less*," "half," "next," "sometimes," "last," "hours by hours"—as

[6] *John Keats*, p. 582.

well as by the movement and diversity implied by such different positioning prepositions and adverbs as "amid,"
"abroad," "across."

It is in the last stanza that these various oppositions
achieve a resolution unlike any in the odes of the spring. The
questioning with which the stanza begins becomes more direct and pressing, forcing into conscious recognition[7] the
knowledge that has all the while been growing latently
throughout the ode:

> Where are the songs of Spring? Ay, where are they?
> *Think not* of them, thou hast thy music too.
>
> (23-24)

The awareness of impermanence and ultimately of death is
no less moving because it must be momentarily suppressed
in a way that makes us recognize the impossibility of any
direct confrontation. Still, such awareness is not finally
rejected but rather tempered and reflected in the light of
the "soft-dying day," where the imagery of the spring
("bloom," "rosy") is briefly reborn amid the tonalities of
autumn, just as it is echoed in the "wailful choir" of gnats
that "mourn" and in the distant "bleat[ing]" of the lambs.
For it is, in the end, the *music* of autumn that works within
the poem its saving mediation, that gathers together and
resolves the various antinomies within a larger movement.
It is a music that is alternately "borne *aloft*" or "*sinking*" as
the "light wind *lives* or *dies*." It composes itself from the
sounds of the "*small* gnats" as well as from those of "*full-
grown* lambs," from the "*loud*" bleating of the sheep to the
"*soft*" treble of the robin. It draws together the song of the
redbreast, as Arnold Davenport has noted, "characteristically
a winter bird," and the call of the swallow, "proverbially the

---

[7] See James Lott's interesting and subtle reading of the ode in
"Keats's *To Autumn*: The Poetic Consciousness and the Awareness of
Process," *Studies in Romanticism*, IX (1970), 71-81. Lott's argument is
that the ode records a change from unthinking empathy with natural
process to a consciousness of time and the speaker's separation from
the season.

bird of summer [who] leaves the country when summer is over."[8] It combines the cadences of change and continuity, of life and death. It rises from earth, *"from* hilly bourn" and *"from* a garden-croft" to ascend *"in* the skies." In its gradual withdrawal and attenuation ("treble," "whistles," "twitter"), it suggests the inevitable end of a natural cycle of growth, maturity and distillment in a ghostly and ethereal dissipation.

One aspect of the ode, especially of its final stanza, deserves to be commented on in more detail: the way it returns for a major element of its technique to the early verse, to sonnets like "How Many Bards" and "After Dark Vapours." The connection is suggested by Reuben Brower's remark that "To Autumn" reveals "how a succession of images, becoming something more than mere succession, imperceptibly blends into metaphor."[9] For the final stanza of the ode remains the most perfect expression of the poet's habit of cataloguing (though the latter term now seems crude and inadequate to describe the effect "To Autumn" achieves). The beginning of the stanza deliberately eschews the invitation to conscious reflection, avoiding the moral sentiment or epitaph that constitutes the chief resolution of a whole tradition of the pastoral mode. Instead the stanza gains its end by offering us one more succession of precise impressions, a series of images that extends its texture of associations and reverberations as it unfolds. It elaborates a music that is entirely earthly and natural, yet filled with further implications. It never removes us from the characteristic world of Keats's poetry, a world of

> leaves
> Budding—fruit ripening in stillness—autumn suns
> Smiling at eve upon the quiet sheaves.
> ("After Dark Vapours," 9-11)

Yet it imperceptibly creates a further range of meaning, the final awareness, if not of "a Poet's death," of a settled ripe-

[8] "A Note on 'To Autumn,'" *John Keats: A Reassessment*, ed. Kenneth Muir (Liverpool, 1958), p. 99.
[9] *The Fields of Light* (New York, 1951), p. 39.

ness of experience we strive to articulate within such set terms as "maturity" or "resignation" or "acceptance." It preserves decorum by remaining to the last a poetry of sensation; yet it leaves us with a full sense of the ultimate values. It takes us as far as we have any right to require toward a poetry of thought.

AFTERWORD (1994)

THE PRINCIPAL contribution to Keats studies during the interval between the first publication of this book, twenty years ago, and its present reappearance has been Jack Stillinger's definitive edition of *The Poems of John Keats* (Harvard, 1978). That edition, together with Stillinger's facsimile reproductions of the original holographs and transcripts in *The Manuscripts of the Younger Romantics* series under the general editorship of Donald H. Reiman (Garland, 1985–1988), has made available virtually all the materials for the study of Keats's text with a new accuracy and sophistication. Stillinger's full annotations (mostly textual) and John Barnard's in his edition of *The Complete Poems* (Penguin, 1973) have supplemented the valuable commentary of Douglas Bush in his edition of *The Selected Poems and Letters* and of Miriam Allott in her edition of the complete poetry. There has been no major successor to the brilliant biographies by Walter Jackson Bate, Aileen Ward, and Robert Gittings, so rich and varied in their views and approaches. However, Wolf Z. Hirst's *John Keats* (Twayne, 1981) joined Douglas Bush's brief critical biography as a useful introduction to the life and poetry. The chief scholarly need at the moment is a new edition of *The Letters* in order to incorporate the wealth of scholarship and commentary that has accumulated since the publication of Hyder Edward Rollins's great edition thirty-five years ago. Perhaps Stillinger, who contributed so much to that effort, could be persuaded to undertake the task, though I can imagine his reluctance to displace a name so revered.

Criticism of the thought and poetry over the last two decades has taken several, at times contrary, directions. Robert M. Ryan's *Keats: The Religious Sense* (Princeton, 1976), Stuart A. Ende's *Keats and the Sublime* (Yale, 1976), and Ronald A. Sharp's *Keats, Skepticism, and the Religion of Beauty* (Georgia, 1979) extended our knowledge of the poet by tracing his development in terms of some long-established intellectual and aesthetic criteria. In *Keats and the Silent Work of Imagination* (Illinois, 1985) Leon Waldoff

343

AFTERWORD

analyzed the poet's creative processes with psychological insight
and acuity; while Donald C. Goellnich in *The Poet-Physician:
Keats and Medical Science* (Pittsburgh, 1984) and Hermione de
Almeida in *Romantic Medicine and John Keats* (Oxford, 1991)
demonstrated the importance not just of Keats's medical training
but of his knowledge of the sciences generally. With the publication of Helen Vendler's *The Odes of John Keats* (Harvard, 1983), a
work that takes not just the odes but most of Keats's major work into
its ken, Keats studies reached a major watershed. Vendler's command of poetic convention and topoi was so powerful, her reading
of the verse and letters so richly and densely textured, that the
question arose as to how much further criticism, at least of the kind
of close reading and analysis, could go, especially in the case of a
poet with so severely limited a canon.

Interesting attempts have been made to strike off into new or
neglected directions. A number of distinguished critics contributed
to a forum on "Keats and Politics" published in *Studies in Romanticism* 25 (Summer 1986). It remains questionable, however,
whether the results were so much to redefine the poet's well-known
allegiance to "the liberal side of the question" as to confirm his
relative aloofness from politics. Among a group of versatile and
gifted younger scholar-critics, Susan Wolfson has freshly illuminated the poetry by searching, subtle forms of rhetorical analysis
in *The Questioning Presence: Wordsworth, Keats, and the Inter-
rogative Mode in Romantic Poetry* (Cornell, 1986). She has also
stimulated interest in neglected portions of the canon ("Composition and 'Unrest': The Dynamics of Form in Keats's Last Lyrics,"
Keats-Shelley Journal 34 [1985]) and sensitively reconsidered the
delicate balance between the masculine and feminine sides of the
poet's temperament ("Feminizing Keats," *Critical Essays on John
Keats*, ed. Hermione de Almeida [G. K. Hall, 1990]). Throughout
the period there has been the occasional essay devoted to some
aspect of the verse or to a major poem that has broken new ground,
most recently Andrew J. Bennett's "'Hazardous Magic': Vision and
Inscription in Keats's 'The Eve of St. Agnes,'" *Keats-Shelley Journal* 41 (1992). Nevertheless the sense of a hiatus remains.

At the same time there has been a remarkable resurgence in what

344

AFTERWORD

might be called the countertradition of Keats criticism. Years ago Arnold and Yeats, both dedicated admirers, commented in different ways on a strain of vulgarity in the poet's nature. Partly this impression was owing to the poet's "cockney" origins (the word of opprobrium that goes back to the earliest reviews) and the undeniable limitations (at least by comparison with the likes of Byron and Shelley) of his social and intellectual upbringing. In part the perception had to do with the poet's extraordinarily sensuous, at times voluptuous apprehension of existence. In his seminal British Academy lecture, "Keats and Reality" (first published 1962; revised and expanded in his *The Uses of Division: Unity and Disharmony in Literature* [Chatto & Windus, 1976]), John Bayley demonstrated how much the supposed weaknesses and excesses of the poet's temperament were inseparable from his essential strengths. Following up this line of perception, Christopher Ricks produced in *Keats and Embarrassment* (Oxford, 1974) arguably the most stimulating and lively study of the last twenty years. In his necessary concentration on the earlier, immature verse, Ricks admittedly neglected (and, like Bayley, partly depreciated) the kind of self-conscious, disciplined, at times heroic poet Keats sought increasingly to become. Nevertheless Ricks's study of the creative uses of the kinds of embarrassment to which the poetry and the letters often expose us provided new and subtle insights into the physiology of the poet's Romantic temperament. The possibilities as well as the dangers of this line of approach have more recently been explored by Marjorie Levinson whose *Keats's Life of Allegory: The Origins of a Style* (Blackwell, 1988) has made the biggest splash of any book since Vendler's. Armed with the tools of Marxist and New Historicist criticism, Levinson has continued the concentration on the negative aspects of the poet's capabilities in ways ranging well beyond the merely stylistic. For her Keats emerges as a social climber and literary entrepreneur whose alienation from his class and proper subject matter is continuously revealed in his autoerotic fantasizing and who rises toward greatness (as in *Lamia*) only where he dramatizes his consciousness of his estrangement. At times capricious and self-indulgent, Levinson's criticism is also trenchant and germane, exposing larger embarrassments of a kind earlier criticism had mostly ignored or repressed. Her study, however, situates Keats among the great Romantics as a poet of diminished stature.

All in all, in the ongoing stock exchange of literary evaluations, a market where individual standing is determined as much by the volume of transactions as by individual appraisals, over the last twenty years Wordsworth's stock has soared, Shelley's has made a substantial recovery, while Keats's has lagged the market. Keats's case is the more compelling by comparison with that of Shelley, the friend and rival with whom he has been proverbially linked virtually from the outset of their careers. Nineteen ninety-two was the bicentennial anniversary of Shelley's birth, an occasion marked in New York City, Gregynog, and Pretoria by major scholarly conferences. Shelley emerged triumphantly from this process of reappraisal as a poet and thinker in the forefront of the philosophical, social, political, and scientific developments of his age, a writer who anticipated many of the theoretical and polemical concerns of the present day. Nineteen ninety-five will mark the bicentenary of Keats's birth, and I hope that its observances will prove equally happy and successful.

Keats remains an attractive subject for the university undergraduate, nor is there any question that through the years he has held the abiding love of the common reader. I wonder, however, if the poet of "Negative Capability" can prove congenial to most postmodernist criticism with its driving political commitments and theoretical priorities. There is always, as Samuel Johnson declared, an appeal open from criticism to nature; and, as Arnold recognized, it is to the Shakespearean criterion of openness and imaginative intensity, the values Keats sought continuously to perfect in his verse, that Keats directs us. The coming period of reassessment may prove as much a test of the resources of contemporary criticism as of whether we can continue to prize as he deserves the poet who of all the great Romantics was the most pleasure-loving and pleasure-giving, the most generous and humane in his responses, and the most committed to the life of the imagination.

Bloomington, Indiana
May 1993

INDEX

Abrams, M. H., 74n, 85
Adam's dream, 6, 38, 46, 63-64,
 74, 156, 162, 196, 277; in the
 Eve of St. Agnes, 213, 217;
 ironical relation to the allegory
 of *The Fall of Hyperion*,
 320-21, 333-35
aether, see ether
Agrippa, Cornelius, 40n
Alison, Archibald, 15
allegory, Keats's early interest in,
 81, 88; in *Endymion*, 91-96,
 105-106, 108, 114-15; "life of
 Allegory," 88, 145; in "Sleep
 and Poetry," 85-86; in *The Fall
 of Hyperion*, 313-28, 334
Allen, Glen O., 112
Allen, William, 36, 45n, 46n
Allott, Kenneth, 252, 254-55n,
 256
Aristotle, 35n
Arnold, Matthew, 96, 143, 155,
 246; on "natural magic" and
 the Celtic strain, 232-36, 239
association of ideas, importance to
 Keats's conception of poetry,
 56-58; Keats's early reliance on,
 72-73; failure of in the *Epistle
 to Reynolds*, 118-19; Keats's
 parody of during walking tour,
 136; in "Ode to a Nightingale,"
 263; in "To Autumn," 341-42.
 See also associationism
associationism, British,
 16; Tucker's development of,
 23-37. *See also* association of
 ideas

Babington, William, 36, 42, 45n,
 46n

Bailey, Benjamin, 6, 38, 46-47,
 58-59, 63-65, 68-69, 93, 113,
 139, 144-47, 153, 156, 174,
 259, 277
Balslev, Thora, 174n
Bate, Walter Jackson, 4, 23,
 31-32, 37n, 72, 117n, 118, 121,
 125n, 133, 193-95, 219-20,
 234n, 242, 255, 268, 279,
 286n, 288, 337, 339
Beattie, James, 12
Beaumont, Sir George, 130
Berkeley, George, 13, 126; his
 idealism, 20-22
Berlioz, Hector, 219
Blackstone, Bernard, 40n, 92n
Blake, William, 8, 165
Bloom, Harold, 130n, 202n, 256,
 260-61, 286n
Boiardo, Matteo Maria, 158
Bonnycastle, John, 37n
Bornstein, George, 38n
Bostetter, E. E., 173n
Brawne, Frances (Fanny), 5, 189,
 191, 198, 231, 292; connection
 with *Lamia*, 300-301
Bridges, Robert, 48n, 91
Brooks, Cleanth, 271-72, 275-76
Brower, Reuben, 341
Brown, Charles Armitage, 34, 52,
 132-34, 285, 312
Brown, Leonard, 94n
Bunn, James H., 259n
Buonaparte, *see* Napoleon
Burfoot, A. H., 36n
Burgess, C. F., 202n
Burke, Kenneth, 32
Burns, Robert, 134; Hazlitt on,
 142-43; Keats's poetry written
 during visit to the Burns coun-

347

Burns, Robert (*cont.*)
try, 138-49; result of Keats's
confrontation with, 153-54.
See also Keats, poems of, "On
Visiting the Tomb of Burns,"
"Written in the Cottage Where
Burns was Born," "Lines Written in the Highlands"
Burton, Robert, 40n; *The Anatomy of Melancholy* and *Lamia*,
293-95; Keats's annotation in
his copy of, 300-301
Bush, Douglas, 40n, 77, 82n, 95n,
111, 156n, 174n, 222n, 226,
234, 252n, 281n, 287n, 296n,
300n, 317n, 337
Byron, George Gordon, Lord,
220n, 279; Byronic titanism in
Hyperion, 186-87; contempt
for wish-fulfillment, 202-203;
and Romantic irony, 245-46

Caldwell, James R., 58n
Carr, Arthur, 202n, 217
Cary, Henry Francis, 134, 312
Chapman, George, 74
Charmian, see Cox (Jane)
Chatterton, Thomas, 139
Chaucer, Geoffrey, 34, 37, 224n
chemistry, Hazlitt's use of analogy
from, 36-37; in Hermes episode
in *Lamia*, 301-307; Keats's
knowledge of, 36-37; Keats's
use of analogies from, 38-54;
Tucker's use of analogy from,
26-27. *See also* "ether,"
"intensity"
Clarke, Charles Cowden, 73n
Claude Lorrain, his painting and
Keats's *Epistle to Reynolds*,
120-26, 129-31; Hazlitt on,
120, 122
Cohen, I. Bernard, 39n
Coleridge, Samuel Taylor, 21, 24,
34, 39, 64, 124, 140, 155, 217;

Keats's criticism of in the
"Negative Capability" letter,
61-62
Collins, William, 236
Colvin, Sir Sidney, 48n, 91, 95,
120n, 124, 287n
Cortez, Hernando, 74
Cox, Jane, 283n, 301
Cross, T. P., 235n, 239n
Cusac, Marian H., 201n

D'Alembert, Jean Lerond, 17, 27
Dante, Alighieri, influence on
The Fall of Hyperion, 312-14,
323, 326; Keats reads on the
walking tour, 134, 143; source
of the sonnet "On a Dream,"
229
Darwin, Charles, 129
D'Avanzo, Mario L., 31n, 52n,
78n
Davenport, Arnold, 340
Davy, Sir Humphry, 46n, 307n;
and Keats's notion of the opera-
tion of imagination, 37-44
Descartes, René, 38
De Selincourt, Ernest, 48n, 85-86,
91, 95n, 186n, 221n, 296n
Dickie, James, 120n
Dilke, Charles Wentworth, 51n,
61, 64, 168, 189, 191, 285
disinterestedness, Keats's ideal of,
67-68, 139, 143-44, 191
Dryden, John, 164, 294, 311
Dunbar, Georgia S., 297n

Eliade, Mircea, 251n
Eliot, T. S., 197, 271-72, 275, 278
ether, ethereal, Davy on, 39-42;
Hartley on, 20; Keats's sense
of, 33-38, 40, 46-47, 52-53, 55,
59, 68-69, 98, 100, 121, 126,
134-35, 138, 162, 170; Wasserman on, 32
Evert, Walter, 117n, 125n, 131n

INDEX

intensity *(cont.)*
   ancholy," 279-81, 285-86; paro-
   died in *Lamia*, 303, 307
irony, described in its romantic
   sense, 244-47

Jack, Ian, 120n, 338n
James, D. G., 330
Jeffrey, Sarah, 287n
Johnson, Samuel, 21
Jones, Isabella, 223
Jones, John, 202n, 268

Kames, Henry Home, Lord, 14
Kean, Edmund, 56
Keats, George, 46, 80, 90, 93,
   132, 150, 152, 168, 190-91,
   193, 223, 224n, 225, 226n, 229,
   249n, 253, 276, 280, 283, 287,
   291, 314
Keats, Georgiana (Mrs. George),
   46, 132, 150, 152, 168, 190-
   91, 193, 223, 224n, 225, 226n,
   229, 249n, 253, 276, 280,
   283, 287, 301, 314
Keats, John, poems of:
   "After Dark Vapours," 77, 341
   "Bright Star," 135, 208, 301
   Endymion, 40, 48-51, 53, 75,
      81, 83, 86, 88-89, 90-116,
      117, 130-31, 157, 189, 194,
      230, 237-38, 240, 246-47,
      277, 293, 300, 306-307,
      311, 334
   *Epistle to John Hamilton Reyn-
      olds*, 117-31, 132-33, 137-38,
      146, 149, 152
   Eve of Saint Mark, 221-28;
      textual problem in, 221-24;
      disputed dating of, 225-26n
   Eve of St. Agnes, 149, 198-220,
      221, 223-24, 226, 228, 233,
      264, 311
   Fall of Hyperion, 155, 195, 223,
      239, 241, 310-335, 336;

importance of disputed lines
   in, 328-29
"God of the Meridian," 152n
"How Many Bards," 52, 72-73,
   75-76, 341
Hyperion, 109, 115-16 131,
   139, 150, 155-97, 198-99,
   246, 294, 303, 308, 310-11,
   313, 316, 319, 322-23, 326,
   329, 332, 336
Isabella; or The Pot of Basil,
   118, 198-200, 202n, 219,
   220
"I Stood Tip-toe," 80-83, 84,
   88, 96, 100-101, 111, 173,
   250-51, 253
"La Belle Dame sans Merci,"
   108, 214, 219, 231-41
Lamia, 219, 240, 261, 292-309,
   310-11
"Lines Written in the Highlands after a Visit to Burns's
   Country," 145-52, 153
"Ode on a Grecian Urn," 119,
   128, 244, 248, 262, 267-78,
   279, 285, 337
"Ode on Indolence," 248, 286-
   91; date of, 286-87n
"Ode on Melancholy," 248,
   278-86
Ode "To Autumn," 224,
   336-42
"Ode to a Nightingale," 216,
   244, 248, 262-67, 268,
   273-74, 291
"Ode to Psyche," 248, 249-61,
   276
"On a Dream," 228-31
"On First Looking into Chap-
   man's Homer," 72, 74, 88
"On Receiving a Laurel Crown
   from Leigh Hunt," 78
"On the Sea," 75-76, 88, 97
"On Seeing the Elgin Marbles,"
   74

350